I0010322

Mastering Microsoft 365 and SharePoint Online

A complete guide to boosting organizational efficiency with Microsoft 365's real-world solutions

Rodrigo Pinto

Mastering Microsoft 365 and SharePoint Online

Copyright © 2024 Packt Publishing

All rights reserved. No part of this book may be reproduced, stored in a retrieval system, or transmitted in any form or by any means, without the prior written permission of the publisher, except in the case of brief quotations embedded in critical articles or reviews.

Every effort has been made in the preparation of this book to ensure the accuracy of the information presented. However, the information contained in this book is sold without warranty, either express or implied. Neither the author, nor Packt Publishing or its dealers and distributors, will be held liable for any damages caused or alleged to have been caused directly or indirectly by this book.

The author acknowledges the use of cutting-edge AI, such as Microsoft Copilot and ChatGPT, with the sole aim of enhancing and improving the clarity of the language, code, and images within the book, thereby ensuring a smooth reading experience for readers. It's important to note that the content itself has been crafted by the author and edited by a professional publishing team.

Packt Publishing has endeavored to provide trademark information about all of the companies and products mentioned in this book by the appropriate use of capitals. However, Packt Publishing cannot guarantee the accuracy of this information.

Portfolio Manager: Aaron Tanna

Publishing Product Manager: Kushal Dave

Book Project Manager: Manisha Singh

Senior Editor: Aditi Chatterjee

Technical Editor: Vidhisha Patidar

Copy Editor: Safis Editing

Proofreader: Aditi Chatterjee

Indexer: Hemangini Bari

Production Designer: Jyoti Kadam

First published: December 2024

Production reference: 1291024

Published by Packt Publishing Ltd.

Grosvenor House

11 St Paul's Square

Birmingham

B3 1RB, UK

ISBN 978-1-83546-365-9

www.packtpub.com

The writing of this book would not have been possible, without the love, support and encouragement of the light of my life: Lurdes. Thank you for being yourself, your wisdom and love have made this adventure not just possible, but meaningful. This book carries your fingerprints on every page. I'd like to also thank my awesome dad, Armando, who shaped me into the person I am today, making me push the boundaries on each step in the right way. The kids: Ana and Rodrigo for joy, and laughter that kept me going. Even when I was busy working on this book, you reminded me of the most important things in life: love, family, and the simple joy of being together.

I'd like to take a moment to thank all the people who've contributed to this book : special thank you to the Packt publishing team who helped keep the book on track and improve it in so many ways. I'd also like to extend sincere thanks to my technical reviewers, Joel Rodrigues and Stephen Corey, for their commitment and for pushing me to think deeper, ensuring that every aspect of this book was both accurate and clear.

Last, but not least special reference to my professional colleagues/family: Adis Jugo, Maarten Eekels, Eric Shupps, Spencer Harbar, Michael Noel, Paolo Pialorsi, Mustafa Toroman, Sasha Kranjac, Rick Van Rousselt, Erwin van Hunen and Vesa Juvonen: your insights, feedback, and encouragement have shaped my work in countless ways, and I am deeply grateful to each of you. This book is a reflection of the knowledge, experience, and professional relationships we've built together. Thank you for being an integral part of both this book and my life.

– Rodrigo Pinto

Enterprise Architect at Perspective Dragon, CollabDays Portugal Organizer, SharePointPt founder and Microsoft 365 MVP

Contributors

About the author

Rodrigo Pinto is an experienced enterprise architect and a Microsoft 365 MVP since 2011. With over 20 years of experience in the field, he's a globally acknowledged thought leader across *Modern Workplace*. His ground-breaking solutions and development approaches have helped transform both broader tech communities as well as client organizations. He drives productivity through successful implementations and ensures that businesses are getting a real return on their technology investments.

As the organizer of *CollabDays Portugal* and *SharePointPt* user group, he has been a strong advocate for fostering community collaboration efforts. He regularly speaks at community and Microsoft events and loves to connect the dots on development, automation, and cutting-edge solutions. A native of Lisbon, Portugal, he currently lives in Seixal with his wife and kids in a lovely home close to the sea.

About the reviewers

Joel Rodrigues is a Microsoft 365 developer with 15 years of SharePoint and M365 development experience. He focuses mostly on creating SharePoint, Microsoft 365, and Azure solutions. He enjoys using the latest technologies to develop solutions for his clients that extend product capabilities to meet their business requirements and enhance productivity and collaboration. With best practices always in mind, he strives to create solutions that are reliable and easy to maintain in the long term. He is passionate about the M365 development ecosystem and the amazing M365 community.

Outside the technical side of things, he enjoys spending time with his family, be it watching movies, playing games, or doing outdoor activities with the kids.

Stephen Corey is a Microsoft MVP and consultant in Microsoft 365 development. He creates solutions for clients and helps them leverage SharePoint Online to the fullest. Steve has spent most of his career working with SharePoint, going back to the early 2000s. He's worked with SharePoint both as an administrator as well as a software developer, creating solutions to solve problems. He is also a content creator and online instructor producing educational content about SharePoint across multiple platforms including YouTube, LinkedIn, his blog, and more. He's also a speaker at community events around the United States. You can find information, guides, and links to all other platforms on his blog (https://stevecorey.com).

Table of Contents

2

Part 2: Enhancing and Automating

3

4

Enhancing SharePoint – Site Templates, Forms, and Power Apps   117

Part 3: Locking It Down and Moving It Smoothly

5

Data Governance and Compliance   187

6

Navigating the Microsoft 365 Migration Process   225

Part 4: Solving Real-World Challenges and Shaping the Future

7

Real-World Case Studies and Future Trends   261

Part 5: Wrapping Up

8

Implementing Microsoft 365 and SharePoint Solutions – Strategic Blueprints   299

9

Implementing Microsoft 365 and SharePoint Solutions – Implementation Playbooks   327

Preface

Welcome to the digital age, where technology is no longer a choice but an integral part of how all businesses function. As part of this transformation, Microsoft 365 and SharePoint have proven themselves to be the right choice for modern organizations to transform what they need when it matters most.

Mastering Microsoft 365 and SharePoint Online will show you how to navigate these platforms, whether you want operational efficiency, teamwork improvements, or data security and compliance. In recent years, SharePoint has evolved from a simple file-sharing tool into an integral component of Microsoft 365's cloud suite that provides workflow automation and advanced security features. If you run a team, manage IT, or strive for better digital infrastructure within your organization, this material will be helpful.

This book is loaded with real-world examples and situations that simplify the complexity of problems into bite-size steps. From optimizing workflows with Power Automate to creating custom apps that increase user engagement, or tackling compliance in the current regulatory landscape, the idea is to provide practical advice that you can start using today. It embodies the change in how we work and it's not all about software.

This book will empower you to make the most of the tools available in Microsoft 365 and SharePoint. It will teach you to automate tasks so you don't need to carry out repetitive tasks, through customization features, and creating a highly-tuned digital workplace.

It addresses the fine line between technology and practicality, but knowing what these tools are capable of doing is not good enough. You should know how they can function for an organization. Illustrated via case studies and best practices, we will deep-dive into how companies in various sectors have seen success in deploying these solutions to increase productivity at a superluminal pace.

Part 1 gets you started by walking through the basics of setting up and understanding the key tools and features of Microsoft 365 and SharePoint. It's all about building a strong foundation so you feel confident as you move on to more advanced topics. Whether you're just getting started or need a quick refresher, this part covers the core setup and concepts that are essential for making the most of these platforms.

Part 2 dives into the more advanced ways you can make SharePoint your own. It's all about taking customization to the next level: whether it's adding your unique branding, creating custom workflows to streamline processes, or automating tasks to save time and effort. We'll explore how to enhance SharePoint so it works even harder for you, making day-to-day operations smoother and more efficient.

In *Part 3*, we'll take a closer look at the key aspects of governance, compliance, and migration to make sure your data stays secure, and your systems run smoothly, especially when you're upgrading or moving to a new platform. It's all about keeping things safe and ensuring a seamless transition without disrupting your workflow.

In *Part 4*, we'll dive into real-world examples, showing you how Microsoft 365 and SharePoint are being used in business settings today. You'll see what works, what doesn't, and how companies are solving everyday challenges. Plus, we'll take a look ahead at the future of these platforms, such as what trends are on the horizon and how they could impact the way you work.

The final section, *Part 5*, will walk you through hands-on guides and practical solutions, breaking down how to implement these tools in a way that's both strategic and easy to follow. It's designed to help you not just understand the concepts, but to put them into action in real-world scenarios. Whether you're planning your approach or diving into the nuts and bolts of implementation, this part will give you the tools and confidence to make it all work seamlessly.

Who this book is for

We appreciate that there is a broad spectrum of people who may be interested in reading this book, and so we'd like to provide some details for each type of reader to help better prepare you for the material.

Students

If you are a student, this is more than just a learning resource: it's a bridge between theory and practice. You'll gain insights into how Microsoft 365 and SharePoint are applied in real-world settings, giving you a solid foundation that can help set you apart as you prepare to enter the workforce. I break down complex concepts into easy-to-understand examples, making it a valuable resource whether you're new to the subject or building on existing knowledge.

Business/end users

If you are a business/end user, think of this book as your toolkit for streamlining your workday. I focus on practical solutions to help you get the most out of these tools, whether you're managing teams, working on collaborative projects, or looking to improve overall productivity. You'll learn how to simplify workflows and create more effective communication and document-sharing systems, all without getting bogged down in technical jargon.

This book also provides clear, step-by-step guidance to help you feel more confident and self-sufficient with Microsoft 365 and SharePoint. Whether you're handling documents, organizing projects, or just trying to make your workday more efficient, I've kept things approachable and easy to follow. My goal is to help you become more comfortable with these platforms, so you can use them to your advantage, without needing to rely on IT help every step of the way.

Developers

This is where things get really exciting! We're not just scratching the surface: you will dive into customizing SharePoint workflows, building powerful automation with Power Automate, and creating branding solutions that take your setup from standard to something uniquely tailored to any organization's needs. You'll find plenty of practical, hands-on examples that give you room to experiment, tweak, and innovate. This isn't just about following steps; it's about giving you the tools to take creative control, push boundaries, and build something that stands out. Whether you're looking to refine your skills or try out new techniques, this section is designed to empower you to do what you do best: build and innovate.

IT professionals

I've loaded this book with advanced strategies that tackle governance, compliance, security, and migration head-on. I understand that your job isn't just about keeping the systems running; it's about making sure everything stays secure, compliant, and future-proof. Inside, you'll find best practices and practical steps to help you roll out solutions that don't just work for today but can scale as your organization grows. I've made sure to focus on real-world challenges you're probably facing so that you can implement these solutions confidently while protecting your data and keeping everything running smoothly. I know you're juggling a lot, so I've broken it down into actionable advice that'll save you time and headaches.

No matter where you are on your journey, whether you're just starting out or already have years of experience, this book is here to meet you where you are and help you level up. My goal is to give you advice that's not only practical and easy to use right away, but also to build your confidence so you can take on bigger challenges when you're ready. I've packed it with real-world examples and insights that you can actually apply, so whether you're figuring out the basics or diving into more advanced topics, you'll find something useful every step of the way. Think of this book as a guide that grows with you, helping you feel empowered to make the most of Microsoft 365 and SharePoint, now and in the future.

What this book covers

Chapter 1, Configuring Microsoft 365 and SharePoint, walks through the basics of setting up Microsoft 365 and SharePoint.

Chapter 2, SharePoint Essentials, is the go-to guide for the core features of SharePoint.

Chapter 3, Automating with Power Automate, dives into customization – how to tailor branding and build custom workflows that fit specific needs.

Chapter 4, Enhancing SharePoint – Site Templates, Forms, and Power Apps, shows how to use Power Automate to streamline tasks and processes. It covers the basics and then digs into some cool use cases to save time and cut out repetitive tasks.

Chapter 5, Data Governance and Compliance, discusses how to keep data secure, compliant, and well-managed. It is a must-read for anyone handling sensitive or regulated data.

Chapter 6, Navigating the Microsoft 365 Migration Process, covers the ins and outs of migration strategies. Whether you are transitioning to SharePoint or upgrading systems, it provides best practices and practical tips.

Chapter 7, Real-World Case Studies and Future Trends, takes a look at how businesses are actually using Microsoft 365 and SharePoint by exploring real-world examples, showcasing innovative solutions, and exploring expected trends in the future.

Chapter 8, Implementing Microsoft 365 and SharePoint Solutions – Strategic Blueprints, is all about planning and strategy. It walks through step-by-step recipes that align with business goals.

Chapter 9, Implementing Microsoft 365 and SharePoint Solutions – Implementation Playbooks, shows exactly how to implement playbooks. Think of it as a hands-on guide that puts everything we've discussed into action.

To get the most out of this book

To make sure you get the most out of this book, it'll help if you're somewhat familiar with a few key concepts. Don't worry if you're not an expert in all of these areas – having some basic knowledge will make things go more smoothly. Here's what will come in handy:

- **Basic familiarity with Microsoft 365 and SharePoint** (knowing your way around the interface will help, but I'll cover the essentials)
- **Some experience with Power Automate** (or a similar automation tool) will be useful for the automation section
- **General knowledge of data governance and compliance** will be helpful, especially when we get into security and legal considerations
- **Basic understanding of workflows and customization** (not a must, but it will make *Chapter 3* even more valuable)

While this book has been written to be practical and beginner-friendly, a little prior experience will make following along easier.

Tools and platforms covered in the book

Throughout the book, I'll be referring to several tools and features:

- **Microsoft 365**: The central hub for all things discussed.
- **SharePoint**: Both the essentials and the advanced features.

- **Power Platform**: This includes both Power Automate and PowerApps. We'll dive into automation using Power Automate to streamline your workflows and take care of repetitive tasks. PowerApps will be explored for building custom apps tailored to your business needs—no heavy coding is required. You'll learn how these tools can work together to create seamless, integrated solutions.

- **Data governance and compliance features**: For managing security and legal requirements effectively, ensuring your data stays compliant with industry standards and regulations.

The examples in the book are designed to be platform-agnostic, everything is on the web. So, whether you're on Windows, macOS, or Linux, you'll be able to follow along just fine.

Resources and recommendations

To get the full experience, I recommend working through the examples as you read. I've made sure they're easy to follow, and you'll get a much deeper understanding by trying them out yourself.

> **Disclaimer on images**
>
> This title contains many long screenshots. These have been captured to provide readers with an overview of the various features of Microsoft 365 and SharePoint. As a result, the text in these images may appear small at 100% zoom.
>
> Some of the images are only presented for contextual purposes. The readability of the graphic is not crucial to the discussion. Please refer to our free graphic bundle to download the images.
>
> You can download the images from `https://packt.link/gbp/9781835463659`

Conventions used

There are a number of text conventions used throughout this book.

Bold: Indicates a new term, an important word, or words that you see onscreen. For instance, words in menus or dialog boxes appear in **bold**. Here is an example: "Select the user and click the **Manage roles** option."

> **Tips or important notes**
> Appear like this.

Get in touch

Feedback from our readers is always welcome.

General feedback: If you have questions about any aspect of this book, email us at customercare@packtpub.com and mention the book title in the subject of your message.

Errata: Although we have taken every care to ensure the accuracy of our content, mistakes do happen. If you have found a mistake in this book, we would be grateful if you would report this to us. Please visit www.packtpub.com/support/errata and fill in the form.

Piracy: If you come across any illegal copies of our works in any form on the internet, we would be grateful if you would provide us with the location address or website name. Please contact us at copyright@packtpub.com with a link to the material.

If you are interested in becoming an author: If there is a topic that you have expertise in and you are interested in either writing or contributing to a book, please visit authors.packtpub.com.

Share Your Thoughts

Once you've read *Mastering Microsoft 365 and SharePoint Online*, we'd love to hear your thoughts! Scan the QR code below to go straight to the Amazon review page for this book and share your feedback.

https://packt.link/r/1835463657

Your review is important to us and the tech community and will help us make sure we're delivering excellent quality content.

Download a free PDF copy of this book

Thanks for purchasing this book!

Do you like to read on the go but are unable to carry your print books everywhere?

Is your eBook purchase not compatible with the device of your choice?

Don't worry, now with every Packt book you get a DRM-free PDF version of that book at no cost.

Read anywhere, any place, on any device. Search, copy, and paste code from your favorite technical books directly into your application.

The perks don't stop there, you can get exclusive access to discounts, newsletters, and great free content in your inbox daily

Follow these simple steps to get the benefits:

1. Scan the QR code or visit the link below

https://packt.link/free-ebook/9781835463659

2. Submit your proof of purchase
3. That's it! We'll send your free PDF and other benefits to your email directly

Part 1: Starting Up

The first part of this book gets you started by walking through the essentials of setting up and understanding Microsoft 365 and SharePoint, focusing on the key tools and features that will form your foundation.

Whether you are brand new to the platform or just need a refresher, this part ensures you will have everything in place to feel confident as you move forward to more advanced topics.

By the time you are done with this part, you will have built a solid base for working with Microsoft 365 and SharePoint and be ready to make the most of these powerful platforms.

This part contains the following chapters:

- *Chapter 1, Configuring Microsoft 365 and SharePoint*
- *Chapter 2, SharePoint Essentials*

1
Configuring Microsoft 365 and SharePoint

This chapter provides an overview of the Microsoft 365 and SharePoint platforms, emphasizing the importance of effective configuration and implementation in real-world scenarios. By the end of this chapter, you will have a solid understanding of the key components and architecture, preparing you with the skills to enhance productivity and collaboration within your organization.

You will learn how to configure Microsoft 365 tenant settings, provision users, manage access control, and integrate with other Microsoft services.

We will delve into real-world scenarios where the effective implementation of Microsoft 365 and SharePoint has led to increased efficiency and security. You will gain practical insights into configuring Microsoft 365 tenant settings and learn user provisioning and access control. Additionally, you will understand the significance of integrating Microsoft 365 with other Microsoft services to maximize the platform's potential.

In this chapter, we are going to cover the following main topics:

- An overview of Microsoft 365 and the SharePoint platform
- The importance of effective implementation in real-world scenarios
- Configuring Microsoft 365 tenant settings
- User provisioning and access control
- Integrating with other Microsoft services

Through detailed explanations, you will gain the expertise needed to effectively implement and leverage Microsoft 365 in your organization.

By the end of this chapter, you will be able to do the following:

- Understand the functionalities, capabilities, architecture, and components of the Microsoft 365 and SharePoint platforms

- Recognize the importance of effective implementation strategies in real-world scenarios

- Configure Microsoft 365 tenant settings

- Provision for users and implement access control measures effectively

Technical requirements

In this section, you will find the technical requirements for completing the tasks in this chapter. The tasks involve configuring and optimizing Microsoft 365 and SharePoint environments, enhancing collaboration and productivity, and implementing robust security measures.

Here are the technical requirements:

- Microsoft 365 subscription

- Access to SharePoint Online

- Access to Microsoft Azure

- Internet connectivity for accessing online resources and services

- A user assigned with the required roles:

  - For the **Microsoft Admin** portal, the user must have the **Global Administrator** role assigned

  - For the **Microsoft Defender** portal, the user must have the **Security Administrator** or **Global Administrator** role assigned

  - In the **Microsoft Compliance** portal, the user must have the **Compliance Administrator, Compliance Data Administrator, eDiscovery Administrator,** or **Records Management** role assigned

  - For the **Microsoft Purview** portal, the user must have the **Compliance Administrator, Global Administrator, Information Protection Administrator, Records Management, Insider Risk Management,** or **Privacy Management** role assigned

  - For the **Microsoft Entra** portal, the user must have the **Authentication Policy Administrator** or **Global Administrator** role assigned

> Important note
> The configurations outlined in this chapter require the use of a Microsoft 365 E5 license. This advanced licensing option provides access to a comprehensive suite of enterprise-level features and essential tools for implementing these configurations effectively.

An overview of Microsoft 365 and the SharePoint platform

In this section, you will learn the process of configuring Microsoft 365 tenant settings. By understanding and implementing these configurations, you will be equipped to optimize your Microsoft 365 environment for enhanced productivity and collaboration.

Effective configuration of Microsoft 365 tenant settings is essential for aligning the platform with your organization's requirements and objectives.

We will delve into various settings and options available within the Microsoft 365 admin center, ensuring that your tenant is tailored to meet your organization's needs. Furthermore, we will explore best practices for configuring tenant settings to maximize security, compliance, and efficiency. Through practical examples and step-by-step guides, you will gain valuable insights into establishing a solid foundation for your Microsoft 365 environment.

By the end of this section, you will be proficient in configuring Microsoft 365 tenant settings, empowering you to create a customized environment that fosters collaboration and productivity within your organization.

A bit of history

SharePoint has undergone a remarkable evolution, transforming from a standalone collaboration platform to an integral component of the broader **Microsoft 365** ecosystem. Understanding this evolution provides valuable context for comprehending the current capabilities and functionalities of SharePoint and Microsoft 365.

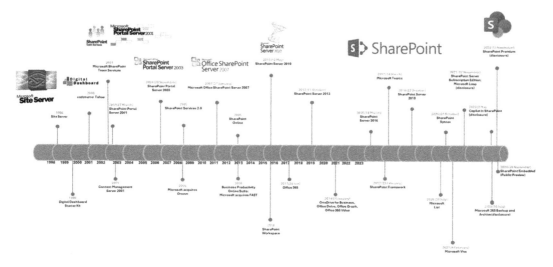

Figure 1.1 – SharePoint history

Originally introduced by Microsoft in 2001, SharePoint emerged as a document management and intranet solution, enabling organizations to store, share, and collaborate on documents and information within a centralized platform. Over the years, SharePoint evolved to encompass a broader range of features, including content management, workflow automation, and business intelligence.

With the advent of cloud computing and the growing demand for more agile and collaborative workplaces, Microsoft recognized the need to modernize SharePoint and integrate it with other productivity tools and services. This led to the development of Microsoft 365, a comprehensive suite of cloud-based applications and services designed to empower modern teamwork and streamline business processes.

Microsoft 365 builds upon the foundation laid by SharePoint, incorporating its core functionalities while introducing new features and capabilities. By integrating SharePoint with other Microsoft products, such as **Teams**, **OneDrive**, and **Office apps**, Microsoft 365 provides a unified platform for communication, collaboration, and content management.

This understanding of SharePoint's evolution to Microsoft 365 will guide our approach to configuring and optimizing the platform for your organization's specific requirements and objectives.

SharePoint Online and SharePoint On-Premises are two different platforms that have been created to meet the needs of their deployment environment. SharePoint Online, which is in the Microsoft 365 bundle, is popular for being easy to access, scalable, and integrating well with other Microsoft Cloud services. This makes it particularly suited to organizations that want to concentrate on reducing IT costs while at the same time improving flexibility. The advantage here is that you can reach the platform from any computer connected to the internet at any time, thus enhancing distant operations and joint working.

SharePoint On-Premises, on the other hand, is deployed on an organization's servers, giving an organization greater control over infrastructure, data, and customization. This version is favored by organizations with particular compliance requirements and data sovereignty fears, as well as those that need customization that is impossible on a cloud platform. Nevertheless, maintaining it requires a lot of IT resources, including hardware and software updates. Servicing it needs a considerable amount of IT resources for hardware and software updates, and security management. This implies that individuals or organizations must be prepared to take more responsibility for managing and securing such an environment, despite the fact that it provides both control and flexibility.

In the following sections, we will look at all Microsoft 365 and SharePoint components and features as well as the configuration of Microsoft 365 tenant settings, making use of the powerful features derived from SharePoint and other Microsoft technologies.

Microsoft 365 components

Microsoft 365 is a suite of services and productivity tools developed by Microsoft that is designed to enhance collaboration, communication, and productivity for individuals and organizations. It is built on a set of essential components and platforms that work together to deliver a seamless and secure user experience across different devices, apps, and locations.

Figure 1.2 – Microsoft 365 key components

Let's look at its key components.

Azure services

Azure services provide a robust cloud computing framework that significantly enhances and integrates with Microsoft 365 and SharePoint Online. This integration includes a variety of infrastructures, such as scalable virtual machines, dedicated virtual networks, and expansive data storage options to ensure that organizations have the necessary computing resources at their disposal. Platform services such as Azure App Service and Azure SQL Database provide environments where businesses can develop, deploy, and manage applications without the complexities of maintaining the underlying servers.

Azure services complement and extend the capabilities of Microsoft 365 and SharePoint Online, such as by providing additional storage, backup, networking, analytics, automation, or artificial intelligence features. You can use Azure services to host, run, or integrate your custom applications, databases, or websites with Microsoft 365 and SharePoint Online.

Microsoft 365 core services

These are the foundational services that enable the functionality and security of Microsoft 365, such as identity and access management, device and app management, threat protection, data governance, and compliance.

They are powered by **Microsoft Entra** (formerly Azure Active Directory), **Microsoft Endpoint Manager**, **Microsoft Defender**, **Microsoft 365 Compliance Center**, and other technologies.

SharePoint Online

This is the cloud-based version of SharePoint that provides a web-based platform for creating and managing sites, pages, libraries, lists, web parts, and apps. SharePoint Online is part of Microsoft 365 and uses the core services and productivity apps to provide a rich and secure content management system. You can use SharePoint Online to store, share, and collaborate on documents, data, and media, as well as to build intranets, extranets, portals, and workflows.

Microsoft 365 productivity apps

These are the cloud-based applications that provide collaboration and communication capabilities for your organization, such as **Word**, **Excel**, **PowerPoint**, **Outlook**, **OneNote**, **Teams**, **Outlook**, **OneDrive**, **Stream**, **Viva**, **Power BI**, **Planner**, **Power Automate**, and **Power Apps**. They are integrated with each other and with the core services to create a seamless user experience across devices and platforms.

The importance of effective implementation of Microsoft 365 in real-world scenarios

In today's fast-paced and increasingly digital business environment, the effective implementation of Microsoft 365 is critical for organizations seeking to enhance productivity, streamline operations, and foster collaboration. Microsoft 365, a comprehensive suite of productivity tools and services, provides numerous advantages, but realizing its full potential requires strategic and thoughtful deployment.

Here are key reasons why effective implementation of Microsoft 365 is vital in real-world scenarios.

Enhanced collaboration and communication

Microsoft 365 provides a range of tools, including Microsoft Teams, SharePoint, and OneDrive, that are designed to improve collaboration and communication within organizations. Effective implementation ensures that these tools are seamlessly integrated, enabling teams to work together in real time, share documents effortlessly, and maintain clear communication channels, regardless of their physical location. This fosters a more connected and efficient workforce, which is essential for success in today's remote and hybrid work environments.

Streamlined operations and increased productivity

With applications such as Word, Excel, PowerPoint, and Outlook, Microsoft 365 provides powerful tools for daily business tasks. When implemented effectively, these tools can be customized to fit the specific needs of the organization, streamlining workflows and automating repetitive tasks. This not only saves time but also reduces errors, leading to increased productivity. Additionally, cloud-based services ensure that employees can access their work from anywhere, at any time, further enhancing operational efficiency.

Robust security and compliance

One of the significant advantages of Microsoft 365 is its robust security features, including Advanced Threat Protection, **Data Loss Prevention** (**DLP**), and compliance solutions. Effective implementation involves configuring these features correctly to protect sensitive data, prevent unauthorized access, and ensure compliance with industry regulations. This is particularly important in sectors such as finance and healthcare, where data security and regulatory compliance are paramount.

Cost efficiency

Microsoft 365's subscription-based model can be cost-effective, but only with proper implementation. Organizations must choose the right plans and licenses based on their specific needs and ensure that all features are utilized to their fullest extent. Effective implementation helps reduce unnecessary costs associated with underutilized services and ensures that the organization gets the best return on its investment.

Improved employee experience and retention

A well-implemented Microsoft 365 environment can significantly enhance the employee experience by providing intuitive, user-friendly tools that support their daily tasks. Features such as **Viva Insights** and **MyAnalytics** provide personalized insights to help employees manage their work-life balance and improve productivity. A positive digital experience can lead to higher job satisfaction, better engagement, and increased retention rates.

Facilitating innovation and growth

By using tools such as Power BI for analytics, Power Apps for custom application development, and Power Automate for workflow automation, organizations can drive innovation and support growth. Effective implementation ensures that these tools are accessible and usable by employees, encouraging a culture of innovation in which innovative ideas can be quickly developed and brought to market.

The effective implementation of Microsoft 365 is essential for organizations looking to harness its full potential. By enhancing collaboration, streamlining operations, ensuring robust security, achieving cost efficiency, improving employee experience, and facilitating innovation, Microsoft 365 can significantly contribute to an organization's success. However, this requires a strategic approach to deployment, ongoing training and support for users, and continuous evaluation and optimization of the tools and services to align with the organization's evolving needs.

Configuring Microsoft 365 tenant settings

Configuring Microsoft 365 tenant settings involves several steps to ensure that your organization's Microsoft 365 environment is set up according to your business requirements and security policies.

Although there are multiple settings that need to be configured in the Microsoft 365 tenant, we will highlight those that align with security policies to protect your tenant, as they are crucial for preventing potential threats to your environment. This includes configuring the **organizational profile**, which is crucial for maintaining an accurate and secure representation of the organization; using **Microsoft Purview**'s data governance capabilities; and utilizing **Microsoft Defender**'s advanced threat protection features to ensure comprehensive security and compliance.

Configure organizational profile

Here are the steps to configure your organization profile:

1. **Log in to Microsoft 365**: Navigate to `https://admin.microsoft.com` and log in with your admin credentials.

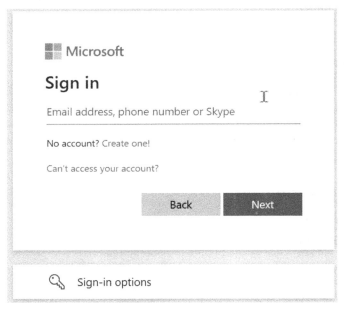

Figure 1.3 – Microsoft 365 login

2. **Access Admin Center**: In the left-hand navigation pane, click on **Admin** to open the Microsoft 365 admin center.

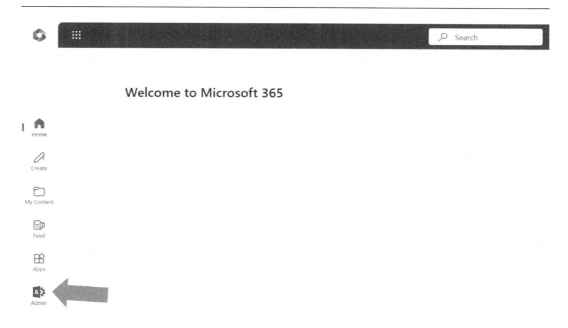

Figure 1.4 – Microsoft 365 portal

3. **Update organizational information**: Go to **Settings** > **Org settings** > **Organization profile**.

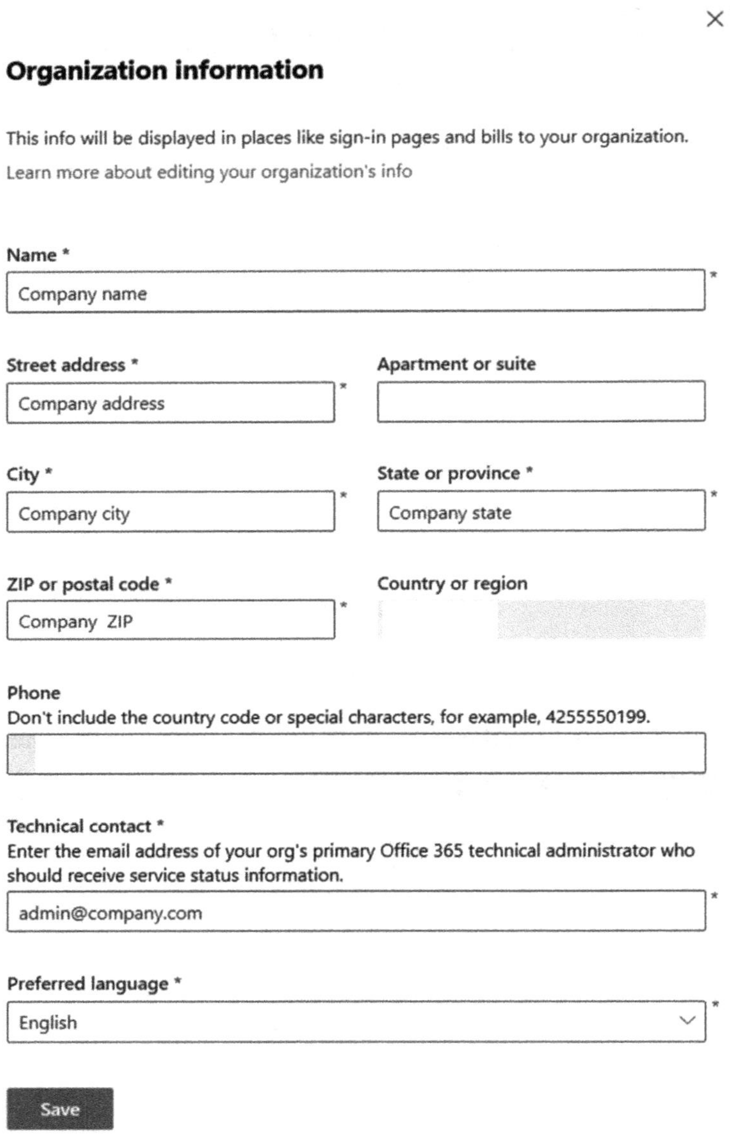

✕

Organization information

This info will be displayed in places like sign-in pages and bills to your organization.
Learn more about editing your organization's info

Name *

```
Company name
```
*

Street address *

```
Company address
```
*

Apartment or suite

```

```

City *

```
Company city
```
*

State or province *

```
Company state
```
*

ZIP or postal code *

```
Company  ZIP
```
*

Country or region

```

```

Phone
Don't include the country code or special characters, for example, 4255550199.

```

```

Technical contact *
Enter the email address of your org's primary Office 365 technical administrator who
should receive service status information.

```
admin@company.com
```
*

Preferred language *

```
English                                                          ⌄
```
*

[Save]

Figure 1.5 – Microsoft 365 admin center settings

4. **Edit details**: Update the basic information, such as organization name, address, technical
    contact, and preferred language.

Security settings

Follow these steps to configure the security settings:

1. **Security**: Access the security center by navigating to **Admin centers > Security**.

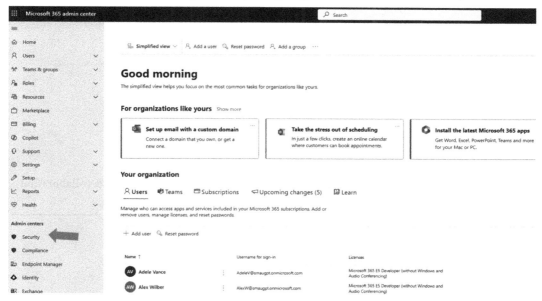

Figure 1.6 – Microsoft 365 admin center

Note

Microsoft Defender is a cloud-based email filtering service that helps protect your organization against advanced threats to email and collaboration tools, such as phishing, business email compromise, and malware attacks.

Figure 1.7 – Microsoft Defender portal

2. **Access email policies and rules**: In the left-hand navigation pane, click on **Email & collaboration** > **Policies & rules** > **Threat policies** > **Preset Security Policies**.

Figure 1.8 – Microsoft Defender Email & collaboration options

You will see the **Preset security policies** screen. Each section outlines specific features and settings:

- **Built-in protection**: This default security policy applied to all users includes additional machine learning models, more aggressive detonation evaluation, and visual indicators in the user interface. It notes that this is available only for paid Microsoft Defender for Office 365 tenants.

- **Standard protection**: Positioned as a baseline protection profile, this defends against spam, phishing, and malware threats. Features include balanced actions for handling malicious content, bulk content, and integration with Safe Links and Safe Attachments. There's an option to manage these protection settings.

- **Strict protection**: Designed for high-value targets or priority users, this provides more aggressive actions on malicious mail, tighter controls over bulk senders, and enhanced machine learning capabilities. Like the standard section, it also provides an option to manage these protection settings.

Figure 1.9 – Microsoft Defender: Preset security policies page

3. Turn on the one you want to configure, and then select **Manage protection settings** to start the configuration wizard.

4. On the **Apply Exchange Online Protection** page (see *Figure 1.10*), identify the internal recipients that the protections apply to (recipient conditions):

- **All recipients**

- **Specific recipients**: Configure one of the following recipient conditions that appear:

  - **Users**: The specified mailboxes, mail users, or mail contacts

  - **Groups**: Members of the specified distribution groups or mail-enabled security groups (dynamic distribution groups aren't supported) or the specified Microsoft 365 Groups

- **Domains:** All recipients in the organization with a primary email address in the specified accepted domain

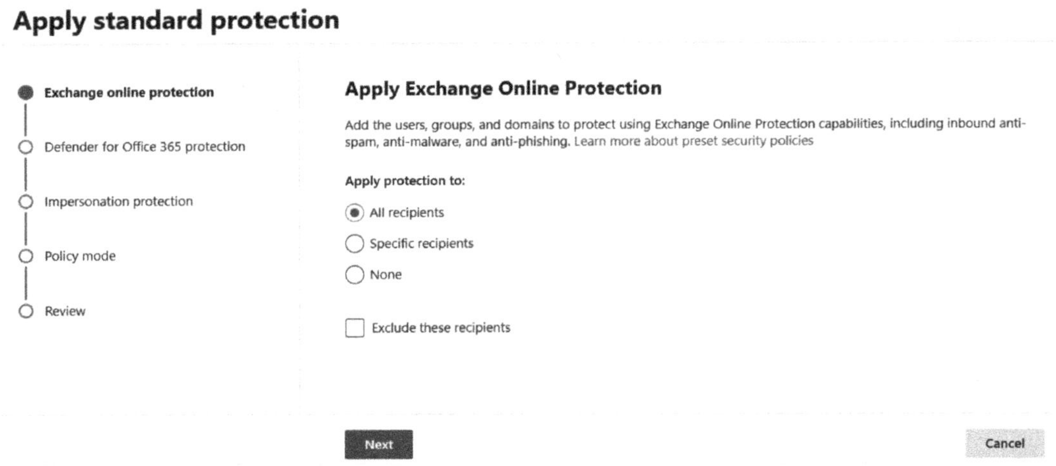

Apply standard protection

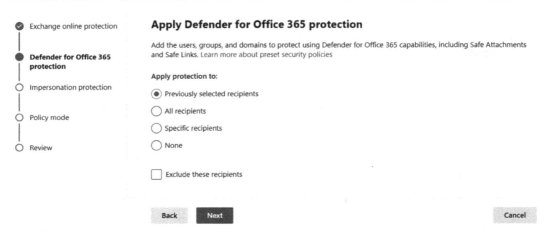

Figure 1.10 – Apply standard protection: Exchange Online Protection option page

Select the appropriate box, begin typing a value, and choose the desired value from the results.

Repeat this process as needed (to remove an existing value, click the **x** next to it). When you're finished on the **Apply Exchange Online Protection** page, select **Next**.

Apply standard protection

Figure 1.11 – Apply standard protection: Defender for Office 365 protection option page

5. On the **Apply Defender for Office 365 protection** page, identify the internal recipients to whom the Defender for Office 365 protections will apply (recipient conditions).

When you're finished on the **Apply Defender for Office 365 protection** page, select **Next**.

Apply standard protection

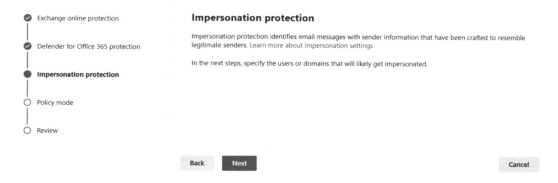

Figure 1.12 – Apply standard protection: Impersonation protection option page

6.   On the **Impersonation protection** page, select **Next**.

Apply standard protection

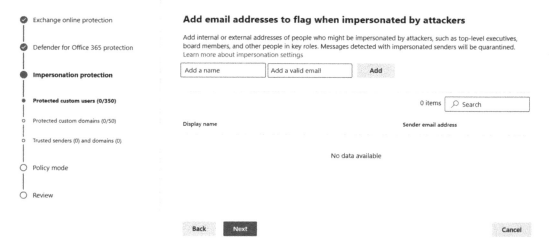

Figure 1.13 – Apply standard protection: Protected custom users option page

7.   On the **Add email addresses to flag when impersonated by attackers** page, add internal and external senders who are protected by user impersonation protection, then select **Next**.

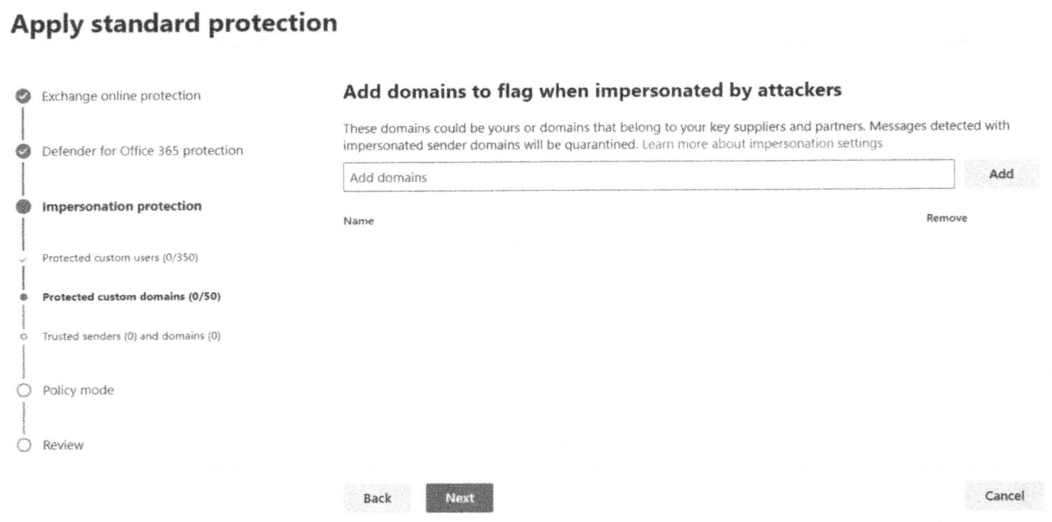

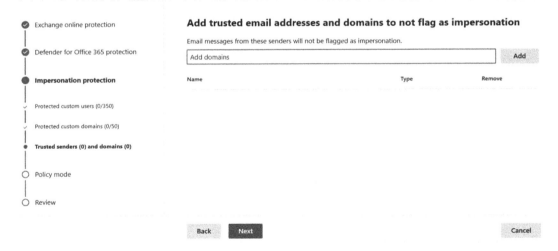

Figure 1.14 – Apply standard protection: Protected custom domains option page

8. On the **Add domains to flag when impersonated by attackers** page, add internal and external domains that are protected by domain impersonation protection, then select **Next**.

Apply standard protection

Figure 1.15 – Apply standard protection: Trusted senders and domains option page

9. On the **Add trusted email addresses and domains to not flag as impersonation** page, enter the sender email addresses and domains that you to exclude from impersonation protection, then select **Next**.

Apply standard protection

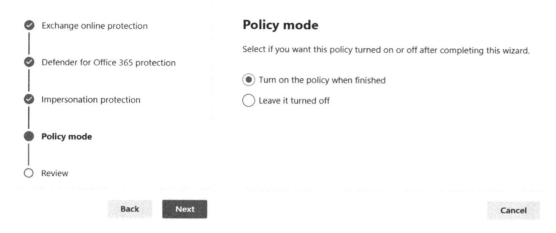

Figure 1.16 – Apply standard protection: Policy mode option page

10. On the **Policy mode** page, select **Next**.

Apply standard protection

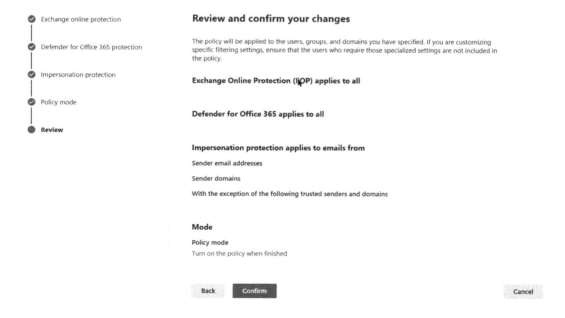

Figure 1.17 – Apply standard protection: Review options page

11. On the **Review and confirm your changes** page, review the settings, and select **Confirm** when you're done.

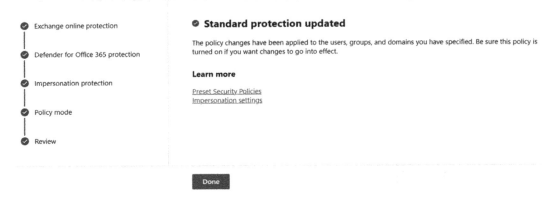

Figure 1.18 – Apply standard protection: Review option page

12. On the **Standard protection updated** or **Strict protection updated** page, select **Done**.

Set up data loss prevention settings

Here are the steps to configure the data loss prevention settings:

1. **Access the compliance portal**: In the left navigation pane, select **Compliance** to open the **Microsoft Purview** compliance portal.

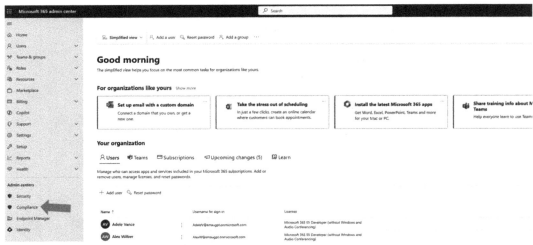

Figure 1.19 – Microsoft 365 admin center settings

> **Note**
>
> **Microsoft Purview** is a cloud-based data governance and compliance solution that helps organizations manage and protect their data across various environments, ensuring regulatory compliance, data security, and effective data management.

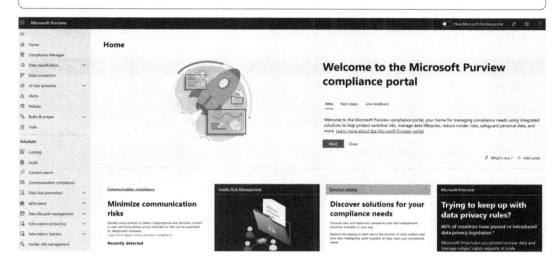

Figure 1.20 – Microsoft Purview portal

2. **Access the data loss prevention policy**: In the left-hand navigation pane, click on **Policies** and select **Data loss prevention**. On the next screen, select the **Policies** tab and click on the **Create policy** option.

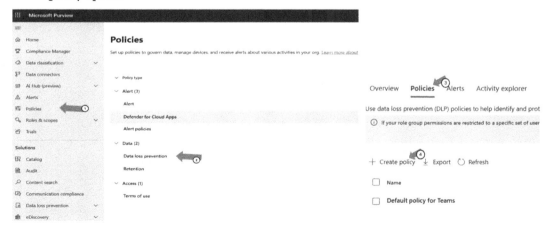

Figure 1.21 – Microsoft Purview Policies settings

3. Follow the DLP policy wizard to create the policy.

    Through predefined or custom templates, choose the type of information to protect based on your needs. Microsoft provides templates for protecting common sensitive information types, such as credit card numbers and social security numbers.

    In this case, we will establish a policy regarding the security of financial data.

4. Choose the type of information to protect.

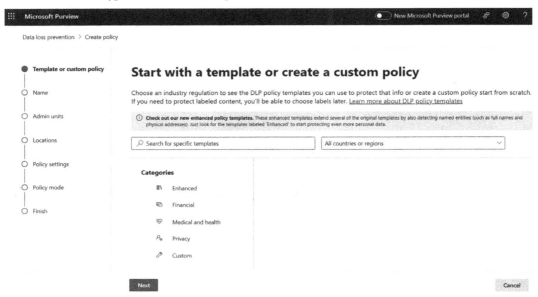

Figure 1.22 – Template or custom policy option page

5. Click **Next** to proceed to the **Name your policy** section, where you will assign a name to the policy.

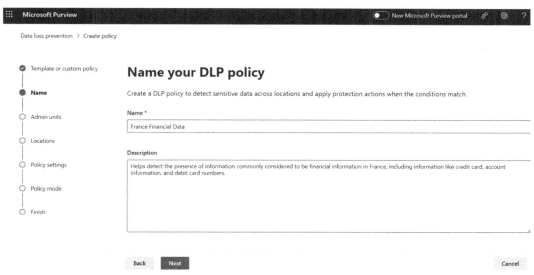

Figure 1.23 – Template or custom policy: Name your DLP policy page

6. Click **Next** and proceed to the **Assign admin units** section.

    *   In this instance, we aim to apply the policy to all users and groups.

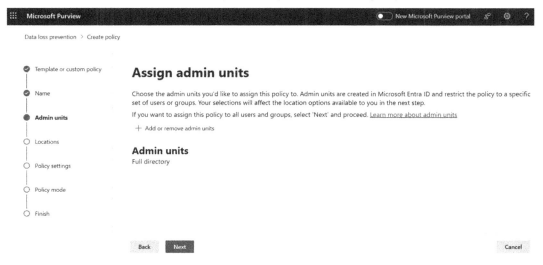

Figure 1.24 – Template or custom policy: Assign admin units option page

7.   Click **Next** and proceed to the **Define policy settings** section.

We can either use the default settings from the template or make our own rules to improve the policy more. In this instance, we aim to use the default settings.

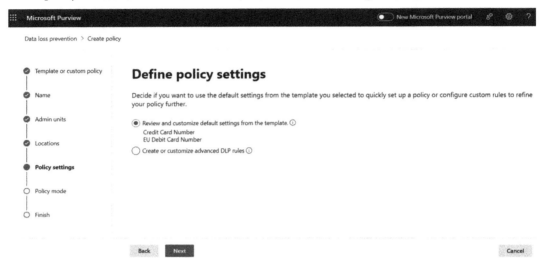

Figure 1.25 – Template or custom policy: Define policy settings page

8.   Click **Next** and proceed to the **Info to protect** section.

This policy will cover content that meets these criteria. Validate and edit them if needed. For example, we can change the criteria to find more sensitive info or content with a certain sensitivity.

Figure 1.26 – Template or custom policy: Info to protect page

9. Click **Next** and proceed to the **Protection actions** section.

This section allows us to configure protection actions that are triggered when content matches the defined policy conditions. These actions help ensure that sensitive information is handled appropriately and that incidents are reported and managed effectively.

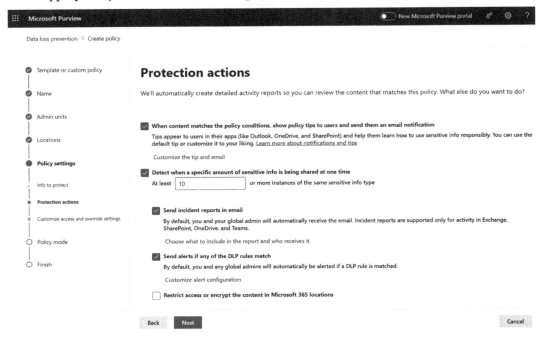

Figure 1.27 – Template or custom policy: Protection actions page

10. Click **Next** and proceed to the **Customize access and override settings** section. These settings allow administrators to configure access restrictions and override settings to protect sensitive content. By default, users are blocked from sending emails and Teams chats that contain the type of content being protected. These configurations will help ensure that sensitive information is securely managed and shared only with authorized individuals.

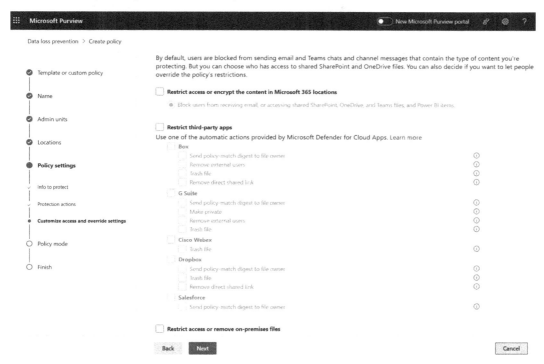

Figure 1.28 – Template or custom policy: Customize access and override settings option page

11. Click **Next** and proceed to the **Policy mode** section. This section allows administrators to choose how and when to activate a newly created or modified DLP policy. We can also use a simulation mode to assess how the policy affects our data. This step is crucial for ensuring that the policy functions as intended without immediately impacting users or workflows.

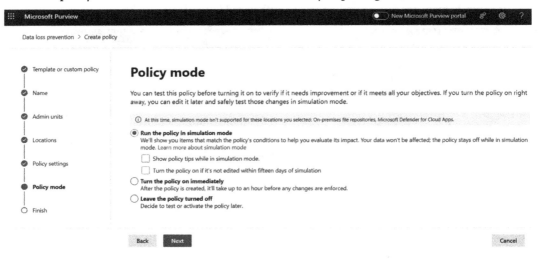

Figure 1.29 – Template or custom policy: Policy mode page

12. Click **Next** and proceed to the **Review and Finish** section. Keep in mind that after the policy is created, it will be applied to the selected locations. Review the settings on this page of the policy wizard and click **Submit** if everything is okay.

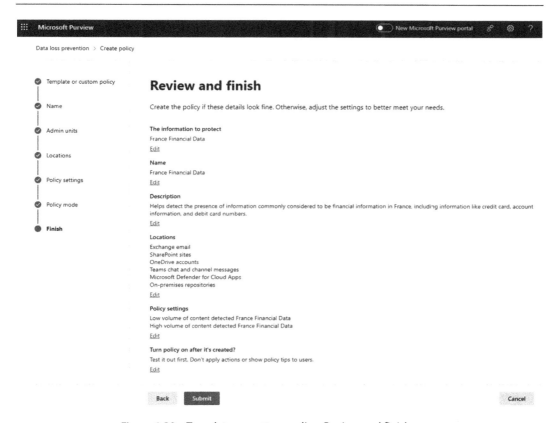

Figure 1.30 – Template or custom policy: Review and finish page

By following these steps, we have successfully activated Microsoft Purview Data Loss Prevention in the Microsoft 365 tenant, which helps to protect sensitive information and comply with data protection regulations by ensuring that the Microsoft 365 tenant is configured correctly and securely. Adjust and revisit settings as needed to accommodate any changes in your organization's requirements.

User provisioning and access control

User provisioning and access control in Microsoft 365 involve creating user accounts, assigning appropriate licenses, configuring permissions, and setting up security measures to manage user access. Keep in mind that settings need to be adjusted and revisited as needed to accommodate any changes in your organization's requirements.

User provisioning

User provisioning involves setting up and managing user accounts and access permissions within a system.

Here are the key steps involved:

1. **Log in to Microsoft 365**: Navigate to `https://admin.microsoft.com` and log in with your admin credentials.

2. Add a new user:

   - Navigate to **Users** > **Active users**

   - Click **Add a user**.

   - Fill in the required information, such as **First name**, **Last name**, **Display name**, and **Username**.

   - In **Password settings**:

     - Choose to automatically generate a password or create one manually

     - Decide if the user should change their password on the first sign-in

3. **Assign product licenses and apps**: On the page, select the licenses you want to assign to the user. You can choose from various Microsoft 365 plans depending on the user's role and needs. Also select the apps to be assigned to the user.

4. **Configure optional user settings**: In Microsoft 365, filling out the user profile with details such as job title, department, office phone, city, and country is important because it significantly enhances collaboration and communication within the organization. Detailed profile information makes it easier for colleagues to find and connect with you, ensuring they have the context needed to understand your role and responsibilities.

   Provide the details for the user profile info, remember this leads to more effective teamwork and efficient communication channels.

5. **Finish adding the user**: Review the details and click **Finish adding**.

Access control

Access control is critical for ensuring that the right individuals have the appropriate access to organizational resources.

Here are the essential elements to consider:

1. **Assign roles and permissions**:

   I.   Go to **Users**> **Active users**.

   II. Select the user and click the **Manage roles** option.

   III. Assign the necessary admin roles (e.g., Global admin, Exchange admin, SharePoint admin) and click **Save Changes**.

2. **Create and manage security groups**:

    I.   Navigate to **Teams & groups** > **Active teams & groups**.

    II.   Click the **Security groups** tab.

    III.   Click **Add a security group**.

    IV.   Name the group and add members.

    V.   In the **Settings** section, select this option if it is intended to allow Azure AD roles to be assigned to the group.

    VI.   Review and finish adding a group by clicking **Create Group**.

3. **Configure access policies**:

    I.   Conditional access:

        i.   Access the Microsoft Entra (formerly Azure AD) portal via the Microsoft 365 Admin Center.

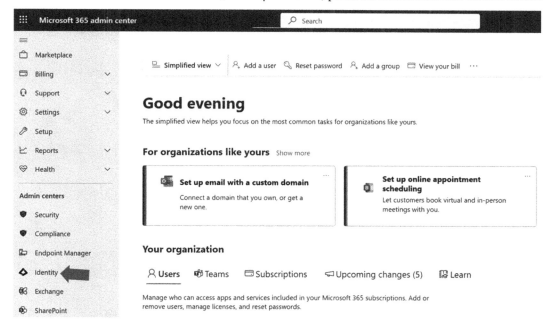

Figure 1.31 – Microsoft 365 Admin center

ii.   Go to **Protection** > **Conditional Access**.

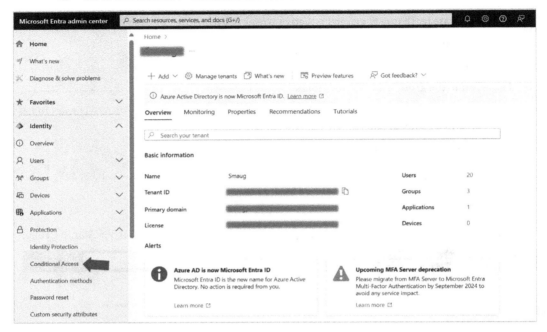

Figure 1.32 – Microsoft Entra Admin Center

iii. Create policies that set up regulations to control access according to your needs and based on factors such as user location, device compliance, and risk level.

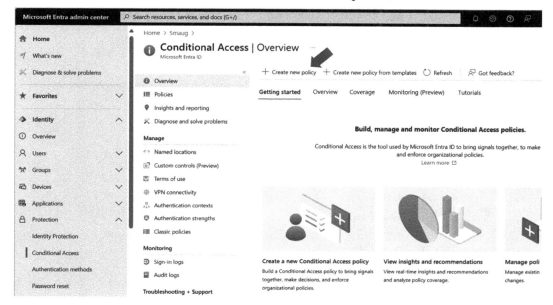

Figure 1.33 – Microsoft Entra Admin Center: Conditional Access options

4. Configure the Microsoft Entra multifactor authentication settings:

I. **Fraud Alerts**:

i. Go to **Protection** > **Multifactor authentication** > **Fraud alert**.

ii. Set **Allow users to submit fraud alerts** to **On**.

iii. Configure the **Automatically block users who report fraud** and **Code to report fraud during initial greeting** settings as needed.

iv. Select **Save**.

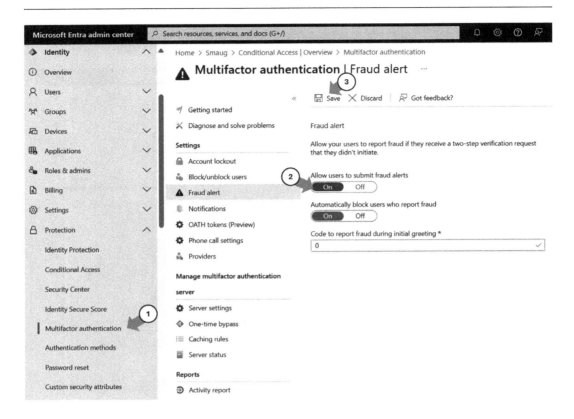

Figure 1.34 – Microsoft Entra Admin Center: Multifactor authentication | Fraud alert options

5. **Report suspicious activity**:

    I.   Go to **Protection** > **Authentication Method** > **Settings**.

    II.   Set **Report suspicious activity** to **Enabled**. The feature remains disabled if you choose **Microsoft managed**.

    III. Select **All users** or a **specific group**.

    IV. Select **Save**.

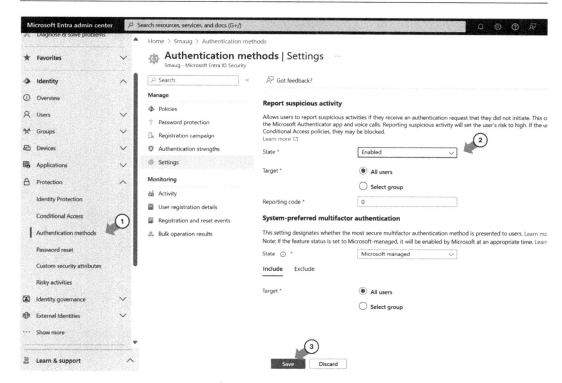

Figure 1.35 – Microsoft Entra Admin Center: Authentication methods

6. **Notifications**:

    I.   Go to **Protection** > **Multifactor authentication** > **Notifications**.

    II.   Enter the email address to send the notification to.

    III. Select **Save**.

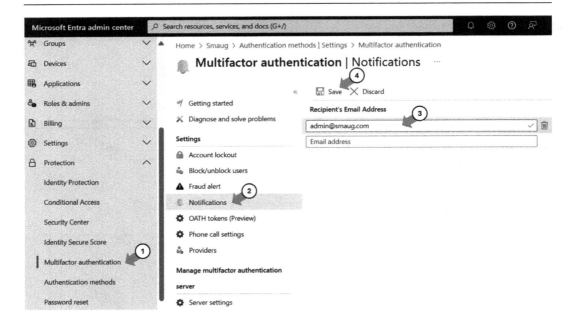

Figure 1.36 – Microsoft Entra Admin Center: Multifactor authentication | Notifications

7. **Enable and disable verification methods**:

    I.   Go to **Identity** > **Users**.

    II.   Select **Per-user MFA**.

    III.   At the top of the page, under **Multifactor authentication**, choose **Service settings**.

    IV.   On the **Service settings** page, choose or uncheck the relevant boxes under **Verification options**.

    V.   Select **Save**.

8. **Remember multifactor authentication**:

    I.   Go to **Identity** > **Users** > **All users**

    II.   Select **Per-user MFA**.

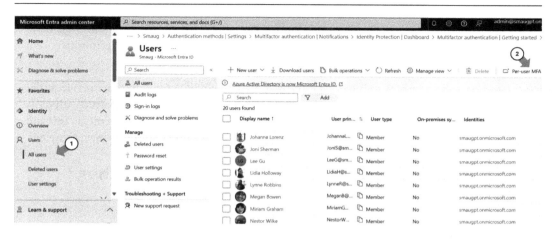

Figure 1.37 – Microsoft Entra Admin Center: Users options

III.   Go to the top of the page and select **service settings** under **Multifactor authentication**.

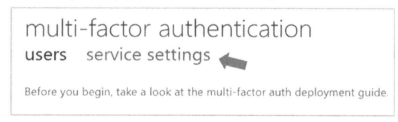

Figure 1.38 – multi-factor authentication options

IV.   On the **service settings** page, find **remember multifactor authentication** and select **Allow users to remember multifactor authentication on devices they trust**. Choose the number of days to let trusted devices skip multifactor authentications. To make the user experience better, increase the duration to 90 days or more.

V.   Select **Save**.

Figure 1.39 – Multi-factor authentication options

By following these steps, we have enhanced the security of Microsoft 365 users and their data, improving the user experience by allowing trusted devices to bypass the extra verification step for a certain period, balancing convenience and protection for the organization.

The next section will show how to integrate Microsoft 365 and SharePoint with other services that can enhance productivity and workflows. We will learn how to connect these platforms with tools and applications supporting collaboration, communication, and efficient task management. This will help us to leverage the full potential of Microsoft 365 and SharePoint and optimize business processes.

Integrating Microsoft 365 and SharePoint with other services

Integrating Microsoft 365 and SharePoint with other services can significantly enhance productivity and streamline your organization's workflow. By connecting these powerful platforms with additional tools and applications, you create a seamless ecosystem that supports collaboration, communication, and efficient task management.

Let's see how to get the maximum benefit from this integration.

Unified communication with Microsoft Teams

Microsoft Teams, part of the Microsoft 365 suite, can be seamlessly integrated with SharePoint to facilitate real-time collaboration. Teams channels can be linked directly to SharePoint document libraries, allowing users to access and share files within their conversation space. This integration ensures that team members can collaborate on documents without switching between platforms, maintaining context and improving efficiency.

Synchronizing tasks with Planner and To-Do

Integrating **Microsoft Planner** and **To-Do** with SharePoint and Microsoft 365 enables effective task management. SharePoint lists can be connected to Planner to convert list items into actionable tasks, providing a visual and interactive way to track progress. Additionally, tasks assigned in Teams can be synchronized with To-Do, ensuring individuals have a consolidated view of their responsibilities, boosting productivity by keeping all tasks in one place.

Enhancing data insights with Power BI

Power BI integration with Microsoft 365 allows advanced data analytics and visualization. By embedding Power BI reports in SharePoint sites or Teams channels, you provide users with interactive dashboards that offer real-time insights into business data. This integration helps teams make informed decisions based on up-to-date information, leading to improved outcomes and operational efficiency.

Automating workflows with Power Automate

Power Automate (formerly Microsoft Flow) can be used to create automated workflows that connect Microsoft 365, SharePoint, and other services. For instance, you can set up workflows that trigger notifications, update records, or collect data across different platforms. Automating repetitive tasks reduces manual effort, minimizes errors, and ensures consistent execution of processes, thereby enhancing productivity.

Integrating third-party applications

Microsoft 365 and SharePoint can be extended with various third-party applications available in the **Microsoft AppSource**. Integrations with popular tools such as Salesforce, Trello, and Dropbox can be configured to ensure data consistency and streamline operations. For example, synchronizing data between Salesforce and SharePoint allows sales teams to access customer documents directly within their CRM, improving response times and customer service quality.

Secure access and compliance

Integrating Microsoft 365 with identity management services such as Microsoft Entra (formerly Azure AD) ensures secure access and compliance. It provides **single sign-on** (**SSO**) capabilities, allowing users to authenticate once and gain access to multiple applications. This integration not only enhances security but also simplifies the user experience, reducing the need for multiple logins and improving productivity.

Custom development with Microsoft Graph

For organizations with specific needs, custom integrations can be developed using **Microsoft Graph**, the API gateway to data in Microsoft 365 (`https://developer.microsoft.com/en-us/graph`). Developers can create custom applications that interact with SharePoint and other Microsoft 365 services, enabling tailored solutions that meet unique business requirements. This flexibility ensures that the integration strategy aligns perfectly with organizational goals, driving productivity through bespoke solutions.

Integrating Microsoft 365 and SharePoint with other services creates a cohesive digital environment that supports seamless collaboration, efficient task management, and advanced data insights. By using built-in tools such as Teams, Planner, Power BI, and Power Automate, along with third-party applications and custom development, organizations can significantly enhance productivity and achieve a higher level of operational efficiency. Investing in these integrations not only simplifies workflows but also empowers employees to work smarter and more effectively.

Summary

This chapter provided a comprehensive overview of the Microsoft 365 and SharePoint platforms, detailing the main components and architecture where we gained practical insights into configuring Microsoft 365 tenant settings and learned about user provisioning and access control. Additionally, we explored effective implementation strategies in real-world scenarios and recognized the significance of integrating Microsoft 365 with other Microsoft services to optimize and maximize the platform's potential and capabilities. Furthermore, the discussion highlighted the role of security measures in maintaining data integrity and compliance across the system, highlighting the use of tools such as Microsoft Defender to safeguard organizational assets. We also examined the impact of seamless collaboration and communication tools within Microsoft 365 on improving operational efficiency and fostering a connected workplace environment. This understanding not only enhances our technical proficiency but also positions us to use Microsoft 365 and SharePoint for strategic business advantages.

In the next chapter, we will dive deep into the core elements of SharePoint and gain a thorough understanding of its architecture and the strategic planning of site collections and site structures, covering essential features such as document libraries, lists, and effective metadata management, which are crucial for organizing and retrieving information efficiently. Additionally, it will guide you on how to tailor the SharePoint environment to deliver a personalized and engaging user experience by exploring options for branding and theming, and enabling the creation of custom workflows and forms that streamline business processes.

2

SharePoint Essentials

This chapter provides an overview of the essential aspects of SharePoint with a comprehensive understanding of its architecture, planning, and management capabilities. The focus will be on practical skills and knowledge that can immediately be applied to enhance the organization's information management and user experience.

You will start by learning about the core components of the SharePoint information architecture and how they influence the organization's information management.

We will delve into the strategic planning of site collections and structures, which are crucial for efficient content organization and scalability, and you'll explore effective management of document libraries, lists, and metadata to streamline information retrieval and enhance productivity. We will then introduce **Power Platform**, a collection of powerful tools that extend SharePoint's functionality and customization capabilities by creating custom workflows and forms, essential for automating collaboration processes and improving efficiency. Additionally, we will cover branding and theming strategies to personalize the user experience, making a SharePoint environment not only functional but also engaging.

In this chapter, we are going to cover the following main topics:

- Understanding SharePoint architecture
- Site collection and site structure planning
- Document libraries, lists, and metadata management
- Introduction to Power Platform
- Creating custom workflows and forms
- Branding and theming for a personalized user experience

Through detailed explanations, you will gain the expertise needed to effectively design, implement, and manage a SharePoint environment that enhances organizational information management, boosts productivity, and creates a tailored user experience.

By the end of this chapter, you will be able to do the following:

- Understand SharePoint information architecture and its impact on information management
- Plan and structure site collections for optimal content organization
- Manage document libraries, lists, and metadata effectively
- Use Power Platform to enhance SharePoint functionality by creating custom workflows and forms to streamline business processes
- Implement branding and theming strategies to personalize the SharePoint user experience

So, let's get started!

Technical requirements

In this section, you will find the technical requirements necessary for completing the tasks in this chapter:

- User assigned with the required roles:
  - For the Microsoft admin portal, the user must have the Global Administrator or SharePoint Administrator role assigned
  - For the SharePoint sites, the user must have the Global Administrator or SharePoint Administrator role assigned
- Microsoft 365 subscription
- Access to SharePoint Online
- Internet connectivity for accessing online resources and services

> **Important note**
> The customizations outlined require the use of at least a Microsoft 365 Business Basic or Microsoft 365 E1 license.

Understanding SharePoint information architecture

Designing and implementing an effective information architecture is crucial for developing a smart and efficient intranet, hub, or site. The crucial first step in developing an effective information architecture is to understand the users and design a system that helps them easily find the information they need to complete their tasks efficiently.

Effective information architecture enhances user adoption, satisfaction, and productivity, helping reduce IT costs, mitigating information overload, and minimizing compliance and security risks.

In this section, you will learn the process of designing and implementing an effective information architecture for SharePoint. This involves analyzing user needs to understand who the users are, what information they require, and how they prefer to navigate and access it.

We will define the mechanisms to ensure consistency and ease of use across the environment by creating a logical site structure that reflects the flow of information and tasks within an organization and design intuitive navigation elements such as site, hub, global, and footer links.

By the end of this section, you will be proficient in designing and implementing an effective SharePoint information architecture that will enhance user experience, improve productivity, and support the organization's goals and objectives within the SharePoint environment.

Information architecture elements

Information architecture involves structuring and labeling the content to facilitate user interaction and task completion. On websites, it encompasses navigation, search functionality, site hierarchy, taxonomy, and security features. In modern SharePoint, information architecture also focuses on ensuring that the appropriate content reaches the right audience while adhering to the organization's content compliance regulations.

Information architecture in SharePoint encompasses six key components related to wayfinding:

- **Global navigation structure**: This is the primary navigation across a SharePoint tenant, organizing sites so users can locate content, including the main site of an intranet

- **Hub structure and organization**: Hubs allow the grouping of related topics, tasks, and content together for better coherence and accessibility

- **Local site and page navigation**: This involves the organization of content within individual sites and pages, enabling users to navigate and consume content efficiently

- **Metadata architecture**: Metadata influences search capabilities, browsing structures, and compliance and retention policies

- **Search experiences**: This aspect focuses on how users interact with and retrieve information through search functionalities in addition to browsing

- **Personalized content experiences**: This entails targeting specific content to particular users or user groups

Designing an effective structure for hubs, sites, and pages requires thorough planning and an understanding of the domain, content, user experience, design strategies, and SharePoint best practices.

However, information architecture is an ongoing process. As organizations, people, and projects evolve, continual learning about user behaviors will enable adjustments to enhance content discoverability.

Information architecture roles

An intranet's information architecture works best when different roles work together, such as intranet owners, departmental business owners, IT administrators, and hub owners, among others:

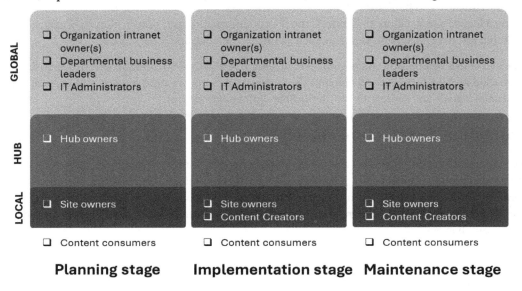

Figure 2.1 – Roles and stages

- **Organization intranet owners**: The organization intranet owners are a group of people who have different roles and responsibilities to oversee and guide the organization's intranet. They collaborate with business owners (departments) and IT admins to set up global and hub-level navigation. They mainly focus on designing and executing global and hub-level navigation.

- **Departmental business leaders**: Departmental business leaders oversee major parts of the organization, such as **human resources** (**HR**), marketing, and engineering. They collaborate with organizational intranet owners to make sure their part of the business is properly reflected in global and hub navigation. Departmental business leaders should be involved early in the planning stage to ensure business and user needs are met.

- **IT admins**: IT admins collaborate with organizational intranet owners and departmental business owners to set up the top-level navigational structure, such as creating the start page and hubs. They also assist in applying some governance policies for site creation and usage. IT admins participate in designing, executing, and sustaining information architecture as the business evolves and grows.

- **Hub owners**: Hub owners manage hub site settings, permissions, and navigation, and can associate or disassociate sites from the hub. They also configure search scopes, approve site association requests, and manage news roll-ups and activity feeds to ensure important updates are visible.

- **Site owners**: Site owners have full control over a site, including managing permissions, site settings, and content organization. They are responsible for configuring the site's structure, ensuring it meets organizational needs, maintaining overall site health, and facilitating collaboration by adding or removing users and managing access to site resources.

- **Content creators**: Content creators are responsible for generating and managing the content within a site. They create documents, pages, and multimedia resources, ensuring that information is accurate, up to date, and well organized. Content creators collaborate with team members, manage versions, and publish content that supports the organization's goals and projects.

- **Content consumers**: Content consumers are the end users who access and utilize the content provided on a site. They navigate through the site's resources, read documents, view pages, and engage with shared information. Content consumers rely on the organized structure and updated content provided by site owners and content creators to stay informed and perform their tasks efficiently.

Core concept – optimizing content management with distinct sites and efficient linking strategies

Creating individual sites for each specific topic, task, or unit of work is beneficial for effective content management and organization. This approach simplifies tracking and management of content collections and allows for easy rearrangement of sites in the navigation without disrupting links. Furthermore, when a topic becomes obsolete, the corresponding site can be easily archived or deleted.

To connect sites and content within this streamlined structure, consider using the following methods from the information architecture toolkit: utilize roll-up web parts such as news, highlighted content, or sites to dynamically display content from other sites, incorporate inline hyperlinks to provide additional details and enrich the user experience, including direct links to related sites in the navigation and use hubs to integrate groups of related sites.

One way to help users locate and access content within their sites is using navigation with different levels, in order to enable the users to quickly find the information for their tasks and collaboration.

Navigation levels

Consider three levels of navigation for modern SharePoint experiences:

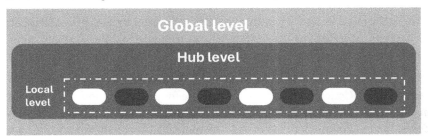

Figure 2.2 – Levels of navigation

- Global navigation for the entire intranet site collection
- Hub navigation for clusters of related sites
- Local navigation for individual sites

Global navigation

Many intranets feature a persistent top navigation bar that appears on every site. This **global navigation** creates a cohesive navigation experience for the intranet, visually connecting all the sites, content, and tools the viewers need to perform their tasks. Each organization has unique requirements for its global navigation, but common categories often include the following:

- *About Us*
- *News*
- *Operations*
- *Benefits*
- *Locations*
- *Administrative Services*
- *Policies and Procedures*

The primary goal of global navigation is to facilitate content browsing. Given the limited space available for global navigation links, these links typically lead to major category navigation pages, sub-links, or a mega menu that provides sufficient information for viewers to find the content they need. Crafting labels that are both comprehensive and useful can be challenging due to the broad context required for global navigation. It's important to test the proposed navigation to ensure it resonates with users.

> **Important note**
> Global navigation is enabled through the SharePoint app bar on the home site. A home site is required to activate global navigation. Once enabled, global navigation will appear on the left side of every site and page.

Hub navigation

SharePoint hubs organize related sites based on projects, departments, divisions, regions, or concepts. They simplify the discovery of related content, such as news and site activities, and enable the application of common navigation, branding, and site structure across associated sites, facilitating search across all linked sites. Hub navigation is displayed above the local navigation on each site, just below the suite bar. This navigation is established in the site designated as the hub, defined by the hub owner, and shared across all associated sites.

A site can be part of only one hub at a time, but hubs can be interconnected through a combination of navigation links and associated hubs to enhance the navigation experience.

Local navigation

Local navigation refers to the menu options and links that help users navigate within a specific site or subsite; it includes the Quick Launch menu (on the left side for Team sites, on the site header for communication sites), which contains links to key sections such as document libraries and lists, and the top navigation bar at the top of the site, which can link to various parts of the current site or other sites within the collection. Additionally, features such as site contents and breadcrumbs provide easy access to all site elements and a trail of links showing the user's navigation path, respectively. Local navigation ensures users can efficiently find and access the content and features relevant to the site they are currently viewing.

Sites

A **site** is a top-level container that houses various content types and functionalities, providing a centralized hub for collaboration and information sharing. Sites can be customized to fit different organizational needs, ranging from team collaboration to project management, departmental communication, or company-wide intranets. Each site can include libraries for storing documents, lists for tracking information, and subsites for specific projects or teams. Sites also support integration with other Office 365 tools, allowing users to create, store, and manage content in a secure and accessible environment.

Pages

Pages are individual content areas within a site where users can present information and content in a structured format: used to display text, images, videos, documents, and other features, making them essential for communicating information and creating engaging user experiences.

Pages can be customized with different layouts and designs to suit various purposes, such as news articles, announcements, or dashboards, playing a critical role in how information is conveyed and consumed within a site, offering flexibility and ease of use for content creators and viewers alike.

Metadata architecture

In SharePoint Online, **metadata architecture** is a structured system that organizes, manages, and tags information to improve content discovery, governance, and collaboration. It involves the creation and use of site columns, content types, term stores, and managed metadata fields. Site columns standardize metadata across sites, while content types group these columns for specific document types, enhancing consistency and reusability. The term store is a centralized repository for managing taxonomy and term sets, ensuring uniformity and controlled vocabulary across the organization. Managed metadata fields link to these term sets, enabling hierarchical data classification and facilitating more efficient search, navigation, and information management.

Search experiences

Finally, we come to **search experiences** on SharePoint Online. It leverages the information architecture investments to help users locate content, even if they are unsure where it resides within the structure. Enhance content discovery and improve search outcomes by utilizing various search features such as acronyms, bookmarks, Q&A, floor plans, and locations.

That's a wrap on this section, which showed the fundamental elements and roles involved in designing and implementing an effective SharePoint information architecture where understanding the users, organizing the content, and structuring the navigation are crucial steps in creating a seamless and efficient SharePoint environment. This is vital information since a well-designed information architecture not only enhances user adoption and satisfaction but also improves productivity, reduces IT costs, and mitigates compliance and security risks. By structuring and labeling content effectively, you ensure that users can easily find the information they need, which is essential for completing their tasks efficiently.

As we move forward, we will delve deeper into the specifics of site collection and site structure planning. Effective site collection planning is fundamental to creating a scalable and manageable SharePoint environment, involving defining the hierarchy and organization of your sites to reflect the business structure and workflows.

Site collection and site structure planning

Strategically planning the SharePoint Online site collections starts with aligning the structure with the organization's objectives. This involves understanding the key goals such as enhancing collaboration, improving information sharing, and streamlining business processes. Engaging with different user groups through surveys and interviews helps uncover their needs and expectations. By setting clear objectives and defining success metrics, such as user adoption rates and productivity improvements, we can ensure that the SharePoint deployment effectively supports the organizational goals:

- **Identify key goals**: Align the SharePoint structure with the strategic goals of the organization, such as improving collaboration, enhancing information sharing, or streamlining business processes

- **Understand user needs**: Conduct surveys and interviews to understand the needs and expectations of different user groups within the organization

- **Set clear objectives**: Define what success looks like for the SharePoint deployment, including specific metrics for user adoption, satisfaction, and productivity improvements

Map out information architecture

Creating an effective information architecture is crucial for a successful SharePoint deployment.

- **Content inventory**: Perform a content inventory to identify all existing content types, their locations, and their owners.

- **Taxonomy development**: Develop a clear taxonomy that includes site collections, libraries, lists, and metadata terms. Ensure it reflects how users think about and search for information.

- **Content life cycle**: Plan for the entire content life cycle, from creation and usage to archiving and disposal, ensuring compliance with regulatory requirements.

Planning site collections

Organizing site collections around business functions, projects, and departments enhances usability and access control.

- **Business function sites**: Create site collections for major business functions (e.g., HR, finance, marketing) to group related content and ensure easy access

- **Project-based sites**: For large or strategic projects, establish dedicated site collections to centralize all project-related documents, tasks, and collaboration

- **Departmental sites**: Set up site collections for each department to facilitate departmental workflows and content management

- **Hub sites**: Use hub sites to connect related site collections and create a cohesive navigation experience across different areas of the organization

Designing for flexibility and scalability

To ensure long-term success, design the SharePoint structure to be flexible and scalable.

- **Modular structure**: Design site collections and libraries to be modular, allowing for easy scaling as the organization grows

- **Adaptability**: Ensure the structure can adapt to changes in organizational needs, such as new departments or shifting business priorities

- **Future-proofing**: Consider upcoming SharePoint features and integrations that may impact site collections and plan accordingly, enabling seamless adaptation to future changes

Leveraging metadata and content types

Effective use of metadata and content types improves searchability and content organization.

- **Standardize metadata**: Implement standardized metadata across site collections, using custom columns to capture specific details such as project names and document types to improve searchability and content organization

- **Content types**: Use content types to define templates and metadata for specific types of documents, ensuring consistency and ease of use

- **Managed metadata service**: Set up a managed metadata service to maintain a consistent set of terms and facilitate accurate tagging and enhanced search results

Implementing effective navigation

Designing intuitive navigation is key to enhancing user experience.

- **Global navigation**: Create a global navigation menu that provides easy access to all major site collections and important resources

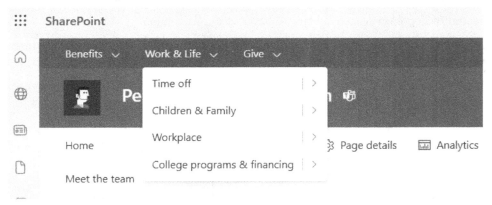

Figure 2.3 – Global navigation

- **Local navigation**: Design intuitive local navigation within each site collection to help users find content quickly

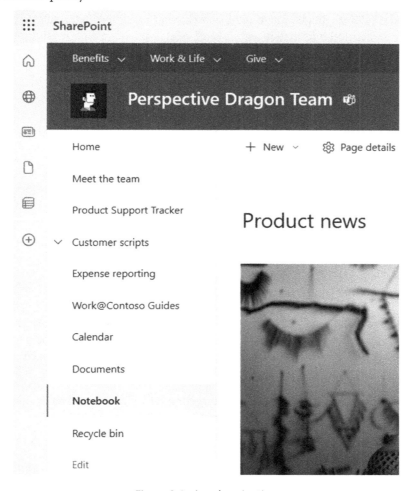

Figure 2.4 – Local navigation

- **Hub and spoke model**: Use the hub and spoke model to connect related sites, providing a seamless navigation experience across the organization

Enhancing search capabilities

Optimizing search functionality helps users find content quickly and accurately.

- **Search configuration**: Customize search settings to enhance content discovery, including configuring search schemas, result sources, and query rules to improve search results

- **Search features**: Utilize advanced search features such as bookmarks, Q&A, acronyms, and locations to improve search outcomes

- **Promoted results**: Highlight important documents and pages in search results to ensure users can easily find critical information

Planning for governance and compliance

Establishing a robust governance framework is essential for managing the SharePoint environment.

- **Governance framework**: Establish a governance framework that defines roles, responsibilities, and policies for managing the SharePoint environment (to control access, site creation, and content life cycle management.)

- **Permissions management**: Clearly define and manage user permissions to control access to content and ensure security

- **Compliance policies**: Implement compliance policies to meet regulatory requirements, protect sensitive information, and provide training and documentation to users and administrators on governance best practices

Enabling personalization and audience targeting

Personalizing the SharePoint experience enhances user engagement and relevance. It ensures that users see the most pertinent information based on their roles or departments. Allow users to customize their views and access frequently used content quickly, creating a more personalized and efficient user experience:

- **Audience targeting**: Configure audience targeting for web parts and navigational links to deliver relevant content to specific user groups

- **Personalized experiences**: Use audience targeting in communication sites and SharePoint news to create personalized user experiences

- **User preferences**: Allow users to customize their views and access frequently used content quickly

Planning for multilingual support

If the organization operates in multiple languages, enabling multilingual capabilities in SharePoint is crucial. Configure language settings and translation options to allow users to switch between languages. This will provide a seamless user experience.

- **Multilingual features**: Enable multilingual capabilities if the organization operates in different languages

- **Translation management**: Set up processes for translating site content and UI elements to ensure all users can access information in their preferred language

- **Consistent updates**: Regularly update translations to reflect changes in content and ensure accuracy

By following these detailed steps, we can strategically plan and structure SharePoint Online site collections, ensuring an organized, scalable, and user-friendly environment that supports the organization's goals and enhances productivity.

Document libraries, lists, and metadata management

Effectively managing content in SharePoint Online requires a solid knowledge of document libraries, lists, and metadata. These components are central to SharePoint's content management system, facilitating the organization, storage, and retrieval of information in a structured manner.

Document libraries

Document libraries in SharePoint Online serve as centralized repositories for storing and managing various types of documents.

These libraries can be customized to handle specific content, such as policy documents, project files, and multimedia.

By organizing documents in libraries, users can easily locate and manage their content, ensuring that important files are accessible and organized:

- **Version control**: SharePoint's version control feature allows users to track changes to documents over time. This is crucial for maintaining a history of document edits, enabling users to revert to previous versions if necessary. Version control ensures that all users are working with the most up-to-date information, while also preserving a record of changes for auditing purposes.

- **Permissions management**: Configuring permissions at the library, folder, and document levels helps secure sensitive information. SharePoint allows administrators to control who can view, edit, or manage specific documents, ensuring that only authorized users have access to confidential content. This granular control helps maintain data security and compliance with organizational policies.

- **Document templates**: Utilizing document templates within libraries standardizes content creation across the organization. Templates ensure that documents adhere to consistent formatting and metadata standards, making it easier to manage and search for content. This consistency is particularly important for documents that require uniformity, such as reports, contracts, and forms.

- **Integration with Microsoft 365 applications**: SharePoint document libraries seamlessly integrate with Microsoft 365 applications, allowing users to open, edit, and save documents directly from SharePoint. This integration enhances productivity by enabling real-time collaboration and editing, reducing the need to switch between different platforms.

Practical examples

The following are some common document libraries that organizations set up to help their business processes:

1. **HR Documents library**:

    - **Purpose**: To store and manage HR-related documents, such as employee records, policies, procedures, and training materials

    - **Structure**:

Figure 2.5 – The HR Documents library

    - **Folders**: Employee Records, Policies, Procedures, and Training Materials

    - **Custom columns: Employee ID, Document Type (Policy, Procedure, Training Material), Status (Draft, Final), Effective Date, Review Date**, and **Document Owner**

    - **Permissions**: Restricted access to HR personnel only, with different permission levels for viewing, editing, and managing documents

    - **Templates**: Standard templates for policy documents, procedure manuals, and training materials

    - **Metadata**: Employee name, department

2. **Project Management document library**:

- **Purpose**: To centralize documents related to specific projects, such as project plans, timelines, reports, and meeting notes

- **Structure**:

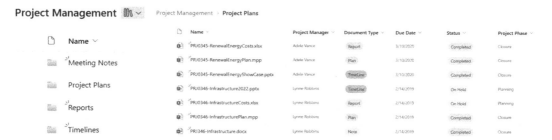

Figure 2.6 – The Project Management document library

- **Folders**: `Meeting Notes`, `Project Plans`, `Reports`, and `Timelines`
- **Custom columns: Name, Project Manager, Document Type (Plan, Report, Note, TimeLine), Due Date**, and **Status (In Progress, Completed, On Hold)**
- **Permissions**: Access for project team members, with specific permissions for project managers and stakeholders
- **Templates**: Project plan templates, report templates, meeting note templates
- **Metadata: Project Phase** (*Initiation*, *Planning*, *Execution*, *Closure*), Priority

3. **The Marketing Documents library**:

- **Purpose**: To manage marketing assets, such as campaigns, promotional materials, brand guidelines, and creative assets.

- **Structure**:

Figure 2.7 – The Marketing Documents library

- **Folders**: `Campaigns`, `Promotional Materials`, `Brand Guidelines`, and `Creative Assets`

- **Custom columns**: CampaignName, AssetType (**Image**, **Video**, **Document**), ApprovalStatus, CampaignStartDate, ExpiryDate, and TargetAudience

- **Permissions**: Marketing team access, with additional permissions for external partners and contractors

- **Templates**: Templates for marketing plans, creative briefs, and promotional content

- **Metadata**: **ContentType** (*Digital*, *Print*), **ApprovedBy**

Creating and structuring these document libraries involves thoughtful planning and customization to ensure that each library serves its intended purpose efficiently. By leveraging custom columns, metadata, templates, and permissions, organizations can ensure that documents are well organized, easily accessible, and secure, thereby enhancing overall productivity and collaboration.

Lists

SharePoint lists are designed to manage structured data, such as tasks, events, contacts, and issues. Lists provide a versatile way to organize and track information, supporting a wide range of business scenarios. By using lists, organizations can capture and manage data in a structured format, making it easier to analyze and report on key information:

- **Custom columns**: Customizing lists with various columns allows organizations to capture relevant data types, including text, choice, date, and lookup columns. This flexibility supports a wide range of business needs, from simple task tracking to complex project management. Custom columns ensure that lists can be tailored to capture the specific data required for different processes.

- **Views and filters**: Creating custom views and filters enhances the accessibility and usability of list data. Users can group, filter, and sort information to display data in ways that meet their specific needs. For example, a project manager might create a view that shows only high-priority tasks, while a team member might filter tasks assigned to them. Custom views and filters make it easier for users to find and focus on the most relevant information.

- **Integration with workflows**: Integrating lists with SharePoint workflows and Power Automate automates business processes, such as approvals, notifications, and data updates. This integration streamlines operations by reducing manual effort and ensuring that processes are consistently followed. Automated workflows enhance efficiency and help ensure that tasks and approvals are completed in a timely manner.

- **Mobile access**: SharePoint lists are accessible via mobile devices, allowing users to view and update information on the go. This mobile access supports remote work and enhances productivity by enabling users to stay connected and manage their tasks from anywhere. Mobile access ensures that critical information is always at users' fingertips, regardless of their location.

Practical examples

Some common types of lists that organizations use to facilitate business processes are as follows:

1. **HR list – employee onboarding checklist**:

   - **Purpose**: To track the progress of new employee onboarding tasks

Employee Onboarding Checklist ☆

Task Name ⌄	Assigned To ⌄	Due Date ⌄	Status ⌄	Priority ⌄	Comments ⌄
Complete HR Paperwork	Joni Sherman	6/19/2024 5:00 PM	Not Started	High	Needs to be completed before the first day.
Setup Workstation	Joni Sherman	6/21/2024 5:00 PM	In Progress	Medium	Ensure all necessary software is installed.
Attend Orientation	Joni Sherman	6/22/2024 5:00 PM	Completed	High	Orientation scheduled for 9 AM.
Meet Team	Joni Sherman	6/23/2024 5:00 PM	Not Started	Low	Arrange a meeting with the team.
Complete Training Modules	Joni Sherman	6/29/2024 5:00 PM	In Progress	Medium	Training modules are accessible online.

Figure 2.8 – Employee Onboarding Checklist

   - **Columns**:

     - **Task Name** (single line of text)
     - **Assigned To** (person or group)
     - **Due Date** (date and time)
     - **Status** (**choice**: Not Started, In Progress, Completed)
     - **Priority** (**choice**: High, Medium, Low)
     - **Comments** (multiple lines of text)

   - **Views**:

     - **Default view**: Group by **Status** to see tasks at different stages
     - **Filtered view**: Show tasks assigned to the current user

- **Integration**: Link with a Power Automate workflow to notify HR staff when tasks are due or completed

- **Usage**: This list helps HR manage and monitor the completion of onboarding tasks for each new employee, ensuring a smooth onboarding process

2. **Project management list – Project Task Tracker**:

- **Purpose**: To manage tasks and deadlines for a specific project

Project Task Tracker ☆

Task Title ∨	Description ∨	Assigned To ∨	Start Date ∨	Due Date ∨	Priority ∨	Status ∨	Project Phase ∨
Define Project Scope	Outline the project scope and objectives.	Adele Vance	5/31/2024 5:00 PM	6/4/2024 5:00 PM	High	Completed	Initiation
Assemble Project Team	Gather team members and assign roles.	Lidia Holloway	6/5/2024 5:00 PM	6/7/2024 5:00 PM	High	In Progress	Planning
Develop Project Plan	Create a detailed project plan.	Adele Vance	6/8/2024 5:00 PM	6/14/2024 5:00 PM	Medium	Not Started	Planning
Resource Allocation	Allocate resources for project tasks.	Lynne Robbins	6/15/2024 5:00 PM	6/17/2024 5:00 PM	Medium	Not Started	Execution
Execute Project Tasks	Carry out project tasks as per the plan.	Lynne Robbins	6/18/2024 5:00 PM	7/14/2024 5:00 PM	High	In Progress	Execution
Monitor and Control	Track project progress and make adjustments.	Johanna Lorenz	7/15/2024 5:00 PM	7/29/2024 5:00 PM	High	Not Started	Monitoring
Project Closure	Close the project and finalize documentation.	Adele Vance	7/31/2024 5:00 PM	8/4/2024 5:00 PM	Medium	Not Started	Closure

Figure 2.9 – The Project Task Tracker list

- **Columns: Task Title, Description, Assigned To, Start Date, Due Date, Priority, Status, and Project Phase**

- **Views**:

  - **Gantt chart view**: Visual representation of tasks over time

  - **Calendar view**: Display tasks by due date

  - **Filtered view**: Show tasks by project phase

- **Integration**: Connect with Microsoft Planner for detailed task management and tracking

- **Usage**: Project managers use this list to assign and track tasks, ensuring that project milestones and deadlines are met efficiently

3. **Marketing list – Campaign Tracker**:

- **Purpose**: To track marketing campaigns and their performance

- **Columns: Campaign Name, Start Date, End Date, Campaign Type, Target Audience, Budget, Status, and Results**

- **Views**:

  - **Calendar view**: Display campaigns by start and end dates
  - **Filtered view**: Show active campaigns
  - **Summary view**: Group by **Campaign Type** to analyze performance by type

- **Integration**: Use Power BI to create dashboards for visualizing campaign performance metrics

- **Usage**: Marketing teams use this list to plan, execute, and review marketing campaigns, tracking their progress and results

Creating and structuring these lists involves understanding the specific needs of each department and tailoring the columns, views, and integrations to meet those needs. By doing so, organizations can enhance their efficiency, streamline workflows, and improve overall productivity.

Metadata management

Metadata management in SharePoint Online involves the strategic organization and maintenance of metadata, which is data about data. Effective metadata management ensures that information is classified consistently, making it easier to find, retrieve, and manage content across the SharePoint environment.

This involves several key components:

- **Custom columns**: Adding custom columns to both document libraries and lists enables organizations to capture specific metadata, such as project names, document types, status, author, and date. Custom columns help classify and organize content, making it easier to search for and retrieve relevant information. This structured approach to metadata ensures that important details are consistently captured across the organization.

- **Content types**: Using content types to define and standardize metadata and templates for specific documents and list items ensures consistency in content management. Content types allow organizations to apply specific metadata fields and templates to different types of content, such as contracts, reports, or meeting minutes. This standardization simplifies content creation and improves the accuracy of metadata tagging.

- **Managed metadata service**: Implementing a managed metadata service helps maintain a consistent set of terms across the SharePoint environment. This service supports the creation and management of term sets and term groups, which can be used to tag and classify content. Consistent metadata terms improve search results and ensure that content is organized in a logical and meaningful way.

- **Tagging and classification**: Allowing users to tag content with relevant metadata terms enhances searchability. Consistent tagging helps users find and filter content efficiently, reducing the time spent searching for information. Metadata-driven classification ensures that content is categorized accurately, making it easier to manage and retrieve.

- **Faceted navigation**: Faceted navigation allows users to filter and sort content based on metadata attributes, providing a dynamic and intuitive way to explore information. Faceted navigation enhances the user experience by enabling users to narrow down search results and find specific content quickly. This feature is particularly useful for large libraries or lists with extensive metadata.

Implementing and managing document libraries, lists, and metadata effectively in SharePoint Online helps create a structured, organized, and user-friendly environment. These tools support content management, improve searchability, and streamline business processes, enhancing overall productivity and collaboration within the organization.

Practical examples

These are some concrete instances of metadata that organizations typically generate to facilitate business operations:

HR metadata for employee records:

- **Employee ID**: A unique identifier for each employee
- **Department:** *HR, Finance, Marketing, IT, Sales*
- **Employment type:** *Full-time, Part-time, Contractor, Intern*
- **Hire date:** The date the employee was hired
- **Manager**: The employee's direct supervisor
- **Status**: *Active, On Leave, Terminated*

Usage: This metadata helps HR track employee information efficiently, making it easy to filter and sort records by department, employment type, or status

Project management metadata for project documents:

- **Project name**: The name of the project
- **Project manager**: The individual responsible for the project
- **Start date**: The project's start date
- **End date**: The project's end date
- **Project phase**: *Initiation, Planning, Execution, Closure*
- **Priority**: *High, Medium, Low*
- **Status**: *Not Started, In Progress, Completed, On Hold*

Usage: This metadata enables project managers to organize and manage project documents, making it easy to track the progress of various projects and prioritize tasks

Marketing metadata for campaign assets:

- **Campaign name**: The name of the marketing campaign

- **Campaign type**: *Digital, Print, Social Media, Email*

- **Start date**: The campaign start date

- **End date**: The campaign end date

- **Target audience**: The intended audience for the campaign

- **Budget**: The allocated budget for the campaign

- **Approval status**: *Pending, Approved, Rejected*

Usage: This metadata helps the marketing team manage and track various campaign assets, ensuring that campaigns are executed smoothly and within budget

Implementing metadata for these specific areas involves understanding the unique needs of each department and tailoring the metadata fields accordingly. By doing so, organizations can enhance their content management, improve searchability, and streamline business processes, leading to increased efficiency and productivity.

Introducing Power Platform

Many organizations face the challenge of building effective solutions for their users. Modernizing systems is tough, and with limited resources, keeping up with the fast-paced business world seems impossible. The demand for custom applications has skyrocketed, often exceeding what departments can deliver by up to five times.

This isn't just about resource shortages; it's also about adapting to a rapidly changing business landscape.

Here are some of the key hurdles:

- **Changing workforce expectations**: Millennials and Gen Z now make up most of the workforce, and they expect the workplace to reflect their tech-savvy lifestyles. They're used to personalized experiences and social media collaboration, so businesses need to offer custom, streamlined, and collaborative digital tools to fully leverage their skills.

- **High costs of custom application development**: Custom apps are pricey and time-consuming, not just to build but also to maintain. The costs quickly add up, making it a significant investment.

- **Need for agility**: Traditional development timelines are too slow. Businesses can't afford to wait months for a solution or weeks for minor changes. They need to adapt quickly to stay competitive.

- **Efficient scaling of development**: Meeting the ever-changing needs requires a new approach to development. By empowering power users (citizen developers) to contribute to the development process, organizations can create hybrid teams that boost overall productivity and growth.

Power Platform offers a practical solution to these challenges. Its low-code tools and enterprise-level development capabilities foster collaboration between citizen developers and professional developers, enabling the creation of targeted solutions tailored to user needs.

Take field technicians as an example. They often need to request mechanical parts to complete jobs. Traditionally, this process involves delays as they wait for inventory managers to respond, only to find out parts aren't in stock. This bottleneck can be eliminated by using Power Apps to create a dedicated app that allows technicians to check inventory levels in real time and request parts on the spot. Technicians, who best understand their needs, can prototype the app using Power Apps, choosing the most intuitive interface and user experience.

Once they have a working prototype, professional developers can step in to add advanced features, such as real-time inventory checks via APIs. These APIs can be seamlessly integrated into Power Apps and Power Automate, ensuring the solution is robust and efficient. This approach, known as **fusion development**, maximizes the strengths of both citizen developers and professional developers, making it a win-win for the entire organization.

Microsoft Power Platform consists of four key products: **Power Apps**, **Power Automate**, **Power BI**, and **Power Pages**.

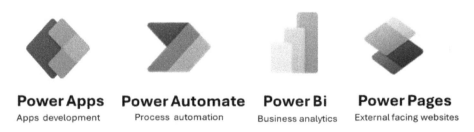

Figure 2.10 – Power Platform

Let us explore these products one by one:

- **Microsoft Power Apps** gives a fast and easy way to build custom apps for business needs with low-code development. It's a powerful suite of app development services that includes a scalable data platform (Microsoft Dataverse) and can connect with both cloud and on-premises data sources. With Power Apps, we can create web and mobile applications that work on any device.

- **Microsoft Power Automate** helps create automated workflows between applications and services. It's perfect for automating repetitive tasks such as sending weekly update emails or managing approval processes. Its user-friendly interface allows anyone, from beginners to experienced developers, to streamline their work.

- **Microsoft Power BI** is the go-to tool for turning data into insights. It helps analyze data and share those insights through visual reports and dashboards, enabling quick, informed decisions. Power BI is scalable across the entire organization and comes with built-in security and governance features. With it, we can share dashboards that track key metrics such as sales data, progress toward goals, or employee performance.

- **Microsoft Power Pages** is a secure, low-code platform for building and managing modern external-facing business websites. Pages allows you to quickly design, configure, and publish websites that work seamlessly across browsers and devices. With rich templates, a fluid design studio, and an integrated learning hub, Power Pages helps to create sites tailored to business needs. It's the latest addition to the Power Platform family, allowing to build sites using the same shared business data from Microsoft Dataverse that can be used for apps, workflows, and analytics.

Power Platform enables organizations to empower their team members to create their own solutions using an intuitive low-code or no-code set of services by simplifying the solution-building process, allowing solutions to be rapidly developed.

Supporting tools

Alongside these main products, several tools enhance Power Platform solutions:

- **Microsoft Copilot Studio**: A low-code tool that brings together powerful conversational AI capabilities, including custom GPTs and generative AI plugins, to customize Microsoft Copilot for Microsoft 365 or build standalone copilots.

- **Connectors**: These allow us to connect apps, data, and devices in the cloud. Think of them as bridges for information and commands. There are over 1,000 prebuilt connectors, including popular ones such as Salesforce, Office 365, Twitter, Dropbox, and Google services.

- **AI Builder**: This tool adds AI capabilities to workflows and Power Apps without needing any coding. It helps predict outcomes and improve business performance easily.

- **Dataverse**: A scalable data service and app platform that lets you securely store and manage data from multiple sources, integrating it into business applications with a common data model for consistency.

- **Power FX**: The low-code programming language used across Power Platform, making it easy to write and understand code for apps.

- **Managed environments**: These are secure and isolated environments within Power Platform where applications can be built, tested, and deployed while maintaining control over data and resources.

These tools make it easy to build tailored solutions that fit specific business needs, empowering everyone in the organization to contribute to development and innovation.

Creating custom workflows and forms

Microsoft Power Automate provides powerful tools for automating business processes and creating custom forms and applications. With Power Automate, we can build workflows to streamline repetitive tasks, integrate data between systems, and trigger actions based on events. Power Apps allows us to rapidly build low-code applications with forms, views, and logic tailored to specific needs.

By combining the capabilities of Power Automate and Power Apps, we can create end-to-end solutions that boost productivity, improve data management, and deliver better user experiences.

Whether we need to automate employee onboarding, track sales leads, or gather customer feedback, these Microsoft 365 tools empower us to build custom solutions without extensive coding knowledge where we can quickly configure workflows and forms to optimize business processes.

Create an approval workflow

To create an approval workflow in Power Automate, follow these steps:

1. **Define the approval process**:

    I.   Identify the specific actions and individuals involved in the approval process.

    II. Determine the triggers for the approval process, such as when a new item is created in a SharePoint list.

2. **Choose the trigger**:

    I.   Select the trigger for the approval workflow in Power Automate. For example, when an item is created in a SharePoint list.

    II. Configure the trigger to initiate the approval process at the right time and in response to the desired events or actions.

3. **Set up the approval process**:

    I.   Choose the approval action. For example, **Start and Wait for an Approval** or **Create an Approval**.

    II. Configure the approval action to include the necessary details, such as the title, description, and assigned approver.

    III. Use dynamic content to include relevant information from the SharePoint list, such as the project title.

4. **Configure approval rules**:

    I.   Determine the approval rules, such as the number of approvers required and the approval process sequence.

    II.   Configure the approval rules to ensure that the approval process proceeds in a linear sequence or parallel, depending on the specific requirements.

5. **Test and refine the workflow**:

    I.   Test the approval workflow to ensure that it functions as expected.

    II.   Refine the workflow by analyzing and optimizing its performance to maximize efficiency and effectiveness.

By following these steps, you can create a comprehensive approval workflow in Power Automate that streamlines a business process and enhances productivity.

Creating a SharePoint list form

Here are the steps to create a SharePoint list form using Power Apps:

1. **Create a SharePoint list**:

   - Create a new SharePoint list or use an existing one.
   - Customize the list columns to match the fields you want to collect in your form.

2. **Customize the form with Power Apps**: In the SharePoint list, click **Integrate | Power Apps | Customize forms**:

   - Power Apps Studio will open, automatically creating a simple app with a form screen connected to the SharePoint list.
   - In Power Apps, you can customize the form by doing the following:
     - Adding, removing, and reordering columns
     - Setting fields to be read-only or conditionally visible
     - Adding conditional formatting and validations
     - Changing the layout, colors, and theme

3. **Publish the custom form**:

   - Save the Power Apps app.
   - Publish the custom form back to SharePoint by selecting **Publish to SharePoint**.

4. **Use the custom form**:

   - The published custom form will now be used whenever the SharePoint list is accessed.
   - Users can interact with the enhanced form within SharePoint without needing to open Power Apps separately.

By following these steps, we can easily create a custom SharePoint list form using Power Apps. This allows you to tailor the form to your specific needs, add advanced functionality, and provide a better user experience all within the SharePoint environment.

Branding and theming for a personalized user experience

Branding and theming in SharePoint Online modern sites are essential for creating a personalized user experience that aligns with your organization's identity and enhances user engagement. By using the robust customization options available, we can tailor the appearance of your SharePoint sites to reflect your company's branding, including logos, color schemes, and fonts. Theming allows for a consistent visual identity across all pages, reinforcing brand recognition and providing a cohesive look and feel. This personalized approach not only enhances aesthetic appeal but also improves usability by ensuring that navigation and content presentation are intuitive and aligned with user expectations.

SharePoint Online's modern experience makes it easy to implement these customizations, enabling organizations to create dynamic, user-friendly sites that support their communication and collaboration goals effectively.

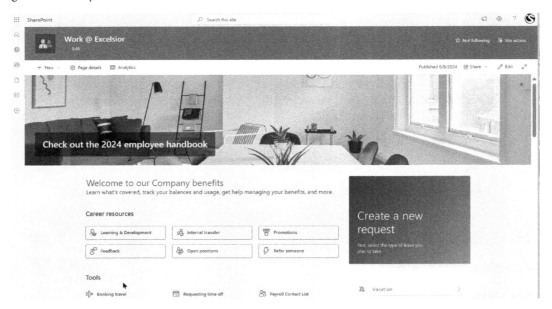

Figure 2.11 – An example of branding

In the modern SharePoint experience, we can effortlessly customize a site's appearance to align with the company or organizational brand. We can modify the logo, colors, and navigation, often without needing to write any code. Branding can be applied to individual sites, groups of sites, or across all sites within your organization.

SharePoint offers a modern and responsive set of default site themes that ensure a consistent look across various devices. With these themes, we can easily customize your site's logo and colors to align with your brand identity.

Additionally, site templates provide pre-designed layouts and functionalities to help you create a unique site experience. The best part is that custom themes and site templates can be used without worrying about compatibility issues when SharePoint is updated.

This means you can create more color schemes beyond the default options using custom themes, and control the site theme, navigation, default applications, and other settings using custom site templates. These custom themes and site templates can be applied to new sites when they are created or to existing sites or groups of sites, ensuring a consistent brand experience across the SharePoint environment.

We can personalize a SharePoint site by selecting and customizing one of the default SharePoint themes, using a company-approved theme that aligns with the branding, or opting for one of the classic experience designs.

Changing the colors of a SharePoint site using a theme

To enhance the visual appeal of a SharePoint site and ensure consistency with the organization's branding, we can easily change the colors by applying a custom theme.

Follow these steps to update the color scheme of your SharePoint site:

1. On the SharePoint site, click **Settings** and then click **Change the look** | **Theme**.

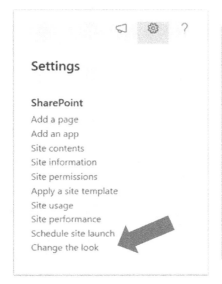
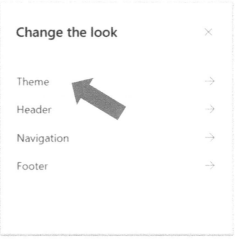

Figure 2.12 – Theme settings

2. Click **Theme**. A preview of the selected theme will show what the site looks like with the theme applied. Click **Save** to apply the theme to the site or click **Cancel** to revert the site to the initial theme configuration.

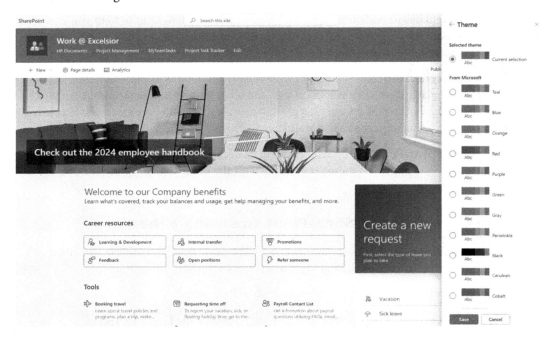

Figure 2.13 – Theme selection

3. To personalize the colors of a SharePoint theme, select the theme and click **Customize**.

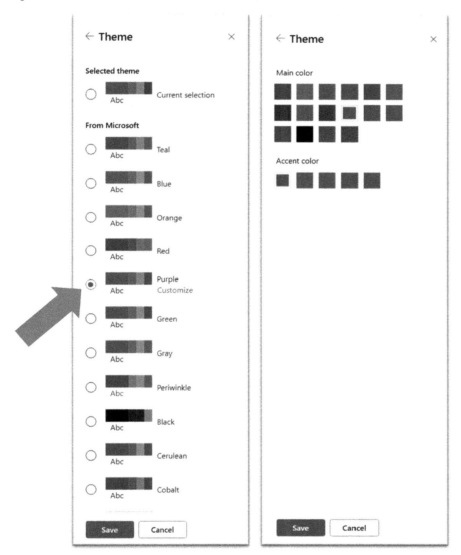

Figure 2.14 – Theme customization

4. Pick main and accent colors, then click **Save** to apply them to the site.

Customizing a SharePoint site header

To create a more personalized and visually appealing SharePoint site, we can customize the site header by following these steps:

1. On the SharePoint site, click **Settings** and then click **Change the look | Header**.

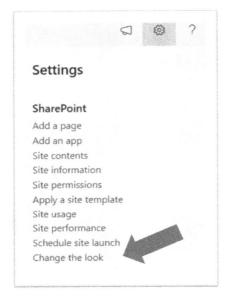 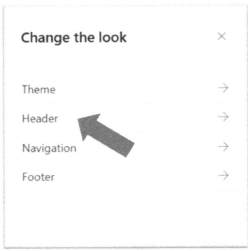

Figure 2.15 – Header customization

2.   Choose a **Layout** option:

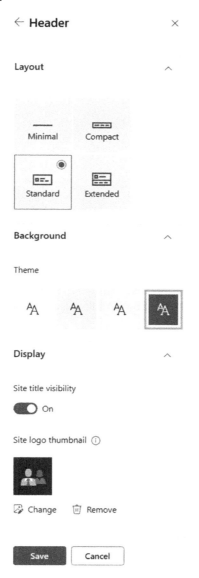

Figure 2.16 – Header customization – Layout

- **Minimal**: Features a compact design with all content aligned in a single line, including the small site logo, site title, site navigation, site actions, and labels.

- **Compact**: Provides a taller layout featuring a full-size site logo, with all content arranged on a single row.

- **Standard**: Features the full-size site logo with content divided into two rows.

- **Extended**: Largest design, with content divided into two sections. The site logo, site title, and an optional background image are positioned above the other contents.

3. In the **Background** section, choose a theme color to change the background color of your site header. Select the **Extended** option to set the focal point for the background image.

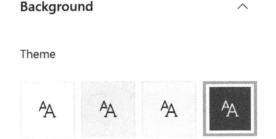

Figure 2.17 – Header customization – Background

4. In the **Display** section, choose **Site title visibility** to show/hide the title from the site header. To modify the site logo and site logo thumbnail, select the **Change** option.

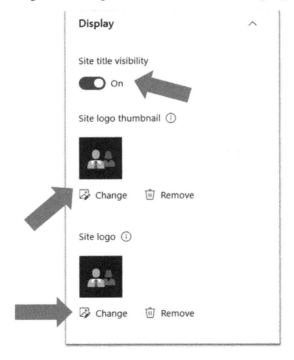

Figure 2.18 – Header customization – Display

5. Once finished, click **Save**.

Customizing SharePoint site navigation

Customizing SharePoint site navigation is a key aspect of enhancing user experience and ensuring that visitors can easily access important content.

Here are some common ways to customize the SharePoint site navigation:

1. On the SharePoint site, click **Settings** and then click **Change the look | Navigation**.

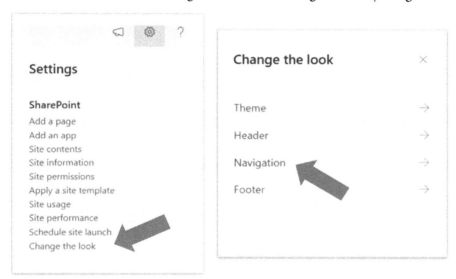

Figure 2.19 – Navigation customization

2. Choose from the following options: choose **Site navigation visibility** to show/hide the navigation. Select the menu style: **Mega menu** or **Cascading**.

Figure 2.20 – Navigation customization – site navigations and menu style

3. Once finished, click **Save**.

Customizing a SharePoint site footer

To enhance the functionality and appearance of a SharePoint site, we can customize the site footer with various elements.

Here are several options for customizing the footer:

1. On the SharePoint site, click **Settings** and then click **Change the look | Footer**.

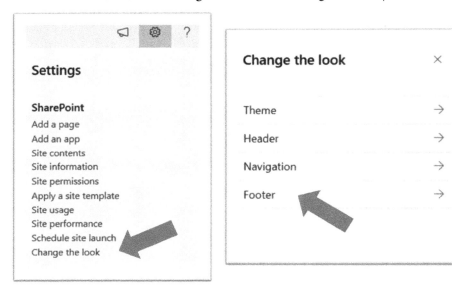

Figure 2.21 – Footer customization

2. Choose from the following options: choose **Enable** to show/hide the footer. Select the layout: **Simple** or **Extended**:

- **Simple**: This shows a single level of links and labels, spanning up to eight columns wide

- **Extended**: This shows two levels of links and labels, spanning also up to eight columns wide

Figure 2.22 – Footer customization: Enable and Layout

3. To add an image of the logo to the footer, click **Upload**, enter a display name to name the footer, and select a color for the background.

Figure 2.23 – Footer customization: Logo, Display name, and Background

4. Once finished, click **Save**.

Customizing the branding and theme of a SharePoint Online site is crucial for reflecting a company's identity. We can create a cohesive visual style that reinforces brand recognition and enhances user engagement with a consistent design that not only makes the site more visually appealing but also helps create easier navigation and user interaction. With it, the organization can significantly improve communication and collaboration within the team, ensuring that the site aligns with the corporate branding, and create a professional/unified appearance.

Summary

In this chapter, we've explored the intricate architecture of SharePoint and its impact on information management. We have learned about the core components of SharePoint information architecture, including site collections, site structure planning, and the management of document libraries, lists, and metadata. The introduction of Power Platform and its powerful tools has shown how SharePoint's functionality can be extended and customized, while branding and theming strategies have been discussed to personalize the user experience.

Looking ahead, the next chapter will delve deeper into the practical application of branding and custom forms. By doing so, we will ensure that we can effectively design, implement, and manage a SharePoint site and business process that meets the organization's needs and enhances productivity.

Part 2: Enhancing and Automating

Once you've mastered the essentials, it's time to explore the more advanced features that take SharePoint and Microsoft 365 environment to the next level. This section is all about pushing the boundaries of what you can do with these platforms: by diving into customization and automation, you can tailor workflows to your needs, streamline operations, and significantly boost productivity. Think of it as turning a solid foundation into a highly efficient machine that works for you.

In this part, we'll be looking at ways to customize SharePoint with branding and custom workflows that fit your unique business needs and will guide you through advanced tools such as Power Automate, helping you build workflows that save time by automating repetitive tasks.

This part contains the following chapters:

- *Chapter 3, Automating with Power Automate*
- *Chapter 4, Enhancing SharePoint – Site Templates, Forms, and Power Apps*

3

Automating with Power Automate

In this chapter, we will explore how to make SharePoint even more powerful by introducing automation and custom workflows. Using Power Automate, we can simplify and optimize various business processes, making them more efficient and productive. You'll learn how to create custom workflows tailored to your specific business needs and automate those repetitive tasks that eat up your time so that you can focus on more important activities. Plus, we'll look at how these automated solutions can boost overall functionality and collaboration in the organization.

As we move through this chapter, you'll get hands-on experience in designing and creating automated workflows with Power Automate. These workflows will not only make things run smoother but also ensure that your processes fit perfectly with your business goals, helping you gain practical skills and tools to bring about significant improvements in operations through automation. By the end of this chapter, you'll be well-versed in best practices for customizing and integrating workflows, enhancing user experiences by streamlining business processes, and increasing efficiency in your organization.

In this chapter, we're going to cover the following main topics:

- Overview and key concepts within Power Automate
- Building workflows
- Automating business processes with a real-life scenario
- Power Automate – best practices

By mastering these topics, you'll be able to leverage the full potential of SharePoint and your business process, driving productivity and improving your workload. This chapter will equip you with the knowledge and skills needed to implement and deploy Power Automate effectively. By following best practices, you'll ensure that automated processes significantly contribute to your organization's success.

Technical requirements

To complete the tasks outlined in this chapter, you'll need the following:

- A Microsoft Office 365 subscription

- Access to SharePoint Online

- Internet connectivity for accessing online resources and services

> **Important note**
> The operations outlined in this chapter require the use of a regular **Microsoft Office 365 license** with a **Power Automate** app license assigned.

Overview and key concepts of Power Automate

Power Automate is an innovative service from Microsoft that's designed to automate workflows between various applications and services. It empowers users to streamline their routine tasks by creating automated workflows, known as flows, which trigger actions based on specified events. By leveraging Power Automate, individuals and organizations can enhance productivity, reduce manual effort, and ensure consistency in their processes:

Figure 3.1 – Power Automate

At its core, Power Automate facilitates the automation of tasks across multiple applications, ranging from email services to social media platforms and data storage solutions.

The primary components of Power Automate are as follows:

- **Flow**: A flow is a sequence of actions that are triggered by specific events. For instance, a flow might be configured to send an email notification whenever a new file is added to a designated folder in OneDrive.

- **Trigger**: A trigger is the event that initiates a flow.

- **Action**: Following the trigger, actions are the tasks that are executed by the flow.

- **Connector**: Connectors enable Power Automate to interact with a wide array of apps and services. There are hundreds of connectors available, including those for Microsoft services such as Office 365, as well as third-party services such as Google Drive, Twitter, and Salesforce.

- **Template**: Templates are pre-built flows that are created by Microsoft and the Power Automate community. These templates serve as excellent starting points for users, providing ready-made solutions that can be customized to meet specific needs.

Power Automate is designed with user-friendliness in mind, featuring a drag-and-drop interface that allows individuals with minimal technical expertise to create robust automations. Moreover, as part of Microsoft Power Platform, it integrates seamlessly with other tools such as Power Apps, Power BI, and Dynamics 365, enhancing its utility across various business functions.

Building workflows

Building workflows is a crucial skill for leveraging automation in various business processes. Creating a flow involves designing the sequence of tasks and setting up triggers and actions that define how the workflow operates. Understanding the mechanisms behind triggers and actions is essential for ensuring that workflows are executed correctly and efficiently. This knowledge allows users to streamline processes, reduce manual intervention, and increase overall productivity.

Utilizing templates for common scenarios can significantly speed up the process, providing pre-built structures that can be easily customized to meet specific needs. Templates offer a starting point, ensuring that users don't have to create workflows from scratch. This is particularly useful for standard processes such as onboarding new employees, managing customer service requests, or processing orders. By modifying these templates so that they suit unique requirements, businesses can quickly deploy effective automated solutions.

Creating an automated flow involves defining the series of tasks or actions that will be executed in response to a specified trigger.

The process typically starts like so:

1. The trigger event must be identified, such as the receipt of an email or the addition of a new file in a designated folder.

2. Following the trigger, a series of actions is defined to fulfill the desired outcome. These actions can include sending notifications, updating records, or performing calculations.

The flow creation process is facilitated by intuitive design interfaces that allow users to build workflows without needing extensive technical knowledge. These interfaces include drag-and-drop functionality, making the process accessible to users with varying levels of expertise.

Understanding triggers and actions

At the core of this automation are two key components: triggers and actions. Knowing how they work together is key to building workflows that are smooth, responsive, and fit needs perfectly.

Triggers

Triggers are the core components of any automated workflow and serve as the initiating events that start the workflow, whereas actions are the steps taken in response. Understanding the interplay between triggers and actions is essential for designing effective workflows, something that makes them responsive and perform the desired tasks seamlessly.

Triggers can be varied and may include events such as receiving an email, a new file being uploaded, a change in data, or even a scheduled time. Each trigger sets off a chain of actions that are designed to accomplish a specific task.

Actions

Actions are another important core component of an automated workflow. Actions within a workflow can range from simple tasks such as sending an email or updating a database to more complex operations, such as executing conditional logic based on previous actions. For instance, an action could involve checking inventory levels before confirming an order, updating the status of an order in a customer relationship management system, or generating reports for management review. The ability to incorporate conditional logic and branching paths in workflows allows for greater flexibility and precision in handling various scenarios.

Advanced workflow techniques

Beyond basic workflows, there are advanced techniques that can further enhance automation capabilities.

These include the use of the following aspects:

- **Conditional logic**: Allows workflows to make decisions based on specific criteria, enabling more complex and dynamic processes

- **Parallel processing**: Enables multiple actions to be executed simultaneously, improving efficiency and reducing processing time.

- **Integration with external systems**: Allows workflows to leverage data and functionality from other applications, creating a more connected and cohesive automation environment.

Testing

To ensure that workflows are robust and reliable, testing them thoroughly before deployment is important. This involves running simulations or pilot tests to identify potential issues and make necessary adjustments. Regularly monitoring and maintaining workflows is also essential to address any changes in business processes or external factors affecting their performance. By continuously optimizing workflows, businesses can adapt to evolving needs and maintain high levels of efficiency.

Security and compliance in workflow automation

Security and compliance are critical considerations in workflow automation as they ensure that workflows adhere to organizational policies and regulatory requirements. They also help protect sensitive data and maintain compliance. This involves implementing access controls, encryption, and audit trails within workflows. Regular reviews and updates to workflows are necessary to address any security vulnerabilities and ensure compliance with evolving regulations.

Future trends in workflow automation

The future of workflow automation is being shaped by advancements in **artificial intelligence** (**AI**) and **machine learning** (**ML**). These technologies are enabling more intelligent and adaptive workflows that can learn from data and make autonomous decisions.

AI-driven workflows can analyze patterns, predict outcomes, and optimize processes in real time, offering new levels of efficiency and innovation.

Additionally, the rise of low-code and no-code platforms is making workflow automation more accessible to a broader range of users, democratizing the ability to create and manage automated processes.

By staying informed about these trends and continuously exploring new possibilities, businesses can harness the full potential of workflow automation to drive growth and innovation.

Scenario – automating email notifications for document library changes

Consider the following scenario: we're a marketing team member responsible for managing project files related to a media campaign that's currently rolling out. All assets are stored in a specific document library, and you need to detect changes and new document entries.

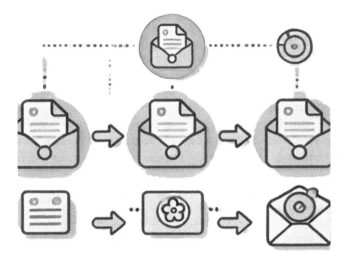

Figure 3.2 – Our "automating email notifications for document library changes" scenario

To achieve this, a flow has been configured with a trigger set to detect changes in the specific SharePoint document library. When a new file is added or an existing file is updated, this trigger activates the flow. The subsequent action in the flow is to email the marketing team member responsible for managing the project files, informing them of the change, including details such as the filename, the type of change (upload or modification), and a link to the file. This automation ensures real-time updates and enhances collaboration by keeping the responsible member informed about the latest document changes. The main goal is not only to learn how to create and configure Power Automate workflows but also to understand how to design efficient flows in line with best practices.

Creating an automated cloud flow

Creating a cloud workflow is a straightforward process, and with a few steps, we can begin enhancing efficiency within an organization.

The following steps outline the process of creating a simple automated cloud flow:

1. The initial step involves logging into your Microsoft account:

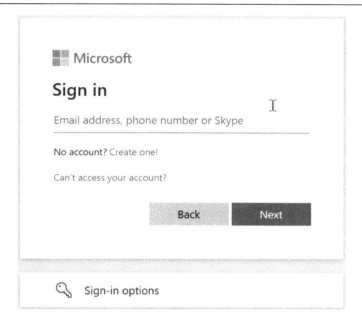

Figure 3.3 – Microsoft Office 365 login

2. Once you've logged in, access Power Automate via the Office 365 app launcher. To do so, click **App Launcher**, then **Power Automate**:

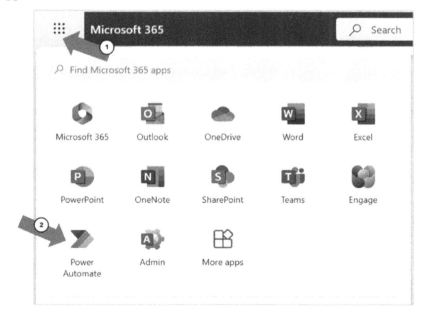

Figure 3.4 – Microsoft Office 365 app launcher

3. You'll be directed to the Power Automate portal. This portal is your central hub for viewing, creating, and managing flows:

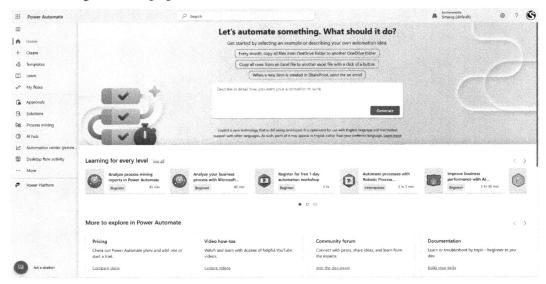

Figure 3.5 – Power Automate portal

When creating a flow, it's considered best practice to start by creating a solution that will contain the flow. Power Automate solutions serve as containers for flows, allowing us to manage and organize automated processes more effectively.

Solutions provide a structured approach to grouping related flows, ensuring that all components are consistently deployed and maintained together, simplifying the process of transferring workflows between different environments, such as development, testing, and production, and supporting version control and change management.

By using solutions, we can also implement governance policies more effectively, ensuring that automation efforts align with organizational standards, thus enhancing the scalability and maintainability of automated workflows.

4. To start creating a solution, click on the **Solutions** option:

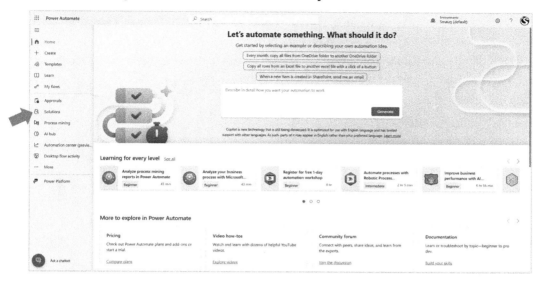

Figure 3.6 – Power Automate portal – Solutions

5. Click on the **New solution** option:

Figure 3.7 – Power Automate portal – New solution

6.   Fill in the values that define the solution:

I.   In the **Display name** field, type the name of the solution. For this scenario, set it to `Marketing Media Campaign`.

II.   The **Name** field will be automatically filled in with the previous value with spaces trimmed down. So, type the name of the solution here.

III. Select the available **Publisher**.

IV.   Click **Create**:

Figure 3.8 – Power Automate portal – New solution

7.   Next, create a flow:

I.   Click on the **New** option to open the menu.

II.   Click the **Automation** option.

III. Click the **Cloud flow** option.

IV.   Click the **Automated** option:

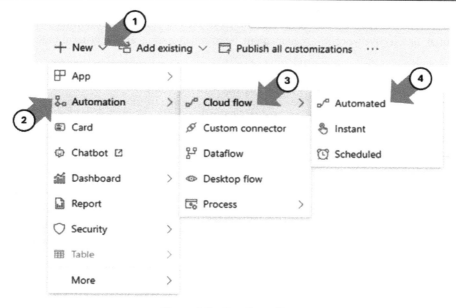

Figure 3.9 – Creating a flow

8.   The **Build an automated cloud flow** screen will be displayed:

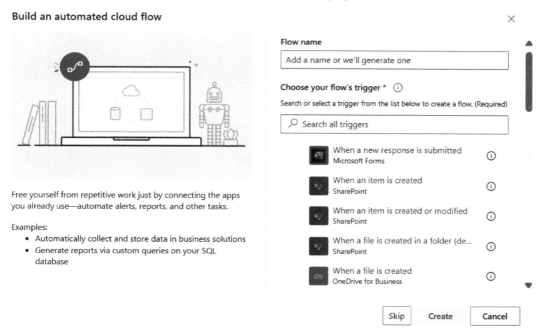

Figure 3.10 – Build an automated cloud flow

9. Enter a value for **Flow name**. Adopting a standardized naming convention for flow names is essential for effective workflow management, team collaboration, and long-term maintainability.

    A flow name should consist of the following elements:

    *   It should start with a category name aligned with the context.

    *   It should include the verb (action word), clearly describing the intended outcome of the flow.

    *   It should include the trigger type. Use proper capitalization and keep it as concise as possible.

Important note

The importance of a proper naming convention for the flow name in Power Automate can't be overstated. A well-thought-out naming convention enhances clarity, organization, and efficiency in managing automation workflows. It ensures that team members can quickly identify the purpose and functionality of each flow, reducing the time spent searching for the correct flow to modify or troubleshoot.

Consistent naming conventions also facilitate better collaboration and communication among team members as everyone can easily understand the context and objectives of each flow.

Moreover, as the number of flows grows, a clear naming convention becomes crucial for maintaining an organized and scalable workflow environment, preventing confusion and errors.

In this scenario, the flow name should be `Monitor Campaign: Monitor Documents Changes in Media Campaign (Automated)`:

Flow name

> Monitor Campaign: Monitor Documents Changes in Med...

Figure 3.11 – Flow name

10. At this stage, you need to choose the flow's trigger:

    I.   Type **sharepoint** in the available search textbox.

    II.   Click **When an item or file is modified SharePoint**.

    III. Click **Create**:

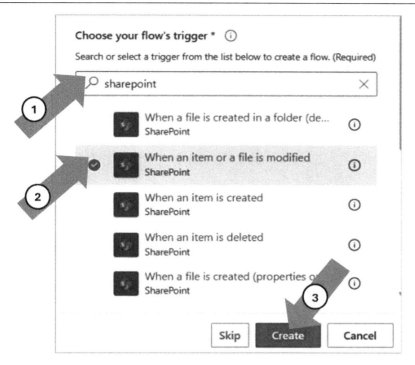

Figure 3.12 – Flow trigger selection

11. You'll be directed to the Power Automate editor portal. This page serves as the central workplace for creating/editing the flow:

Figure 3.13 – Power Automate editor

If we encounter the old Power Automate designer instead of the new one, we'll be able to find a toggle button in the top-right corner so that we can switch between the old and new designer. Microsoft 365 is constantly updating its services, and the new designer is being rolled out gradually. Depending on our tenant settings or regional availability, we might still see the older version, but rest assured the functionality remains the same, although the interface may look slightly different.

12. Next, configure the flow's trigger:

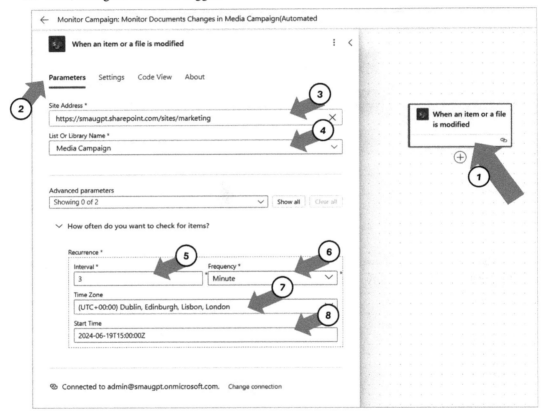

Figure 3.14 – Power Automate editor – trigger options

I.   Click **When an item or a file is modified**.

II.   Select the **Parameters** tab.

III. Select the SharePoint site where the document library is available. In this scenario, the site is `https://smaugpt.sharepoint.com/sites/marketing`.

IV.   Click the **List Or Library Name** dropdown. In this scenario, the site should be set to **Media Campaign**.

V.   In the **How often do you want to check for items?** section, enter the values that will define the trigger's recurrence.

VI.   Set **Interval** to 3.

VII. Set **Frequency** to **Minute**.

VIII. Set **Time Zone** to **(UTC+00:00)**.

IX.   Input a **Start Time** value. This value is in **Coordinated Universal Time (UTC)**, a standard that's used to set all time zones around the world. In this scenario, set it to 2024-06-19T15:00:00Z.

13. Add an action flow:

I.   Clicking on the + button.

II.   Click **Add an action**:

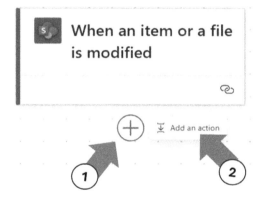

Figure 3.15 – Add an action

III. Select the **Office 365 Outlook** action. If you don't see the Office 365 Outlook connector, you can use the search bar to find it:

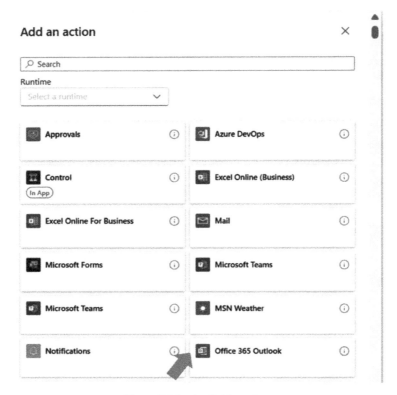

Figure 3.16 – Available actions

14. Select **Send an email (V2)**:

Figure 3.17 – Available Office 365 Outlook actions

15. On the **Send an email (V2)** page, click in the **To** field and type the email for the user that will receive the notification. In this scenario, Adele Vance is the owner of the media campaign, so we'll enter her email – that is, `AdeleV@smaugpt.onmicrosoft.com`:

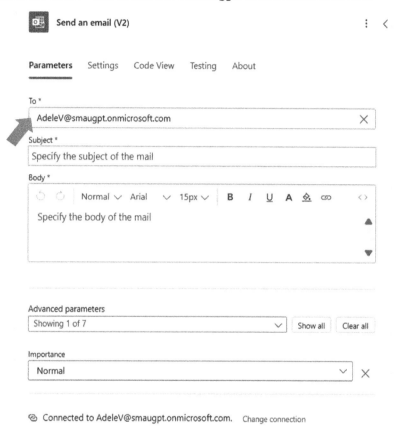

Figure 3.18 – Send an email (v2) configuration

16. In the **Subject** field, type The file and click the **Lightning Bolt** icon. This will give you the option to select fields from the previous step (in this case, we want to select the SharePoint trigger):

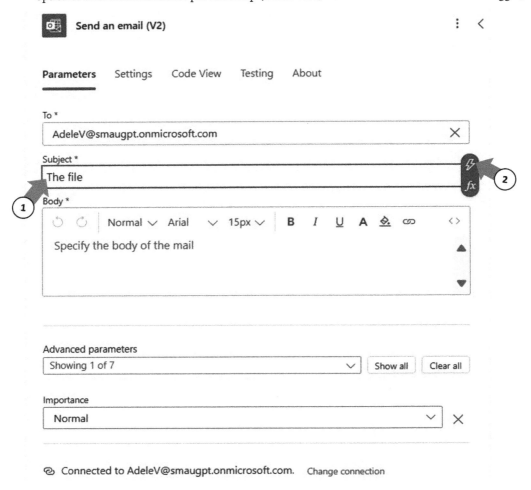

Figure 3.19 – Send an email (v2) configuration

17. From the available trigger fields, click **Title**:

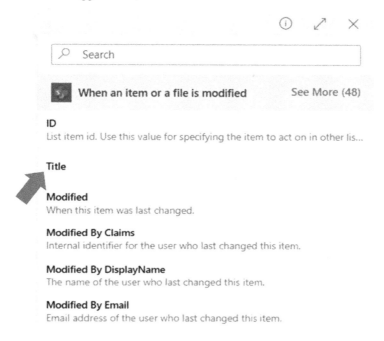

Figure 3.20 – Trigger fields

18. For **Send an email (V2) configuration**, notice that the **Title** field has been added to the **Subject** textbox.

19. Next, enter was created\modified in the **Subject** textbox:

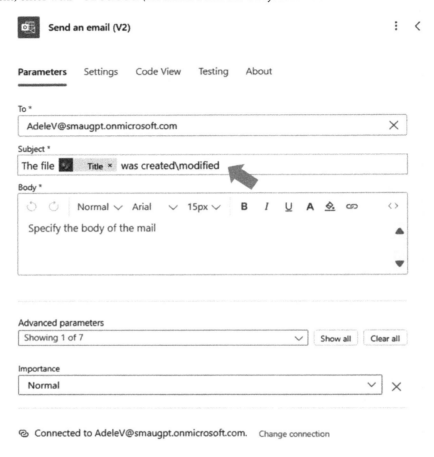

Figure 3.21 – Send an email (v2) configuration

20. Click inside the **Body** field and click the **Lightning Bolt** icon:

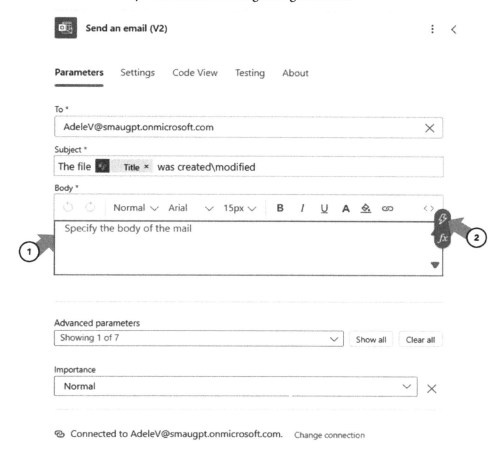

Figure 3.22 – Send an email (v2) configuration

21. Using the same procedure that we used previously, select the **Title**, **Link to Item**, and **Modified by DisplayName** fields:

Figure 3.23 – Trigger fields

For **Send an email (V2) configuration**, notice that the **Title**, **Link to Item**, and **Modified by DisplayName** fields, have been added to the **Body** textbox:

Figure 3.24 – Send an email (v2) configuration

22. Next, add the relevant text:

    - `Hi,`

    - `A filename was created\modified by`

    - `Here's the file link:`

    - Make sure the three fields you added previously are aligned within the sentence. The result should look something like this:

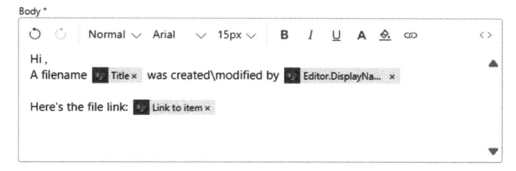

Figure 3.25 – Send an email (v2) configuration – the Body field

- Add a hyperlink to the **Link to item** field:
- Position the text cursor at the end of the text **Link to item**.
- Click the **Insert Link** option and edit the link.
- Type `@{triggerBody()?['{Link}']}` in the textbox.
- Click **Accept**:

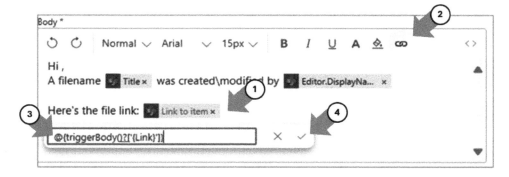

Figure 3.26 – Send an email (v2) configuration – adding a link

23. Now that the configuration is complete, we can save the cloud flow. To do so, click **Save**:

Figure 3.27 – Flow editor

24. As a best practice, we need to check for flow errors. To do so, click on the **Flow checker** button:

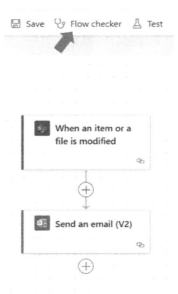

Figure 3.28 – Flow editor

If everything is OK, we should see the no entries in the **Errors** and **Warnings** sections:

Figure 3.29 – Flow Checker

25. As another best practice, we also need to see whether the flow is working properly. To do so, click on the **Test Flow** button.

26. Next, click on the **Manually** option and click **Test**:

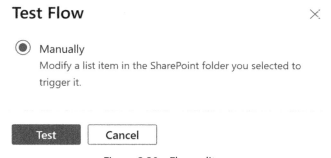

Figure 3.30 – Flow editor

Now, the automated flow is ready to be tested.

27. To test the flow, we can upload a file to the SharePoint document library we're monitoring. To do so, drag and drop a file into the document library. In this case, we'll be using the `MediaCampaign.pptx` file:

Figure 3.31 – Dragging and dropping a file into the Media Campaign document library

28. As the upload operation is executing, we'll see that the flow editor is demarked with **checkmark green icons**, stating that all the steps were executed correctly.

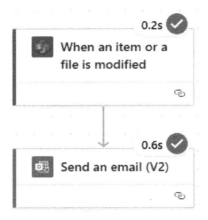

Figure 3.32 – Flow editor

As a final confirmation, Adele received an email stating that a file was created/modified within the Media Campaign document library:

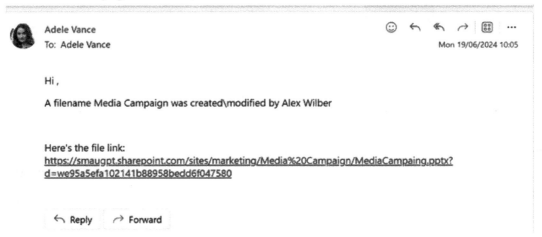

Figure 3.33 – Email

In this section, you learned how to create an automated cloud flow in Power Automate to monitor changes in a SharePoint document library and notify the responsible marketing team member via email. The main idea was to provide a step-by-step guide for this process that highlights naming conventions, best practices, and the most efficient methods. It's essential to apply all the techniques you've learned here to create an effective flow.

This information is crucial for ensuring real-time updates and enhancing collaboration by keeping team members informed about the latest document changes. Understanding this process lays the groundwork for optimizing workflow automation and improving team efficiency.

In the next section, we'll delve into key considerations for creating Power Automate flows. This will include essential best practices, common pitfalls to avoid, and advanced tips to ensure your flows are efficient, reliable, and maintainable.

Power Automate – best practices

Power Automate can save us time by streamlining processes that would otherwise be manual and repetitive. However, to unlock its full potential and ensure everything runs smoothly, it's crucial to follow the best practices. Why bother with best practices? Well, they help us to avoid common pitfalls, making the automations more efficient, and ensuring they're reliable and secure. Keep in mind that well-structured workflows are easier to manage and troubleshoot. Let's explore some essential best practices that can enhance the Power Automate experience and ensure optimal performance and reliability.

Flow planning

Before jumping into building a flow, you need to take a step back and think through what you want to achieve. Understanding the requirements and mapping out the process can save a lot of headaches down the line. Whether it's automating a routine task or integrating multiple services, having a clear picture of the end goal will help you design a more efficient and effective flow. Sketching out the workflow on paper or using a digital tool can help you visualize the steps and identify any potential issues before they become problems:

Figure 3.34 – Planning an automated flow

By planning your flows, you can also anticipate and accommodate any future changes or expansions. This proactive approach ensures that the automation solution is not just a quick fix but a robust, scalable system that grows with the evolving requirements. Plus, having a well-documented plan makes it easier to communicate the ideas with team members and get their buy-in.

Use naming conventions

As we mentioned in the previous section, a well-organized flow starts with clear and consistent naming conventions. It might seem trivial, but giving meaningful names to our automated flows, triggers, and actions can make a huge difference when we need to debug or update them later. Instead of leaving default names such as *Condition 1* or *Action 2*, use descriptive names such as *Check Order Status* or *Send Email Notification*. This way, anyone looking at the automation flow will understand what each part does without needing to dive deep into the details:

Figure 3.35 – Naming conventions

Consistency is key here. You should decide on a naming convention and stick to it throughout your flows. This not only makes the flows easier to understand but also simplifies collaboration with others. When team members see familiar naming patterns, they can quickly get up to speed and contribute more effectively. It's a small step that pays off big in terms of efficiency and clarity.

Optimize performance

Performance optimization is crucial for ensuring that the automated flows run smoothly and efficiently. One way to do this is by limiting the scope of the operations by using filters and conditions to process only the relevant data, which can significantly reduce execution time and resource usage. For instance, applying filters to narrow down the data before performing actions can make the flow much faster if you're working with a large dataset:

Figure 3.36 – Performance

Avoiding unnecessary loops is another important aspect of optimization since loops can be resource-intensive, especially when dealing with large datasets. Where possible, use built-in actions that perform bulk operations or explore alternative designs that minimize the need for looping. By optimizing your flows, you'll not only improve performance but also enhance the user experience by ensuring faster and more reliable automations.

Modular design

Breaking down complex flows into smaller, reusable components is a smart way to manage your automations. By creating child flows, you can encapsulate specific tasks and reuse them in multiple parent flows. This modular approach not only makes your flows easier to understand and maintain but also promotes reuse, saving time and effort in the long run:

Figure 3.37 – Modular design

Standardizing actions for common tasks is another aspect of modular design. For example, if you have a routine process for sending emails or logging data, you can create a template or a reusable flow component for those actions. This ensures consistency and reduces the likelihood of errors since you don't need to recreate these actions from scratch every time.

Documentation

Good documentation is the backbone of any well-maintained system, and Power Automate is no exception: adding comments within your flows helps explain the purpose and functionality of each step, making it easier for others to understand the flow's logic when they revisit it later. Clear comments can significantly reduce the time spent deciphering complex flows, especially when there's a need to debug or update them:

Figure 3.38 – Documentation

In addition to in-flow comments, maintaining external documentation is crucial. This should include an overview of the flow architecture, design decisions, and any troubleshooting tips.

Detailed documentation serves as a valuable resource for training new team members, providing them with the context and information they need to work effectively with your flows. Plus, it helps ensure continuity and consistency, even as team members come and go.

Testing and debugging

Thorough testing is essential to ensure that your flows work as expected in all scenarios. You need to test your flows with different inputs and conditions to identify any potential issues or edge cases. This comprehensive approach helps catch and address problems before they impact end users. Power Automate provides built-in debugging tools, such as the ability to view run history and step-by-step execution, which can be invaluable for troubleshooting and fine-tuning flows. Debugging can sometimes be a tedious process, but taking the time to do it right pays off in the long run:

Figure 3.39 – Testing and debugging

Also, use the logs and error messages provided by Power Automate to pinpoint issues and understand what went wrong. By systematically testing and debugging your flows, you can ensure they're robust, reliable, and capable of handling real-world usage without hiccups.

Monitoring and maintenance

Regular monitoring and maintenance are key to keeping flows running smoothly over time. Power Automate offers analytics, which provides insights into the performance and execution of your flows.

Regularly reviewing these metrics can help you identify any bottlenecks or issues that need attention as you can set up alerts to notify you of any anomalies or failures so that you can address them promptly:

Figure 3.40 – Monitoring and maintenance

Establishing a maintenance schedule ensures that the flows remain up-to-date and aligned with changing requirements as you can review and update flows periodically, make necessary adjustments, and retire obsolete flows.

Proactive maintenance helps prevent issues from arising and keeps the automation solutions efficient and effective.

Use Power Automate templates

Power Automate offers a wide range of templates for common tasks and workflows, which can serve as a great starting point for automation:

Figure 3.41 – Templates

Leveraging the pre-built templates can save you a lot of time and effort. It not only speeds up the development process but also ensures adherence to best practices from the outset. These templates underwent rigorous validation and testing before being published within the platform.

Governance

Establishing governance policies is crucial for managing the creation, usage, and life cycle of flows within an organization. Define clear guidelines on who can create and manage flows, what types of flows are allowed, and how flows should be documented and maintained. This helps ensure that automation efforts are aligned with organizational goals and standards:

Figure 3.42 – Governance

Providing usage guidelines and training for users promotes the effective and responsible use of Power Automate: educate users on best practices, common pitfalls, and how to get the most out of the tool. This not only empowers them to create their automations but also helps maintain a high standard of quality and consistency across all flows within the organization.

Solutions

Using solutions for deployment helps streamline the process of transferring workflows across environments. Solutions in Power Automate package workflows and their dependencies, making it easier to move them between development, testing, and production environments. This method ensures that all components are configured correctly and reduces the likelihood of deployment errors:

Figure 3.43 – Solutions

Solutions also support version control and change management, providing a structured approach to workflow deployment.

Ownership

In Power Automation, having more than one owner for a flow is crucial for ensuring continuity and operational stability: when a flow has multiple owners, it reduces the risk of disruption being caused by the unavailability of a single owner.

For instance, if the sole owner of a flow is unavailable due to vacation, illness, or leaving the organization, the flow could face significant downtime or issues that remain unresolved. By having multiple owners, other designated individuals can step in to manage, troubleshoot, and maintain the flow, ensuring that business processes remain uninterrupted and are handled efficiently:

Figure 3.44 – Ownership

Also, assigning multiple owners to a flow enhances collaboration and knowledge sharing within the team. Different owners bring diverse perspectives and expertise, which can lead to better optimization and innovation in the flow's design and functionality, fostering a collaborative environment where team members can learn from each other, share responsibilities, and develop a deeper understanding of the workflows.

This approach not only strengthens the team's overall capability but also builds resilience into the organization's automation strategy, making it more robust against individual absences or transitions.

Using Power Automate in multi-factor authenticated-enforced environments

When using Power Automate to connect to SharePoint, each connection is typically tied to a user account. In environments where **multi-factor authentication** (**MFA**) is enforced, the user is required to provide additional verification (such as a one-time password, mobile confirmation, or a hardware token) beyond the usual username and password.

Here are some strategies and best practices for using MFA efficiently in Power Automate:

Figure 3.45 – MFA-enforced environments

- **Use service accounts with conditional access**: Instead of regular user accounts, use service accounts specifically designed for automation. Apply conditional access policies to these accounts to ensure security without the need for MFA. Restrict access based on IP addresses, device compliance, or other criteria to maintain a secure environment.

- **Implement certificate-based authentication**: For critical workflows, consider using certificate-based authentication. This method provides a secure, non-interactive authentication process that aligns well with automated systems, eliminating the need for frequent user intervention.

- **Employ OAuth tokens with long lifetimes**: Where possible, configure OAuth tokens with extended lifetimes and ensure they can be refreshed programmatically without user interaction. This approach reduces the frequency of authentication interruptions, ensuring the smoother operation of automated workflows.

- **Regularly monitor and refresh connections**: Establish procedures to regularly check the status of connections and refresh them proactively. Automated scripts or tools can be used to handle token refreshments before they expire, minimizing the risk of workflow interruptions.

By following these best practices, organizations can mitigate the challenges posed by MFA in Power Automate, ensuring more reliable and secure automation for business-critical workflows.

An important remark on SharePoint connections and MFA considers why having a user with MFA in a connection can disrupt the flow:

- **Token expiration**: MFA tokens have a limited lifespan, usually ranging from a few seconds to several minutes. Once a token expires, the authentication session is no longer valid. If Power Automate is using a connection authenticated via MFA, the session token must be refreshed regularly. This can be problematic because automated flows might not be able to handle the re-authentication process required by MFA.

- **The requirement for interactive authentication**: MFA typically requires user interaction to confirm a user's identity. Automated flows run in the background without user intervention. If a flow needs to re-authenticate, it cannot proceed because it cannot perform the interactive steps required by MFA, such as entering a code that's been sent to a mobile device or approving a prompt in an authenticator application.

- **Connection interruption**: If the MFA token expires while a flow is running, the connection to SharePoint can break, causing the flow to fail. This means that the flow will not be able to complete its tasks, such as reading from or writing to SharePoint lists or libraries, as it cannot re-establish the connection without user input.

- **Complexity in token management**: Handling token refresh for MFA in an automated manner is complex and often requires custom solutions or additional services. Standard Power Automate connectors do not natively support the automation of MFA token refreshes, leading to potential interruptions in service.

The reliance on MFA for a SharePoint connection in Power Automate introduces several issues primarily centered around the requirement for user interaction and the expiration of authentication tokens. These challenges make it difficult for automated flows to maintain a stable and continuous connection, leading to disruptions and failures in the flow's execution.

This inherent incompatibility with MFA's interactive authentication undermines the reliability and continuity required for business-critical processes, making Power Automate an unsuitable choice for some scenarios.

Keeping up with Power Automate updates

Keeping up with Power Automate updates is essential for leveraging new features and improvements. Microsoft regularly releases updates that enhance the platform's capabilities, security, and performance:

Figure 3.46 – Updates

Staying informed about these updates allows users to take advantage of new functionalities, optimize existing workflows, and maintain compliance with security standards. Regularly updating workflows so that they incorporate new features ensures that they remain efficient, secure, and effective. As an example, one of Microsoft's latest updates for Power Automate makes it super easy to use with Microsoft Teams, where we can set up and run our workflows right from within the Microsoft Teams application. This means we can start automations directly in the chat channels, get instant notifications, and handle approvals without leaving Teams, making teamwork smoother and boosting productivity.

Summary

In this chapter, we explored how Power Automate can significantly enhance SharePoint by automating workflows and business processes, making operations more efficient and productive. We covered the core components of Power Automate, including flows, triggers, actions, connectors, and templates, and demonstrated how to create and customize automated workflows tailored to specific business needs. We emphasized best practices such as planning, using naming conventions, optimizing performance, and ensuring security and compliance. Through practical examples and advanced techniques, this chapter provided the knowledge and skills necessary to help you implement Power Automate effectively, driving productivity and improving collaboration within your organization.

Looking ahead, the next chapter will delve deeper into the practical application of enhancing SharePoint by exploring techniques and tools that can be used to fully leverage forms and customizations in SharePoint. By doing so, we can ensure a more efficient and powerful SharePoint environment tailored to meet specific business needs.

4

Enhancing SharePoint – Site Templates, Forms, and Power Apps

In this chapter, we'll delve into the art of enhancing SharePoint by utilizing custom forms and site templates, as well as integrating Power Apps for improved functionality. Our journey begins with an introduction to site templates, followed by a detailed guide on creating custom forms, developing applications with Power Apps, and integrating these elements seamlessly with SharePoint.

By the end of this chapter, you'll have the skills to design and implement custom forms that improve user experience and efficiency, apply predefined corporate site templates, and extend SharePoint through tailored custom applications with Power Apps, which will boost the platform's overall functionality and collaborative properties.

This chapter is incredibly useful for those looking to streamline processes and increase productivity within their organization by enhancing SharePoint capabilities. You will gain practical insights and step-by-step instructions that you can apply directly to your projects, ensuring that your SharePoint environment is both user-friendly and highly functional.

In this chapter, we're going to cover the following main topics:

- Site templates
- Creating custom forms
- Integrating Power Apps applications with SharePoint for enhanced functionality
- Best practices in Power Apps

By mastering these areas, you'll be well-equipped to tackle real-world challenges and implement solutions that drive efficiency and user satisfaction. This includes being able to rapidly prototype and deploy custom forms that meet the specific needs of your users, thereby reducing the time and effort required for data collection and processing. You'll also be able to create customized applications using Power Apps, enabling you to automate tasks and processes that were previously manual and time-consuming. Furthermore, you'll learn how to integrate these custom solutions with SharePoint in a way that enhances overall functionality and ensures a seamless user experience. This will allow you to build a cohesive digital workspace where information flows smoothly between different tools and platforms, fostering better collaboration and communication within a team.

Technical requirements

You'll require the following to complete the tasks outlined in this chapter:

- A Microsoft Office 365 subscription
- Access to SharePoint Online
- Internet connectivity for accessing online resources and services

> **Important note**
> The operations outlined require the use of a regular **Microsoft Office 365 license** with a **Power Apps** application license assigned.

SharePoint and customizations in Microsoft Office 365

SharePoint has evolved significantly since its inception, transitioning from an on-premises solution to a robust cloud-based platform within Microsoft Office 365. This evolution has expanded the customization capabilities available to users, particularly in the realm of form customization. Understanding this journey and the level of form customizations possible across different versions of SharePoint is crucial for leveraging the platform effectively.

SharePoint On-Premises – customizations

In the earlier versions of SharePoint, customization options were somewhat limited but still powerful for their time. Users typically relied on tools such as InfoPath for form customization, which allowed users to design complex forms with advanced logic, custom branding, and integration with other systems. However, it required a good deal of technical knowledge and wasn't always user-friendly for non-developers:

Figure 4.1 – Customizations

The following are some of the key features of SharePoint On-Premises (all on-premises versions):

- **InfoPath forms**: Advanced form design capabilities with custom logic and branding
- **Custom web parts**: Ability to create and add custom web parts to pages
- **Server-side code**: Extensive use of server-side code to create complex functionalities
- **Limited user accessibility**: Customizations often required IT intervention and were less accessible to everyday users

Now, let's look at the customizations available in SharePoint Online.

SharePoint Online – customizations

With the introduction of SharePoint Online as part of the Microsoft Office 365 suite, the approach to customizations, especially form customizations, has evolved dramatically. SharePoint Online offers a more user-friendly, accessible, and powerful set of tools that allow both technical and non-technical users to create customized forms and workflows.

This evolution is characterized by a shift toward low-code and no-code solutions, making it easier for users to tailor their SharePoint environments to meet specific business needs without extensive programming knowledge.

Users can leverage Power Apps to create rich, interactive forms and integrate them seamlessly with SharePoint lists and libraries. Additionally, Power Automate (formerly Microsoft Flow) enables the creation of complex workflows that can automate business processes and enhance productivity.

The flexibility of SharePoint Online allows for a wide range of customizations, from simple changes in list views and form layouts to more sophisticated solutions involving custom web parts and **SharePoint Framework (SPFx)** components.

The platform's integration with other Microsoft 365 services, such as Teams and Power BI, further extends its customization capabilities, allowing for a more cohesive and efficient user experience.

SharePoint Online empowers organizations to adapt their digital workplaces to better support collaboration, data management, and process automation, all while reducing the dependency on traditional development approaches.

Here are some of the key features of SharePoint Online:

- **Power Apps integration**: This allows users to create custom forms and applications without writing code. Power Apps is highly intuitive and integrates seamlessly with SharePoint, enabling users to design forms with complex logic, rich data integration, and custom branding.

- **Microsoft Forms**: This provides a simple way to create surveys and forms with basic customization options, ideal for quick data collection and analysis.

- **SPFx**: This enables developers to build custom web parts and extensions using modern web technologies, providing a flexible and scalable way to extend SharePoint functionalities and create tailored solutions.

- **Modern UI**: The modern user interface in SharePoint Online is more responsive and user-friendly, making customization easier and more visually appealing. This responsiveness is evident through its adaptive design, which ensures that the interface adjusts seamlessly to different screen sizes and devices, providing a consistent experience, regardless of whether it's accessed on a desktop, tablet, or smartphone.

  For example, the modern SharePoint experience includes improved navigation and editing features. The simplified navigation allows users to find content quickly, with a clean and intuitive menu structure that reduces clutter, and the inline editing capabilities enable users to make changes directly on the page without having to switch to a separate editing mode, saving time and enhancing productivity.

The user-friendly design tools allow for easy customization of site layouts and themes. Users can personalize their sites with a variety of pre-designed templates and style options, ensuring a professional appearance with minimal effort. The drag-and-drop functionality and real-time preview features make it simple to see how changes will look before they're applied, giving users confidence in their design choices.

Complementing these customization capabilities are SharePoint site templates, which provide pre-configured frameworks for quickly creating sites with a predefined structure, layout, and content.

These templates streamline the setup process while still allowing for extensive customizations, ensuring that the sites can meet specific business needs and maintain a consistent, cohesive design across the organization.

What is a SharePoint site template?

A **SharePoint site template** is a pre-configured framework that's designed to help users quickly create sites with a predefined structure, layout, and content, streamlining the process of setting up new sites:

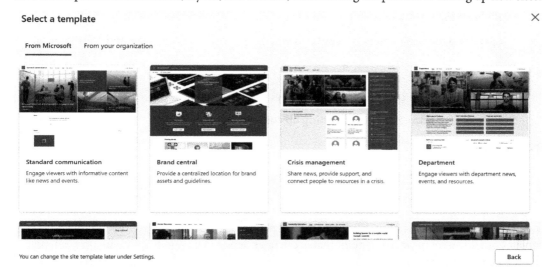

Figure 4.2 – SharePoint site templates

These templates offer a consistent design and functionality tailored to specific business needs, making it easier for organizations to deploy sites that meet their unique requirements where users can choose from a variety of options that cater to different purposes, such as team collaboration, project management, document sharing, and community engagement.

Each template includes a set of pre-built pages, libraries, lists, and features that are relevant to the intended use case, ensuring that the necessary components are in place right from the start. This not only saves time and effort but also ensures that best practices are followed in site design and configuration.

SharePoint site templates can be customized further to fit the exact needs of the organization, allowing for adjustments in branding, layout, and functionality, thus ensuring a consistent user experience across the SharePoint environment and facilitating better collaboration and productivity.

Here are some of the benefits of using site templates:

- **Consistency and uniformity**:

  - Ensures all sites follow a uniform structure and design

  - Promotes a consistent user experience across your organization

- **Time efficiency**:

  - Reduces the time needed to create and configure new sites from scratch

  - Speeds up the deployment process, allowing teams to focus on content and collaboration

- **Ease of use**:

  - Simplifies the site creation process for users with less technical expertise

  - Provides a guided approach to setting up complex site features

- **Scalability**:

  - Facilitates the rapid creation of new sites as your organization grows

  - Supports the implementation of organizational standards across multiple sites

Whether we're setting up a new project site, an intranet portal, or a knowledge base, SharePoint site templates provide a robust starting point that accelerates deployment and helps maintain a cohesive structure across all sites.

Applying a SharePoint site template

Applying a SharePoint site template for creating an initial site is straightforward and involves a few key steps:

1. **Navigate to your SharePoint home page**: Access SharePoint via the Office 365 app launcher, click on **App Launcher**, and then click on **SharePoint**:

Figure 4.3 – Microsoft 365 App Launcher

2.   Click **Create site**:

Figure 4.4 – The Create site option

3.   Choose between **Team Site** and **Communication site**. For this example, we'll choose **Communication site**:

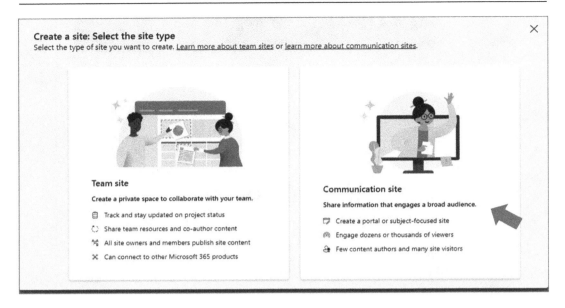

Figure 4.5 – Choosing a site type

4.   Browse through the available templates and select the one that best fits your needs. For this example, we'll choose the **Department** template:

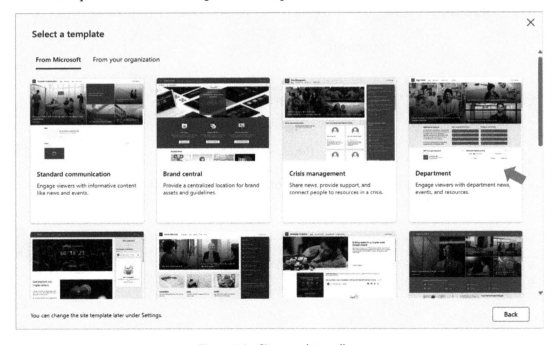

Figure 4.6 – Site template gallery

5. The preview template page shows the site's capabilities and content that will be included. Click **Use template** to apply the chosen template to the site:

Figure 4.7 – The preview template page

6.   Enter the necessary details, such as **Site name**, **Site description**, and **Site address**. Then, click **Next**:

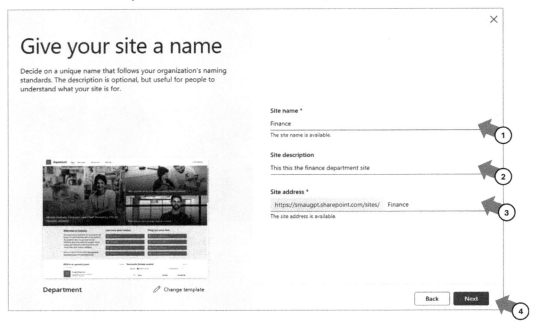

Figure 4.8 – Site details

7.   Select the language of the site by clicking the **Select a language** drop-down box. Then, click **Create Site** to create the site:

Figure 4.9 – Selecting a language

8.   The site will be created with the selected template applied:

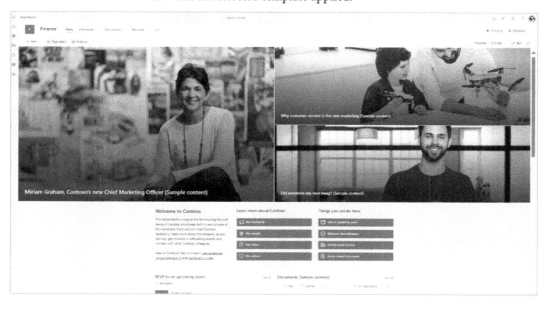

Figure 4.10 – Finance site

Let's take a closer look at the templates that are available in SharePoint Online. SharePoint offers a wide range of templates, each designed to cater to specific business scenarios:

- **Communication site templates**: Ideal for publishing news and announcements.
- **Team site templates**: Designed to facilitate collaboration among team members:
  - **Project management**: For managing project tasks, documents, and timelines
  - **Team collaboration**: To enhance team collaboration and document sharing
- **Custom templates**: Created by the organization to address specific needs and workflows. These templates can be tailored so that they include custom lists, libraries, and site settings.

Let's explore the communication sites templates list in greater detail.

Communication site templates list

Here's a comprehensive list of templates that are designed for communication sites and team collaboration:

- **Standard Communication**: This template delivers engaging content such as updates, announcements, and events to keep the audience informed:

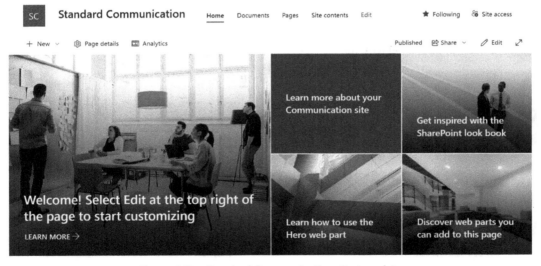

Figure 4.11 – Standard Communication site template

- **Brand Central**: This template offers a unified repository for brand assets and guidelines to ensure consistency:

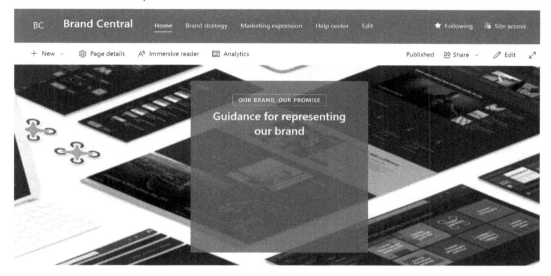

Figure 4.12 – Brand Central site template

- **Crisis Management**: You can use this template to disseminate critical information, offer support, and connect people to resources during emergencies:

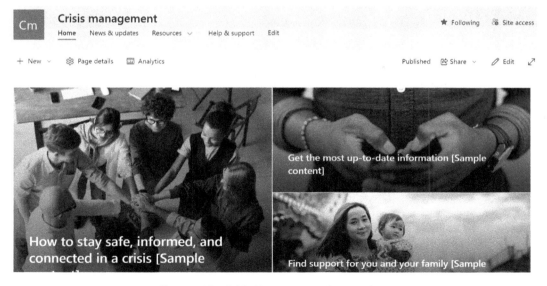

Figure 4.13 – Crisis Management site template

- **Department**: With this template, you can keep viewers updated with departmental news and upcoming events and provide quick access to essential files:

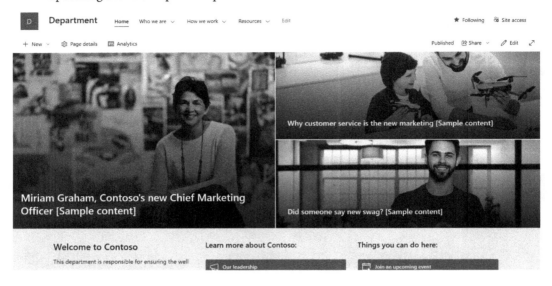

Figure 4.14 – Department site template

- **Event**: With this template, you can supply attendees with details on speakers, schedules, registration, and FAQs:

Figure 4.15 – Event site template

- **Human Resources**: With this template, you can give employees easy access to information about benefits, careers, compensation, and company policies:

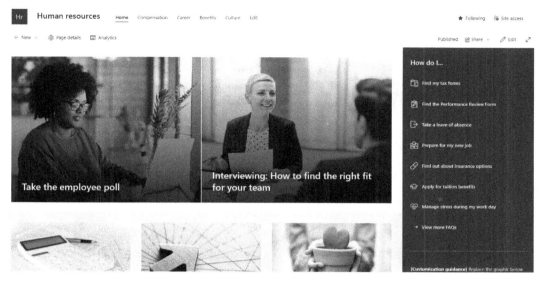

Figure 4.16 – Human Resources site template

- **Leadership Connection**: This template can foster organizational culture by facilitating communication between leadership and team members through news and events:

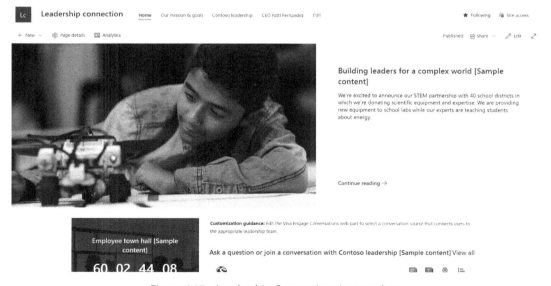

Figure 4.17 – Leadership Connection site template

- **Learning Central**: With this template, you can create a central hub for your organization that features events, news, and additional resources:

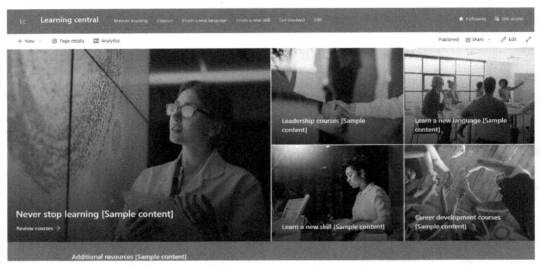

Figure 4.18 – Learning Central site template

- **New Employee Onboarding**: With this template, you can enhance the onboarding process for new hires by guiding them through each step:

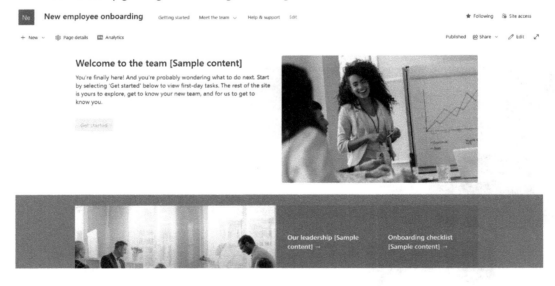

Figure 4.19 – New Employee Onboarding site template

- **Organization Home**: Using this template, you can establish an online headquarters for your organization with news, resources, and tailored content:

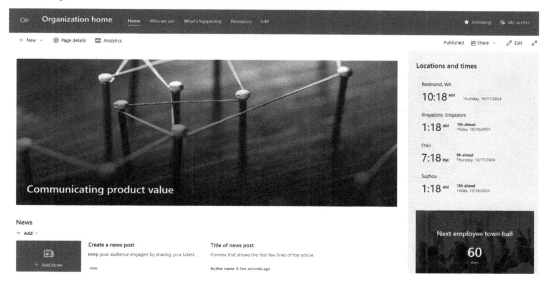

Figure 4.20 – Organization Home site template

- **Showcase**: This template can be used to highlight products, events, or teams using visual media such as images and videos:

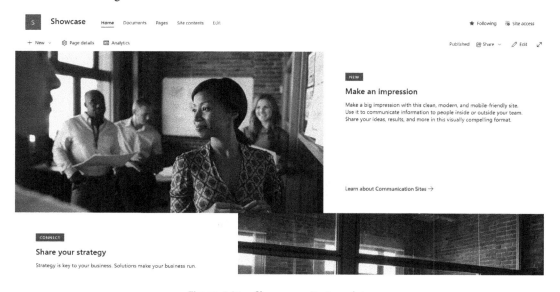

Figure 4.21 – Showcase site template

- **Volunteer Center**: This template provides a centralized hub for volunteers to access training, onboarding information, event details, and more:

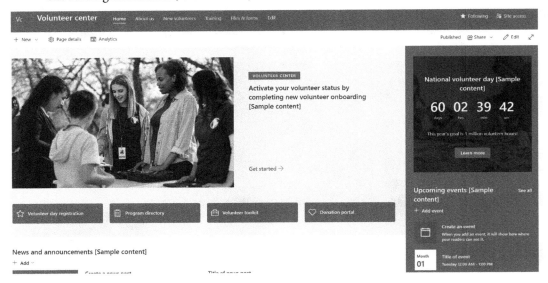

Figure 4.22 – Volunteer Center site template

- **Blank**: With this template, you start with a blank page. Here, you can create a custom site tailored to your user's specific needs:

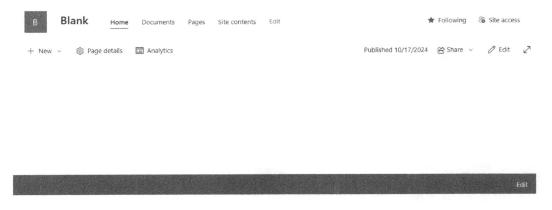

Figure 4.23 – Blank site template

Now, let's explore the Teams sites templates list in greater detail.

Teams site templates list

Teams consists of the following templates:

- **Standard Team**: With this template, you can oversee projects, share resources, and maintain communication with your team members:

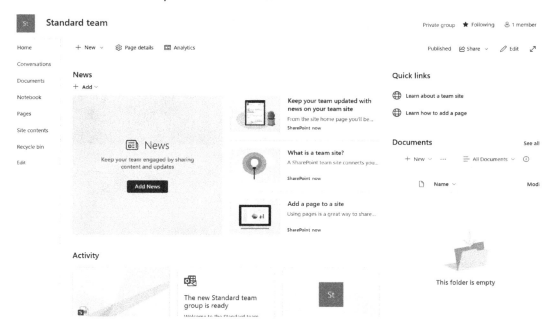

Figure 4.24 – Standard Team site template

- **Crisis Communication Team**: This template allows you to centralize information, resources, and strategies for handling crises effectively:

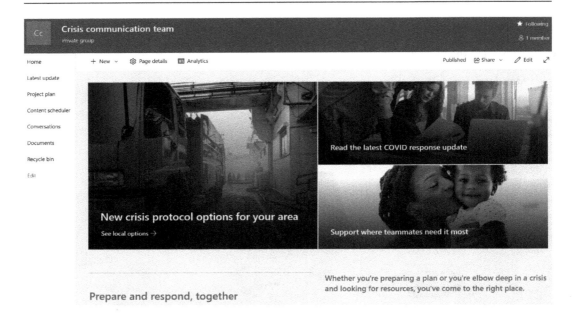

Figure 4.25 – Crisis Communication Team site template

- **Employee Onboarding Team**: With this template, you can assist new hires through your team's onboarding procedures:

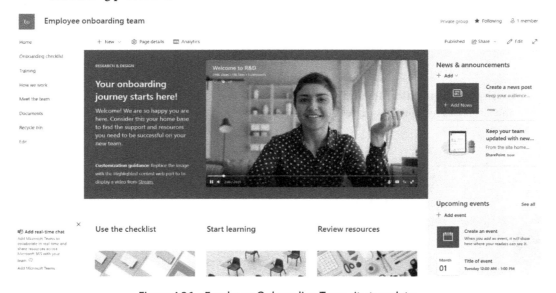

Figure 4.26 – Employee Onboarding Team site template

- **Event Planning**: This template allows you to organize and manage event details collaboratively. Here, you can use ready-made templates for event summaries and status updates to keep your team informed:

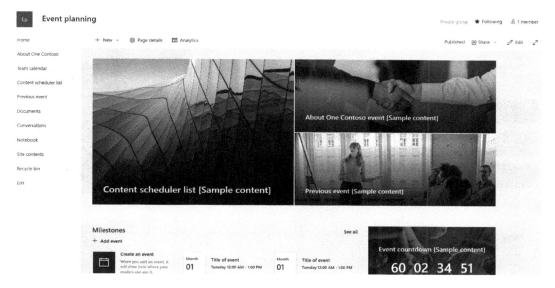

Figure 4.27 – Event Planning site template

- **IT Help Desk**: With this template, you can handle technical issues, keep track of devices, and share training materials efficiently:

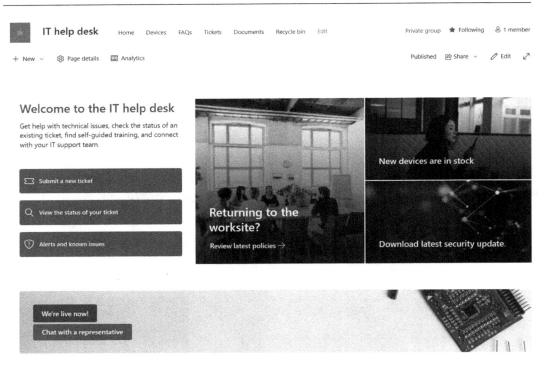

Figure 4.28 – IT Help Desk site template

- **Project Management**: This template allows you to create a collaborative workspace where your team can access tools, share project updates, post meeting notes, and store team documents:

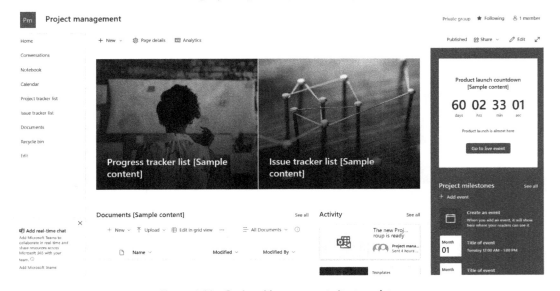

Figure 4.29 – Project Management site template

- **Retail Management Team**: Using this template, you can connect retail managers, keep them informed, and provide access to key resources:

Figure 4.30 – Retail Management Team site template

- **Store Collaboration**: This template lets you coordinate and prepare retail teams by sharing news, resources, and training materials:

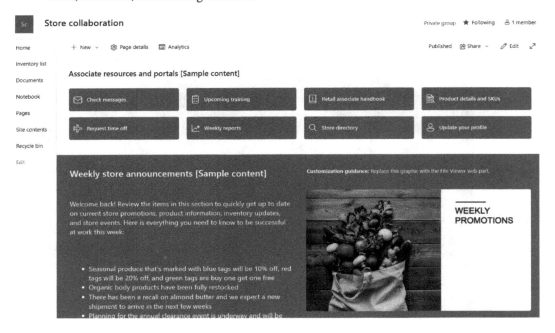

Figure 4.31 – Store Collaboration site template

- **Training Course**: With this template, you can equip participants and students with the necessary resources, news, and event information for specific learning opportunities:

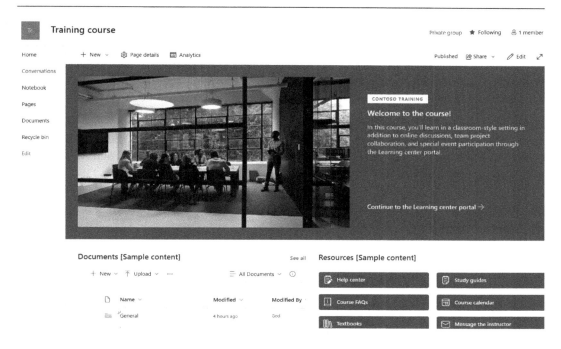

Figure 4.32 – Training Course site template

- **Training Design Team**: Using this template, you can brainstorm and plan educational opportunities to facilitate learning and development:

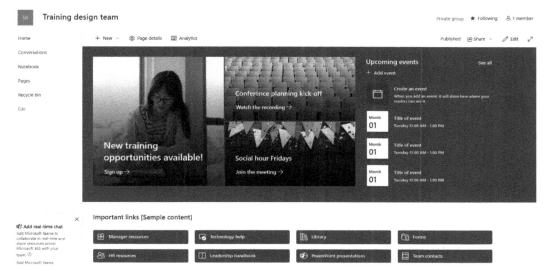

Figure 4.33 – Training Design Team site template

In this section, you learned about the importance and application of SharePoint site templates, which streamline the process of setting up new sites by providing a predefined structure and layout. This ensures consistency, saves time, and promotes ease of use, making it an invaluable tool for organizational growth and productivity. Understanding how to apply these templates effectively is crucial for maintaining a cohesive structure across your SharePoint environment.

Next, we'll explore how to create forms, an essential feature for gathering information and enhancing user interaction within your SharePoint sites. This will build on the foundational knowledge of site templates, ensuring you have a comprehensive understanding of how to leverage SharePoint's capabilities to meet your organization's needs.

Creating custom forms – why are forms indispensable in an enterprise setting?

Forms play a crucial role in the day-to-day operations of any enterprise – they streamline processes, ensure consistency, and enhance data collection efficiency:

Figure 4.34 – Custom forms

In the next few sections, we'll dive into the benefits associated with using custom forms.

Streamlined processes

Forms help standardize procedures, reducing the time employees spend on repetitive tasks. Automated workflows triggered by form submissions can route data and documents to the right departments without manual intervention, enhancing overall efficiency.

Standardized forms reduce confusion and improve workflow by providing a consistent method for data input and processing. When employees know exactly what information is required and how it should be submitted, it significantly speeds up how requests, orders, and approvals are handled. This not only saves time but also ensures that processes are followed correctly and consistently.

Consistency and accuracy

Using standardized forms ensures that all the necessary information is collected consistently across the organization. This minimizes errors and omissions, leading to more reliable data and better decision-making. Forms eliminate the guesswork involved in data collection. By ensuring that all employees use the same format, organizations can reduce variability in data entries. This uniformity is critical for maintaining accurate records, which, in turn, enhances the reliability of data analytics and reporting. Consistent data collection helps in identifying patterns and making informed decisions based on comprehensive and accurate information.

Enhanced data collection and analysis

Forms facilitate the systematic collection of data, which can be easily analyzed to gain insights into business operations. This data can be used to identify trends, measure performance, and make informed strategic decisions.

Well-designed forms allow relevant and comprehensive data to be collected. This data, when aggregated and analyzed, can reveal important trends and insights about business performance. For example, customer feedback forms can highlight common areas of satisfaction or dissatisfaction, enabling businesses to make targeted improvements. Similarly, internal forms can track productivity, helping managers to optimize workflows and resource allocation.

Building forms

Creating effective forms involves careful planning and consideration of the user experience.

The form should be intuitive and easy to complete, with clear instructions and logical flow.

Doing this involves several key elements, including the following:

- **Clear labels and instructions**: Ensure that each field is clearly labeled and provide instructions where necessary to help users understand what information is required.

- **A logical layout**: Arrange fields in a logical order that mirrors the user's thought process. Group related fields together to make the form easier to navigate.

- **Mandatory fields**: Indicate mandatory fields clearly to ensure critical information isn't missed. Use validation rules to enforce this.

- **Simplifying input**: Use appropriate field types (for example, dropdowns and checkboxes) to simplify data entry and reduce errors.

- **Workflow integration**: Forms should be integrated with automated workflows to streamline processes. For example, a leave request form can be designed to automatically route to the employee's manager for approval and then to HR for processing, reducing manual intervention and speeding up the approval process.

- **Data security**: When building forms, it's essential to consider data security. Implement measures such as data encryption, access controls, and regular audits to protect sensitive information. Ensure that forms comply with relevant data protection regulations to safeguard user privacy and maintain trust.

By implementing forms in the enterprise, organizations can achieve significant improvements in terms of efficiency, consistency, and data accuracy, all of which are critical for maintaining a competitive advantage.

Forms not only streamline processes but also enhance the quality of the data that's been collected, providing valuable insights for decision-making. Well-designed forms, integrated with automated workflows and robust security measures, can transform the way businesses operate, driving productivity and growth.

Forms in SharePoint Online

Creating forms in SharePoint Online is an essential task for businesses looking to streamline their data collection and processing workflows.

Forms are crucial in SharePoint as they facilitate user input, data collection, and workflow initiation. The platform supports various form-creation tools, including Microsoft Forms and Power Apps.

Microsoft Forms

Microsoft Forms is an easy-to-use tool that's integrated with SharePoint Online and is suitable for creating simple forms such as surveys, quizzes, and feedback forms:

Figure 4.35 – Microsoft Forms

It offers a user-friendly interface that requires no coding skills, making it accessible to a broad range of users.

The advantages of Microsoft Forms are as follows:

- **Simplicity**: The tool's straightforward design ensures quick form creation without the need for technical expertise.

- **Integration**: Seamless integration with SharePoint Online, Excel, and other Microsoft 365 apps.

- **Real-time responses**: You can view responses in real time. These are automatically saved to an Excel spreadsheet for easy analysis.

Here are some of the limitations of Microsoft Forms:

- **Basic customization**: There are limited options for advanced customization and complex logic

- **Form logic**: It has basic conditional logic capabilities compared to more advanced tools such as Power Apps

To create a form using Microsoft Forms, follow these simple steps for a seamless experience:

1. Navigate to the list in the SharePoint site where you want to create the form.
2. Click **Forms** and select **New form**.
3. Name your form and add your questions using the intuitive drag-and-drop interface.
4. Customize the form with various question types, such as multiple choice, text, rating, and date.
5. Share the form by generating a link or embedding it directly into a SharePoint page.

Now, let's explore Power Apps forms.

Power Apps forms

Power Apps is a powerful low-code platform that enables users to create custom applications with minimal coding effort, enhancing productivity and making it an essential tool for solving complex business challenges efficiently:

Figure 4.36 – Forms in Power Apps

Power Apps also allows users to create custom forms tailored to their specific needs. These forms can be seamlessly integrated into business processes, allowing you to capture and manage data with ease.

This versatility makes Power Apps an invaluable asset for both application creation and form customization since it supports a wide range of business functions and enhances overall operational efficiency.

It's suitable for organizations that require highly tailored solutions that integrate with various data sources.

Here are the advantages of Power Apps forms:

- **Customization**: There are extensive customization options to tailor the form to specific business needs
- **Integration**: Power Apps forms can connect with numerous data sources, including SharePoint lists, Microsoft Dataverse, and external databases
- **Complex logic**: The forms support advanced business logic, calculations, and automation

However, Power Apps forms have some limitations:

- **Learning curve**: They require having some familiarity with Power Apps and formula language for advanced features
- **Cost**: You may incur additional costs, depending on licensing and usage.
- **Limited modern features**: They lack modern functionalities and the user experience that can be found in newer tools, such as Power Apps

To create a form using Power Apps, follow these simple steps for a seamless experience:

1. Open Power Apps Studio from the SharePoint site or Microsoft 365 app launcher.

2. Select **Canvas app from blank** or use a template to get a head start.

3. Connect to your data source, such as an Excel file or SQL database.

4. Design your form using the drag-and-drop interface, adding text inputs, drop-downs, galleries, and other controls.

5. Implement complex logic and workflows using Power Apps formulas and connectors.

6. **Publish** the application and integrate it into your SharePoint site.

Next, let's turn our attention to Microsoft Lists.

Microsoft Lists

Microsoft Lists is a versatile tool that's designed to help users organize, collaborate, and manage information effectively:

Figure 4.37 – Microsoft Lists

This platform provides a range of features that enhance productivity and streamline business processes, making it an essential tool for handling complex data management tasks efficiently.

Microsoft Lists also allows users to create custom forms tailored to their specific needs. These forms can be seamlessly integrated into business processes, capturing and managing data with ease. This versatility makes Microsoft Lists an invaluable asset for both data management and form customization; it also supports a wide range of business functions and enhances overall operational efficiency.

It's suitable for organizations requiring highly tailored solutions that integrate with various data sources.

Here are the advantages of Microsoft Lists:

- **Customization**: Its extensive customization options allow you to tailor forms to specific business needs

- **Integration**: It connects with numerous data sources, including SharePoint lists, Microsoft Dataverse, and external databases

- **Complex logic**: It supports advanced business logic, calculations, and automation

However, Microsoft Lists does have some limitations:

- **Learning curve**: It requires having some familiarity with Microsoft Lists and its features for advanced functionality

- **Cost**: You may incur additional costs, depending on licensing and usage

- **Limited modern features**: It lacks modern functionalities and user experience found in newer tools

To create a form using Microsoft Lists, follow these simple steps for a seamless experience:

1. Open **Microsoft Lists** from the SharePoint site or Microsoft 365 app launcher.
2. Select **New List** to start from scratch or choose a template to get a head start.
3. Click **Forms** and select **New form**.
4. Name your form and add your questions using the intuitive drag-and-drop interface.
5. Customize the form with various question types, such as multiple choice, text, rating, and date.
6. Share the form by generating a link or embedding it directly into a SharePoint page.

Choosing the right tool

Choosing the right tool for creating forms in SharePoint Online depends on the organization's specific needs, technical expertise, and budget.

Microsoft Forms is ideal for simple, quick forms, while **Power Apps** offers extensive customization for complex solutions. Alternatively, **Microsoft Lists** provides a versatile solution for structured data.

By understanding the strengths and limitations of each method, we can select the most suitable approach for optimizing our form creation process in SharePoint Online.

In this section, you learned about various tools you can use to create custom forms in SharePoint Online, including Microsoft Forms, Power Apps, and Microsoft Lists. These tools help streamline processes, ensure consistency, and enhance data collection efficiency, making them indispensable for modern enterprises.

By understanding the advantages and limitations of each tool, you can make informed decisions that best suit your organization's needs.

Moving forward, we'll explore how to integrate these forms with SharePoint for enhanced functionality by creating Power Apps applications. This integration will further optimize your business processes, drive productivity, and enable seamless data management across your organization.

Integrating Power Apps applications with SharePoint for enhanced functionality

Power Apps is a robust platform within the Microsoft Power Platform suite that allows users to create custom applications tailored to their business needs without the need for extensive coding:

Figure 4.38 – Power Apps and SharePoint applications

This section will explore the various capabilities of Power Apps, the steps involved in creating custom applications, cover best practices, and provide a real-world example. The goal is to provide a comprehensive guide to leveraging Power Apps in developing fully SharePoint-integrated solutions that streamline operations, enhance productivity, and drive innovation.

Understanding Power Apps and its features

Power Apps provides a low-code environment for building applications that can connect to various data sources, including Microsoft Dataverse, SharePoint, SQL Server, and third-party services. It empowers users to create business applications with rich functionality, including data entry forms, workflows, and dashboards, with minimal reliance on traditional software development.

Let's consider some of the key features of Power Apps:

- **Low-code development**: It provides a low-code platform for building apps. This means that we can develop applications with minimal hand-coding, relying instead on a user-friendly drag-and-drop interface.

- **Integration**: It seamlessly integrates with various Microsoft services and third-party applications, enabling robust data connectivity and streamlined business processes.

- **Mobile-friendly**: Apps built with Power Apps are responsive by default, ensuring they work well on both desktop and mobile devices.

- **Security and compliance**: Power Apps supports role-based access control and complies with Microsoft's robust security and compliance standards.

- **Extensibility**: Developers can extend Power Apps with custom connectors, controls, and integrations with external systems.

Canvas apps and model-driven apps

Power Apps offers two primary types of apps: canvas apps and model-driven apps. Both types serve different purposes and are suited for different scenarios.

Canvas apps

Canvas apps provide a high degree of control over the application's design and user experience. They are ideal for applications where the look and feel are of utmost importance and where a pixel-perfect design is required.

Here are the key characteristics of canvas apps:

- **Design flexibility**: Canvas apps allow us to start with a blank canvas and design the application's interface from scratch, giving us complete control over the layout and functionality

- **Data sources**: We can connect to multiple data sources, including SharePoint, SQL Server, Excel, and more, using integrated connectors

- **Customization**: With a wide range of controls and formatting options, canvas apps offer extensive customization to match specific requirements

- **User experience**: Canvas apps provide a highly tailored user experience, making them suitable for scenarios where the user interface and interaction are critical

Example use case: A retail company needs an application for its store managers to track daily sales and inventory. The application should have a customized layout that matches the company's branding and provides a user-friendly interface for data entry and reporting.

Model-driven apps

Model-driven apps follow a data-first approach and are built on top of **Microsoft Dataverse** (Microsoft Cloud's scalable data platform). These applications are designed based on the data model and business processes, offering a more standardized and consistent user experience.

Here are the key characteristics of model-driven apps:

- **Data-first approach**: Model-driven apps start with the data model. The structure of the application is based on the data entities defined in Microsoft Dataverse.

- **Components**: These applications use components such as forms, views, charts, and dashboards, all of which are automatically generated based on the data model.

- **Consistency**: Model-driven apps provide a consistent user experience, making them suitable for complex business processes that require standardized workflows.

xModel-driven apps are tightly integrated with Dynamics 365, making them ideal for scenarios that require complex **customer relationship management** (**CRM**) and **enterprise resource planning** (**ERP**) functionalities.

Creating, testing, deploying, and maintaining a Power Apps application

Creating custom applications with Power Apps is a straightforward process that allows us to build powerful applications tailored to our business needs.

Creating the application

Here are the key steps:

1. **Planning and requirements gathering**: Before diving into application development, it's essential to understand the business requirements and define the application's purpose. This phase involves the following aspects:

   - Identifying the problem the application will solve

   - Determining the target users

   - Defining the data sources and integrations needed

   - Outlining the key features and functionality

2. **Designing the application**: The design phase includes creating wireframes and mockups of the application. Power Apps provides canvas apps for designing highly customized user interfaces and model-driven apps for data-centric applications with standardized layouts.

   - **Canvas apps**:
     - Start with a blank canvas and drag and drop elements to create the user interface
     - Customize every aspect of the application, from its layout to the behavior of individual controls

   - **Model-driven apps**:
     - Begin with a data model defined in Microsoft Dataverse
     - Automatically generate forms, views, and dashboards based on the data structure
     - Focus on business processes and workflows

3. **Setting up the environment**: To begin developing an application, set up your environment in Power Apps. This involves the following aspects:

   - Creating or selecting an environment in the **Power Platform Admin Center area**
   - Ensuring the necessary permissions and roles have been assigned
   - Connecting to required data sources such as SharePoint, SQL Server, or Microsoft Dataverse

4. **Building the application**:

   - **Canvas Apps development**:
     - **Add controls**: Use the insert menu to add textboxes, drop-down lists, buttons, galleries, and other controls.
     - **Data connections**: Connect to data sources using the **Data** tab. Common sources include SharePoint lists, Excel files, and SQL databases.
     - **Formulas**: Implement business logic and control behavior using Power Apps formulas, such as Excel functions. You can use these to filter a gallery based on user input, for example.

   - **Model-driven apps development**:
     - **Define entities**: Create entities in Microsoft Dataverse that represent the data structure
     - **Design forms**: Customize forms for data entry and display them using the form editor
     - **Views and dashboards**: Configure views to display data in tabular format and design dashboards for at-a-glance insights
     - **Business rules**: Implement business logic using business rules and workflows

With a comprehensive understanding of the different types of Power Apps and the steps involved in creating them, we're now equipped to leverage Power Apps so that we can build robust, customized applications that can be integrated with SharePoint.

Testing the application

Before deploying the application, test it thoroughly to ensure it meets the requirements and functions as expected. This involves doing the following:

- **Conducting functional testing** to verify each feature
- **Performing usability testing** with end users to gather feedback
- **Ensuring data integrity and security** measures are in place

Deploying the application

Once testing is complete, deploy the application to the intended users. Power Apps provides multiple options for sharing and deploying applications:

- **Share with users**: Share the application directly with specific users or groups within the organization
- **Publish to Microsoft AppSource**: For wider distribution, publish the application to Microsoft AppSource
- **Embed in SharePoint or Teams**: Integrate the application within SharePoint Online or Microsoft Teams for seamless access

Maintaining and updating the application

After deployment, it's crucial to maintain and update the application regularly. This includes doing the following:

- Monitoring performance and usage
- Addressing any bugs or issues reported by users
- Adding new features and enhancements based on user feedback
- Keeping data connections and integrations up to date

By following these steps, we can ensure the successful creation, testing, deployment, and maintenance of Power Apps applications that have been integrated with SharePoint. This process not only enhances functionality but also streamlines business operations and improves productivity. Next, we'll explore the best practices associated with Power Apps to ensure optimal performance and user satisfaction.

Best practices associated with Power Apps

Power Apps can significantly enhance productivity by enabling us to create custom applications that streamline otherwise manual and repetitive tasks. However, to fully leverage its capabilities and ensure seamless operation, it's essential to adhere to best practices. Why focus on best practices? They help us avoid common pitfalls, making the applications more efficient, reliable, and secure. Keep in mind that well-structured applications are easier to manage and troubleshoot.

Let's explore some crucial best practices you can implement to enhance your Power Apps experience and ensure optimal performance and reliability.

Application planning

Before diving into application development, it's important to pause and consider our objectives. Understanding the requirements and mapping out the process can prevent many issues down the line. Whether it's developing a simple application or integrating multiple systems, having a clear vision of the end goal helps in designing a more efficient and effective application. Drafting the application's structure on paper or using a digital tool can help you visualize the steps and spot potential problems before they arise:

Figure 4.39 – Planning a Power App

By thoroughly planning the application development process, we can foresee and integrate future changes or expansions. This proactive strategy ensures that the application isn't merely a temporary solution but a durable, scalable system that adapts to evolving needs. Furthermore, a detailed plan facilitates clearer communication with team members and helps gain their support.

Use naming conventions

While it may seem trivial, assigning meaningful names to the application's components – such as screens, controls, and variables – can significantly ease the debugging and updating process. So, rather than sticking with default names such as *Screen1* and *Button2*, opt for descriptive names such as *HomeScreen* and *SubmitButton*.

This approach ensures that anyone reviewing the application can immediately understand the function of each element without delving into the specifics:

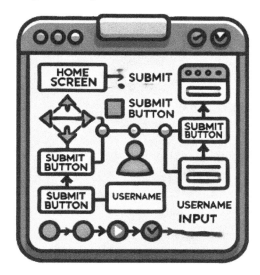

Figure 4.40 – Naming conventions

Consistency is the key factor. Establish a naming convention and adhere to it throughout the entire application development process. This practice not only enhances the clarity and readability of the application but also facilitates collaboration. When team members encounter familiar naming patterns, they can quickly comprehend the structure and contribute more effectively.

Implementing consistent naming conventions is a small but impactful step toward improving efficiency and ensuring seamless teamwork.

Here are some examples of naming conventions that you should consider:

- **Screens**:

    - *HomeScreen*: The main landing page of the application

    - *DetailScreen*: A screen that shows detailed information

    - *EditScreen*: A screen where users can edit data

- **Buttons**:

  - *SubmitButton*: A button to submit forms

  - *CancelButton*: A button to cancel an action

  - *RefreshButton*: A button to refresh data

- **Text inputs**:

  - *UsernameInput*: A textbox for entering a username

  - *EmailInput*: A textbox for entering an email address

  - *SearchInput*: A textbox for entering search queries

- **Labels**:

  - *TitleLabel*: A label for the title text

  - *DescriptionLabel*: A label for descriptive text

  - *ErrorLabel*: A label for displaying error messages

- **Collections and variables**:

  - *colUserData*: A collection for holding user data

  - *varTotalCount*: A variable for storing the total count

  - *colOrders*: A collection of order data

- **Dropdowns and combo boxes**:

  - *StatusDropdown*: A dropdown for selecting status options

  - *CategoryComboBox*: A combo box for selecting categories

  - *CountryDropdown*: A dropdown for selecting a country

- **Galleries and data tables**:

  - *UserGallery*: A gallery displaying a list of users

  - *OrderTable*: A data table showing order details

  - *ProductGallery*: A gallery listing products

- **Forms**:

  - *UserForm*: A form for user input

  - *OrderForm*: A form for order details

  - *FeedbackForm*: A form for collecting feedback

By consistently applying these naming conventions, you can create Power Apps that are not only easier to understand and maintain but also foster better collaboration among team members.

Optimize performance

Enhancing the performance of Power Apps is essential to ensure they operate seamlessly and efficiently. A key strategy is to refine data operations by employing filters and conditions that handle only pertinent data, thereby significantly cutting down on execution time and resource consumption:

Figure 4.41 – Performance

Instead of loading large datasets all at once, use delegation to handle data operations directly on the server side. This approach reduces the amount of data that needs to be processed and transferred to the application, significantly enhancing speed and responsiveness. For instance, implementing filters to streamline data before executing actions can substantially boost performance, particularly when you're managing extensive datasets.

Modular design

Dividing complex applications into smaller, reusable parts is an effective strategy for managing application development. By developing modular elements such as reusable screens, controls, and functions, we can isolate specific tasks and use them in various applications. This approach not only simplifies our understanding of our applications and how we maintain them but also encourages reuse, ultimately saving time and effort in the long run:

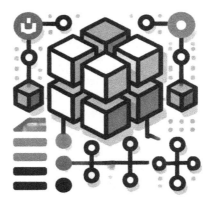

Figure 4.42 – Modular design

Creating standardized components for recurring tasks is a key aspect of modular design. For instance, if we frequently use data entry forms or navigation menus, developing templates or reusable components for these purposes can be highly beneficial. This practice guarantees uniformity and minimizes errors since there's no need to design these elements from the ground up each time. Implementing a modular design strategy in Power Apps significantly improves the efficiency, upkeep, and scalability of our applications.

Documentation

Thorough documentation is essential for maintaining any system effectively, and Power Apps is no different. Including comments within the application components helps explain their purpose and functionality, making it easier for others to understand the application's logic when they revisit it later. Clear annotations can greatly reduce the time spent deciphering complex parts, especially when debugging or updating is necessary:

Figure 4.43 – Documentation

Alongside in-app comments, maintaining external documentation is also critical. This should encompass an overview of the application architecture, design decisions, and any troubleshooting tips. Detailed documentation serves as a valuable resource for training new team members, providing them with the context and information they need to work effectively with our applications. Additionally, it helps ensure continuity and consistency, even as team members change.

Testing and debugging

Rigorous testing is crucial to confirm that your Power Apps perform as intended across various scenarios. It's important to test the applications with diverse inputs and conditions to uncover any potential issues or edge cases. This thorough approach helps identify and fix problems before they affect end users. Power Apps offers built-in debugging tools, such as the ability to monitor application performance and step through code execution, which are invaluable for troubleshooting and refining applications. Although debugging can be time-consuming, investing the effort to do it correctly produces significant benefits:

Figure 4.44 – Testing and debugging

Use logs and error messages provided by Power Apps to locate issues and understand their causes. By systematically testing and debugging our applications, we can ensure they are robust, reliable, and ready to handle real-world use without problems. This process enhances the overall quality and user experience of the applications.

Monitoring and maintenance

Continuous monitoring and upkeep are essential to ensure that your Power Apps operate efficiently over time.

Power Apps provides analytics capabilities that offer valuable insights into application performance and usage. Regularly examining these metrics can help you identify any potential issues or bottlenecks. Setting up alerts to notify you of anomalies or failures allows for prompt resolution:

Figure 4.45 – Monitoring and maintenance

Creating a maintenance schedule is crucial for keeping applications current and aligned with evolving requirements. Periodically review and update your applications, make necessary adjustments, and retire any outdated components.

Proactive maintenance helps prevent issues and ensures that the Power App remains efficient and effective.

Use Power Apps templates

Power Apps provides a variety of templates for frequently needed application functionalities, making them an excellent foundation for Power App application development:

Figure 4.46 – Templates

Taking advantage of these pre-designed templates can significantly reduce the time and effort required for development. They not only accelerate the creation process but also help ensure adherence to best practices from the beginning. These templates have been thoroughly validated and tested, ensuring their reliability and effectiveness within the platform.

Governance

Implementing governance policies is essential for managing the development, use, and life cycle of Power Apps within an organization. Establish clear rules on who can create and oversee applications, what types of applications are permissible, and how they should be documented and maintained. This ensures that development efforts align with organizational objectives and standards:

Figure 4.47 – Governance

Providing guidelines and training for users encourages the effective and responsible use of Power Apps. Educate users on best practices, common mistakes, and how to maximize the tool's potential. This not only enables them to develop their own applications but also helps maintain a high level of quality and consistency across all applications within the organization.

Solutions

Using solutions for deployment in Power Apps simplifies the process of transferring applications across different environments. Solutions in Power Apps bundle applications and their dependencies, facilitating the movement between development, testing, and production stages.

This approach ensures that all components are configured properly, minimizing the risk of deployment issues:

Figure 4.48 – Solutions

Solutions also facilitate version control and change management, offering a systematic method for deploying applications.

Ownership

Ownership is crucial in Power Apps development as it ensures accountability, responsibility, and control over the application life cycle. When a specific individual or team is designated as the owner, they can oversee the development process, ensure adherence to best practices, and maintain the application's quality and performance:

Figure 4.49 – Ownership

Ownership fosters a sense of responsibility, encouraging proactive management of updates, bug fixes, and user feedback. It also simplifies governance and compliance as the designated owner can implement and monitor security measures, data integrity, and user access controls.

Ultimately, clear ownership leads to more reliable, efficient, and sustainable Power Apps solutions.

Keeping up with Power Apps updates

Staying current with Power Apps updates is crucial for maximizing the platform's potential and benefiting from the latest enhancements. Microsoft frequently introduces updates that improve functionality, security, and performance:

Figure 4.50 – Updates

Being aware of these updates enables users to utilize new features, refine existing applications, and adhere to security protocols.

Regularly refreshing applications to integrate new capabilities ensures they remain efficient, secure, and effective. Keeping Power Apps up to date is essential for maintaining optimal performance and leveraging the latest technological advancements.

As an example, one of Microsoft's latest updates for Power Apps introduced AI Builder capabilities. This allows users to integrate AI models directly into their Power Apps applications without needing extensive coding knowledge. With AI Builder, users can add features such as form processing, object detection, and text recognition, making their applications smarter and more efficient.

This enhancement significantly expands the potential use cases for Power Apps, enabling users to automate more complex processes and extract valuable insights from their data.

Example use case: A service company needs a CRM system to manage customer relationships, sales processes, and service delivery. A model-driven app would provide the necessary structure and integration with Dynamics 365 to support these business processes.

Scenario – creating an application to track your department's tasks

Consider the following scenario: as a member of the **human resources** (**HR**) team responsible for the employee onboarding process, you need to create an application to track your team's daily tasks. The goal is to enhance the team's productivity, ensure that all critical tasks are completed on time, and provide a centralized platform for task management and collaboration. By efficiently tracking and managing daily tasks, the HR team can better support new hires, streamline processes, and improve overall efficiency.

Keep in mind that some foundational concepts of Power Apps are assumed to be understood, so not every step will be explained from the ground up. Instead, approach the instructions with a problem-solving mindset and be ready to explore on your own where needed.

Let's learn how to create a *Team Daily Tasks* Power App:

Figure 4.51 – Creating an application to track your department's tasks

The following steps outline the process of creating a *Team Daily Tasks* Power App:

1. The first step involves logging into your Microsoft account:

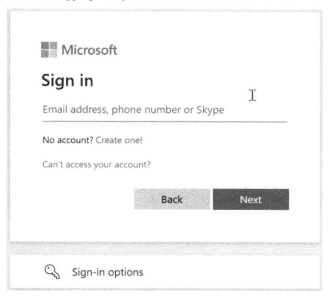

Figure 4.52 – Microsoft Office 365 login

2. Once you've logged in, access the SharePoint site where the list of tasks will be provisioned. In this scenario, we'll access the **Human Resources** SharePoint site:

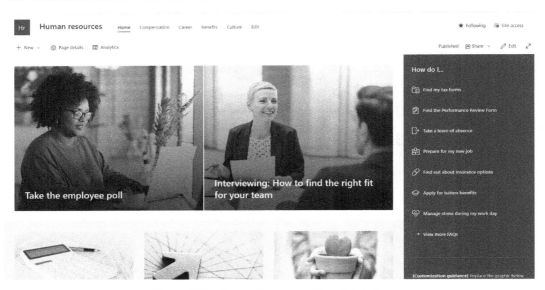

Figure 4.53 – Human Resources SharePoint site

3.   Create a MyTeamTasks list. To do so, click **New**, then **List**:

4.   Choose **Blank list**, name your list `MyTeamTasks`, and then click **Create**.

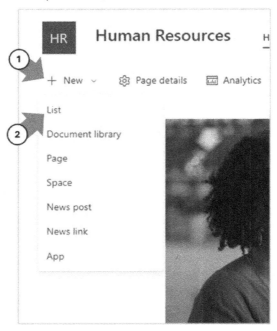

Figure 4.54 – Creating the MyTeamTasks list

5. Create the following **Columns**:

- Task Name (single line of text)

- Assigned To (person)

- Due Date (date and time)

- Status (choice: Not Started, In Progress, Completed)

- Priority (choice: High, Medium, Low)

- Comments (multiple lines of text)

Your **MyTeamTasks** list should look something like this:

Figure 4.55 – The MyTeamTasks list

With our list created, it's time to start creating our Power App. Follow these steps:

1. Access the Power Apps portal by typing https://make.powerapps.com in your browser.

2. You will be directed to the Power Apps portal. This portal is your central hub for viewing, creating, and managing Power Apps:

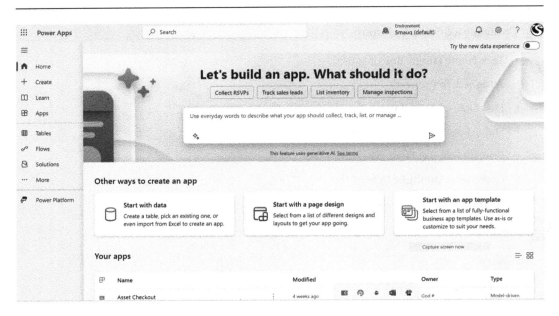

Figure 4.56 – Power Apps portal

When creating a Power App, it's considered best practice to start by creating a solution that will contain the Power App. Power Platform solutions serve as containers for applications, allowing us to manage and organize our applications more effectively.

Solutions provide a structured approach to grouping related applications, ensuring that all components are consistently deployed and maintained together, simplifying the process of transferring applications between different environments, such as development, testing, and production, and supporting version control and change management.

By using solutions, we can also implement governance policies more effectively, ensuring that the application creation efforts align with organizational standards, thus enhancing scalability and applicational maintainability.

Follow these steps:

1. To start creating a solution, click on the **Solutions** option:

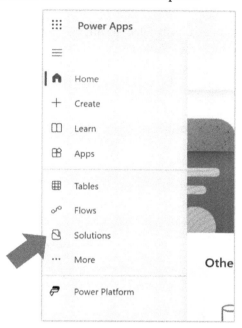

Figure 4.57 – Power Apps portal – creating a solution

2. Click on the **New Solution** option:

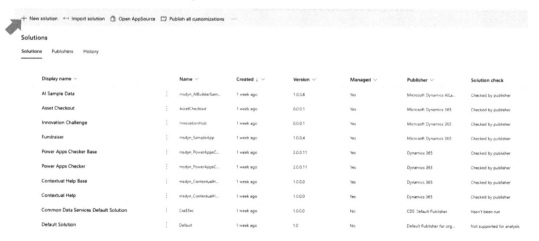

Figure 4.58 – Power Apps portal – New solution

3. Fill in the values that define the solution.

    I.   In the **Display name** field, type the name of the solution. In this scenario, this is MyTeamTasks.

    II.   The **Name** field is automatically filled in with the previous value with spaces trimmed down. Type the name of the solution here.

    III. Select the available **Publisher**.

    IV.   Click **Create**:

Figure 4.59 – Power Apps portal – creating a solution

4. At this stage, you need to create a Power App:

    I.   Click on the **New** option to open the menu.

    II.   Click **App**.

III.   Click **Canvas app**:

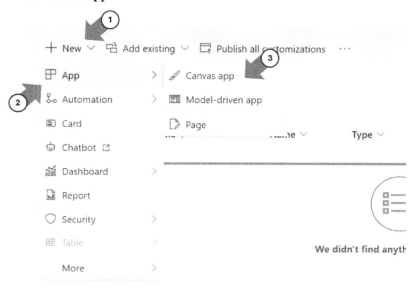

Figure 4.60 – Creating a canvas app

5.   The **Canvas app from blank** screen will be displayed. Enter a value for **App name** and click **Create**:

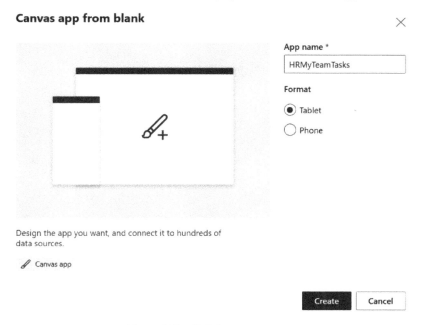

Figure 4.61 – Building a canvas app

Keep in mind that adopting a standardized naming convention for Power App names and all components is essential for effective management, as well as long-term maintainability.

A Power App name should have a name aligned with the context.

> **Important note**
>
> The importance of a proper naming convention for the application's name in Power Apps can't be overstated. A well-thought-out naming convention enhances clarity, organization, and efficiency in managing applications. It ensures that team members can quickly identify the purpose and functionality of the Power App, reducing the time spent searching for the correct application to modify or troubleshoot.
>
> Consistent naming conventions also facilitate better collaboration and communication among team members as everyone can easily understand the context and objectives of each application.
>
> Moreover, as the number of applications grows, a clear naming convention becomes crucial for maintaining an organized and scalable applicational environment, preventing confusion and errors.

In this scenario, the Power App's name is **HRMyTeamTasks**. The main idea for this scenario is to create three screens:

- **HomeScreen**, which will display the list of tasks
- **NewTaskScreen**, which will allow HR team users to add a new task
- **EditTaskScreen**, which will allow HR team users to edit a new task

6. Create a new screen by clicking on the **New screen** menu and then on the **Header and table** option:

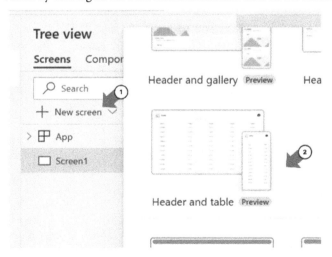

Figure 4.62 – Building a canvas app – New screen

7. Rename it `HomeScreen` by clicking on the ellipse menu and then **Rename**. Hit *Enter* when you're done:

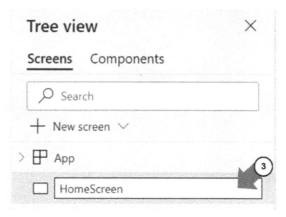

Figure 4.63 – Building a canvas app – the rename screen

8. Using the same approach, create the **NewTaskScreen** and **EditTaskScreen** screens using the **Header and form** option.

In the end, your **HRMyTeamTasks** application will look like this:

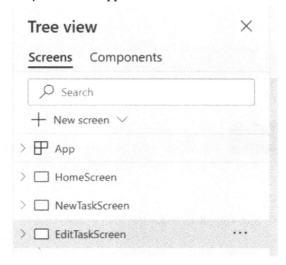

Figure 4.64 – Building a canvas app – Power App screens

9.   Next, create a data source that points to our **MyTeamTasks** SharePoint list:

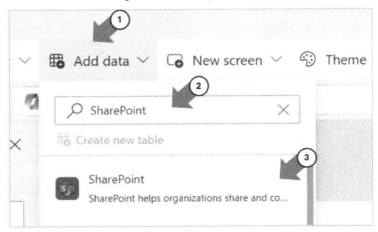

Figure 4.65 – Canvas app

10. Enter the SharePoint URL for the location of the list and click **Connect**:

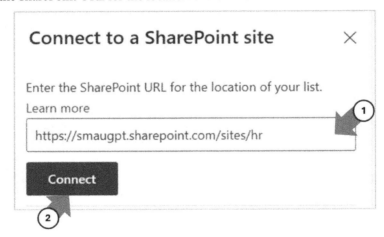

Figure 4.66 – Inserting a data source connection

11. Select the **MyTeamTasks** SharePoint list and click **Connect**:

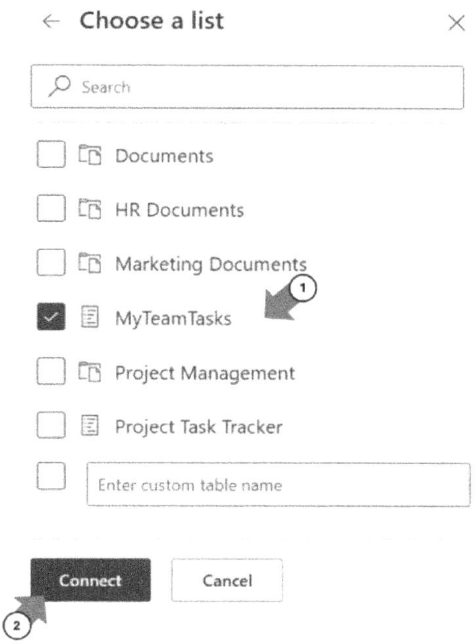

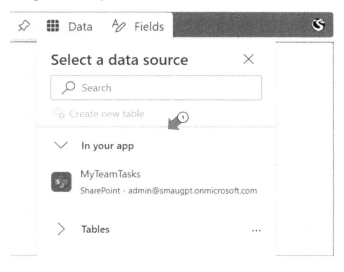

Figure 4.67 – Inserting a data source connection – Choose a list

12. Select **HomeScreen**, select the table in the form, and click the **Data** option to set the data source of the **Table** component to **MyTeamTasks**:

Figure 4.68 – Select a data source

As you may have noticed, all the fields of the list have been exposed. However, we only need the ones that we've defined. So, remove all fields except *Task Name*, *Assigned To*, *Due Date*, *Status*, *Priority*, and *Comments*.

In the end, your **HRMyTeamTasks** application's fields will look like this:

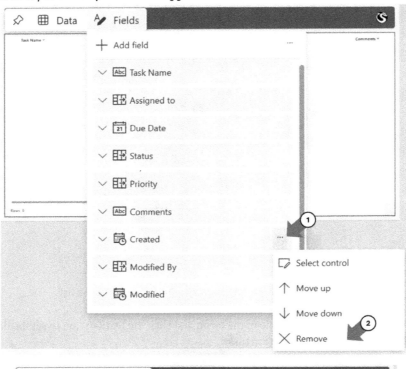

Figure 4.69 – HomeScreen

13. Use the same approach for **NewTaskScreen** and **EditTaskScreen**.

14. At this point, you need to enforce naming conventions in all components by using the prefix of the screen's name. By doing this, it will be easy to identify, change, and use each of them.

   In the end, your **HRMyTeamTasks** application's screens and components will look like this:

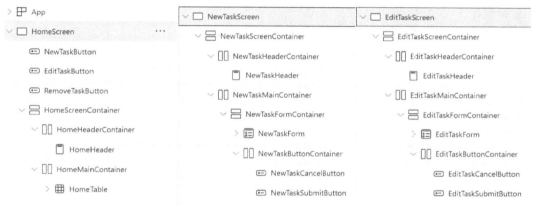

Figure 4.70 – Screens and components

15. Now, select **HomeScreen** and create three buttons:

   • **NewTaskButton**, with the text set to **New Task**

   • **EditTaskButton**, with the text set to **Edit Task**

   • **RemoveTaskButton**, with the text set to **Remove Task**

Align all the buttons on the right-hand side of the screen.

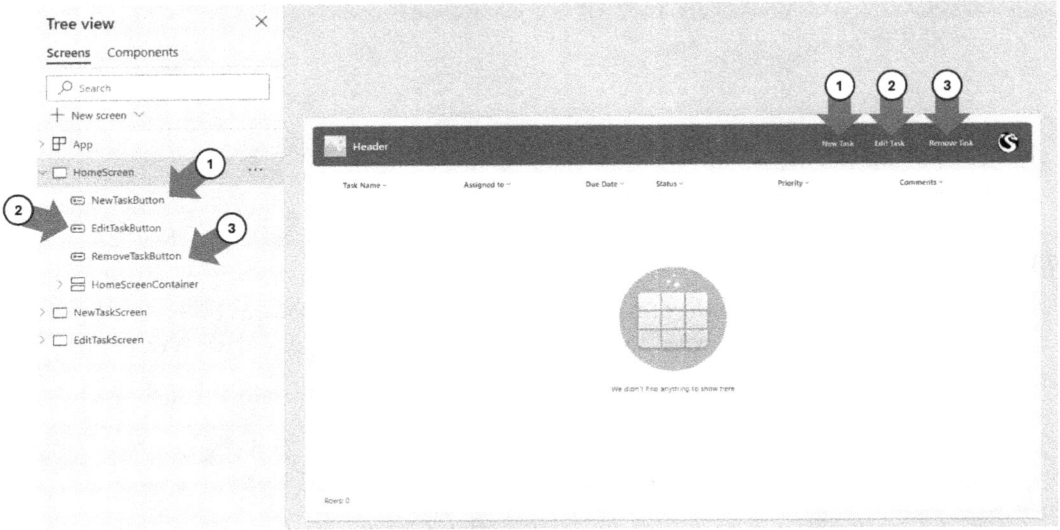

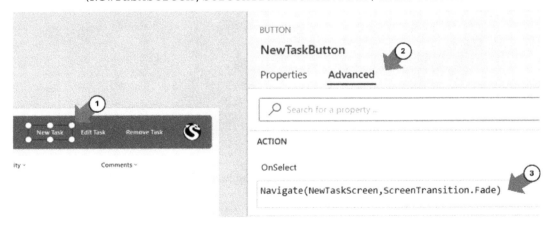

Figure 4.71 – NewTaskButton, EditTaskButton, and RemoveTaskButton

16. Next, create\edit\remove tasks in the MyTeamTasks list:

I. Select **NewTaskButton**, click on the **Advanced** tab, and enter `Navigate` `(NewTaskScreen, ScreenTransition.Fade)` in the **OnSelect** textbox:

Figure 4.72 – NewTaskButton properties

When a user clicks on **NewTaskButton**, they will be redirected to **NewTaskScreen**, ready to create a new task in our SharePoint list.

II.   Using the same approach, select **EditTaskButton**, click on the **Advanced** tab, and enter `Navigate(EditTaskScreen,ScreenTransition.Fade)` in the **OnSelect** textbox:

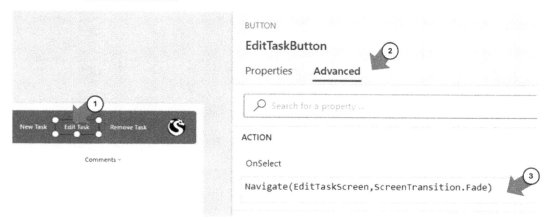

Figure 4.73 – EditTaskButton properties

When a user clicks on **EditTaskButton**, they will be redirected to **EditTaskScreen**, ready to edit a task in our SharePoint list.

III.   Using the same approach, we're going to remove items from the table. Select **RemoveTaskButton**, click on the **Advanced** tab, and enter `Remove(MyTeamTasks, HomeTable.Selected)` in the **OnSelect** textbox. We need to rename the table as appropriate:

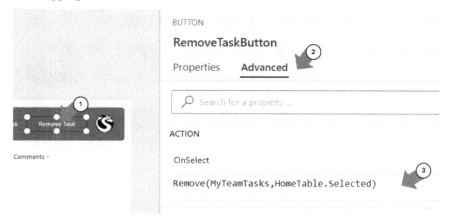

Figure 4.74 – RemoveTaskButton properties

When a user clicks on **RemoveTaskButton**, the selected task will be deleted.

IV.   Select the **HomeTable** component, click on the **Advanced** tab, and enter `Set`
       `(vActiveRecord,HomeTable.Selected)` in the **OnSelect** textbox:

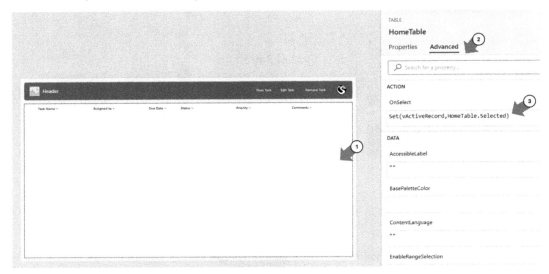

Figure 4.75 – HomeTable properties

This procedure sets a **vActiveRecord** variable that will be used in **EditTaskScreen**, allowing
us to edit the active task that's been selected.

17. Select the **HomeHeader** component, enter `HRTeams Tasks` in the **Title** property, and set
     Show logo to **Off**. This will change the header and show the title of the application.

     As you may have noticed, there isn't a **HomeHeader** header component, so we must rename
     the header component before editing its properties:

Figure 4.76 – HomeHeader properties

18. Select the **NewTaskScreen** and validate the data source. The data source of the **Table** component
     should be set to **MyTeamTasks**.

19. Select the **NewTaskHeader** component, enter New Task in the **Title** property, and set **Show logo** to **Off**. This will change the header so that it shows the contextualize operation.

    As you may have noticed, there isn't a **NewTaskScreen** header component, so we must rename the header component before editing its properties.

20. Rename the buttons to **NewTaskCancelButton**, **NewTaskSubmitButton**, and **EditTasksCancelButton**, respectively.

21. Select the **NewTaskCancelButton** component, click on the **Advanced** tab, and enter ResetForm(NewTaskForm);Navigate(HomeScreen) in the **OnSelect** textbox. This will navigate the application to **HomeScreen**.

22. Select the **NewTaskSubmitButton** component, click on the **Advanced** tab, and enter SubmitForm(NewTaskForm);ResetForm(NewTaskForm); Navigate(HomeScreen) in the **OnSelect** textbox. This will save the data on the form in the SharePoint list and navigate the application to **HomeScreen**.

23. Select the **EditTaskScreen** component and validate the data source. The data source of the **Table** component should be set to **MyTeamTasks**.

24. Select the **EditTaskHeader** component, enter Edit Task in the **Title** property, and set **Show logo** to **Off**. This will change the header so that it shows the contextualize operation.

25. Select the **EditTaskCancelButton** component, click on the **Advanced** tab, and enter ResetForm(EditTaskForm);Navigate(HomeScreen) in the **OnSelect** textbox. This will navigate the application to **HomeScreen**.

26. Select the **EditTaskSubmitButton** component, click on the **Advanced tab**, and enter SubmitForm(EditTaskForm);ResetForm(EditTaskForm); Navigate(HomeScreen) in the **OnSelect** textbox. This will save the data on the form in the SharePoint list and navigate the application to **HomeScreen**.

27. Select the **EditTaskForm** component, click on the **Advanced** tab, and enter FormMode.Edit for the **DefaultMode** property. This will set the form to edit mode. Enter vActiveRecord for the **Item** property. This will set the form's active record.

28. **Save** the application.

29. At this point, the **HRMyTeamTasks** application is ready, which means HR team members can add, edit, and remove tasks from the SharePoint list. All we need to do now is publish the application.

30. Go back to the **Solutions** page by clicking on the **Back** option and click **Publish all customizations**:

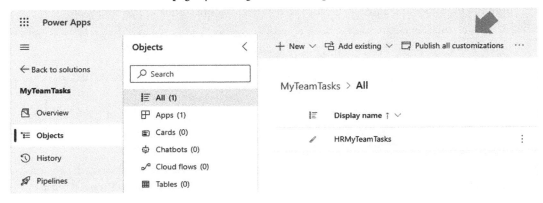

Figure 4.77 – Power Apps Solutions page

Let's look at some screenshots of the Power App when it's using real data.

This is the home screen of the Power App app:

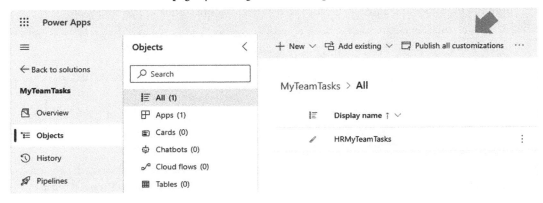

Figure 4.78 – HRMyTeamTasks home

This is the **New Task** screen of the Power App:

Figure 4.79 – HRMyTeamTasks – New Task

This is the **Edit Task** screen of the Power App:

Figure 4.80 – HRMyTeamTasks – Edit Task

In this section, you learned how to create an application in Power Apps to manage the team's tasks provisioned in a SharePoint list. The main idea was to provide a step-by-step guide for this process while highlighting naming conventions, best practices, and the most efficient methods. It's essential to apply all the techniques you've learned so that you can create an effective flow. This information is crucial for enhancing collaboration by keeping HR team members informed about task reassignments and workload changes.

Understanding this process lays the groundwork for optimizing processes and improving team efficiency.

Summary

In this chapter, we learned how to enhance SharePoint through site templates, custom forms, and Power Apps. We covered the benefits and application of SharePoint site templates for consistent and efficient site creation while exploring various tools for creating custom forms. We highlighted Microsoft Forms, Power Apps, and Microsoft Lists, each of which is suited for different needs. Integrating Power Apps with SharePoint was also emphasized for building custom applications that streamline operations and improve productivity by using best practices for Power Apps development.

A practical example of creating a task-tracking Power App integrated with a SharePoint list provided a comprehensive understanding of these enhancements, ultimately aiming to streamline processes, boost productivity, and enhance the user experience within SharePoint.

Looking ahead, the next chapter will delve deeper into data governance and compliance. We'll explore the essential principles and practices that ensure data integrity, security, and regulatory adherence within SharePoint environments.

Part 3: Locking It Down and Moving It Smoothly

Now that you've got the basics and some advanced features under your belt, it's time to get serious about keeping the data safe, staying compliant with regulations, and ensuring a smooth migration to Microsoft 365. This part focuses on the critical aspects of managing the digital environment, things that can make or break your organization if they are not done right.

Securing data and staying compliant are top priorities in today's digital world, and let's be honest, it's easy to get overwhelmed with all the rules and regulations out there. But don't worry; this part will guide you through the best practices, making sure you understand how to keep your organization's data locked down and compliant without losing sleep over it.

And then there's migration. If you've ever been through one, you know that migrating systems can feel like trying to move a fully furnished house across town without breaking anything!

But with the right strategies, you can minimize disruption, keep everything running smoothly, and prevent those dreaded post-migration headaches.

This part contains the following chapters:

- *Chapter 5, Data Governance and Compliance*
- *Chapter 6, Navigating the Microsoft 365 Migration Process*

5

Data Governance and Compliance

Data governance and compliance are critical components of managing any digital platform, especially within Microsoft 365. This chapter focuses on implementing robust security measures, utilizing data classification with sensitivity labels, and leveraging compliance features, including auditing, to ensure an organization's data is protected and regulatory requirements are met.

In this chapter, you'll gain practical insights and hands-on knowledge so that you implement these features effectively in real-world scenarios. By the end of this chapter, you'll be able to set up comprehensive security controls, classify data according to sensitivity levels, and use compliance tools to monitor and audit data usage. These lessons are crucial for minimizing risks, safeguarding sensitive information, and maintaining data integrity and regulatory compliance.

In this chapter, we're going to cover the following main topics:

- Compliance features and auditing
- Implementing security measures in Microsoft 365
- Data classification and sensitivity labels

Throughout this chapter, you'll learn about the following aspects:

- The importance of effective security measures in Microsoft 365 and how to implement them
- How to classify data with sensitivity labels to ensure proper handling and protection
- The compliance features and auditing processes in Microsoft 365 that can be used to meet regulatory requirements and ensure data integrity

This practical guide will equip you with the essential skills to enhance data protection, minimize risks, and ensure your organization remains compliant with industry regulations. You'll discover best practices for setting up access controls such as MFA and role-based access control, establishing policies for effective collaborative governance, and using data classification to handle and protect sensitive information appropriately.

You'll also learn how to leverage Microsoft 365's auditing features to monitor data usage and ensure adherence to regulations, providing a framework for maintaining data integrity and transparency. By mastering these tools and techniques, you'll be well-prepared to manage an organization's data governance and compliance needs, creating a secure and compliant digital workplace.

Technical requirements

To complete the tasks outlined in this chapter, you'll need the following:

- A Microsoft 365 subscription

- Access to SharePoint Online

- Access to Microsoft Azure

- Internet connectivity for accessing online resources and services

- A user assigned with the required roles:

  - In the **Microsoft Admin** portal, the user must have the **Global Administrator** role assigned

  - In the **Microsoft Defender** portal, the user must have the **Security Administrator** or **Global Administrator** role assigned

  - In the **Microsoft Compliance** portal, the user must have the **Compliance Administrator**, **Compliance Data Administrator**, **eDiscovery Administrator**, or **Records Management** role assigned

  - In the **Microsoft Purview** portal, the user must have the **Compliance Administrator**, Global Administrator, **Information Protection Administrator**, **Records Management**, **Insider Risk Management**, or **Privacy Management** role assigned

  - In the **Microsoft Entra** portal, the user must have the **Authentication Policy Administrator** or **Global Administrator** role assigned

---

Important note

The configurations outlined in this chapter require the use of a **Microsoft 365 E5** license. This advanced licensing option provides access to a comprehensive suite of enterprise-level features and tools that are essential for implementing these configurations effectively.

Compliance features and auditing

In today's digital landscape, organizations are increasingly held accountable for how they manage, protect, and utilize data. With the rise of stringent regulatory standards and growing public awareness of data privacy issues, businesses must adopt robust compliance and auditing practices to safeguard sensitive information and maintain trust. Microsoft 365, one of the leading cloud-based platforms for enterprise productivity, offers a comprehensive suite of compliance features and auditing tools designed to meet these demands:

Figure 5.1 – Compliance features and auditing

Compliance within Microsoft 365 is more than just adhering to regulations; it encompasses a strategic approach to managing data integrity, privacy, and security across the organization. The platform's compliance tools help organizations navigate the complexities of regulatory requirements, from global standards such as the **General Data Protection Regulation** (**GDPR**) to industry-specific mandates such as the **Health Insurance Portability and Accountability Act** (**HIPAA**). These tools enable organizations to classify data, protect sensitive information, monitor activities, and respond effectively to legal and compliance inquiries.

Auditing, a critical component of compliance, allows organizations to track and document user activities and data access across their Microsoft 365 environment. This capability is essential for detecting suspicious behavior, conducting internal investigations, and demonstrating compliance with regulatory obligations. Through detailed audit logs and advanced monitoring features, the platform provides the visibility needed to maintain data integrity and prevent unauthorized access or data breaches.

As organizations increasingly rely on cloud services for their daily operations, the need for a robust compliance and auditing framework becomes paramount. Microsoft 365 addresses this need by integrating compliance and auditing features directly into its core services, offering a unified approach to data governance. Whether you're managing sensitive customer data, ensuring secure collaboration, or responding to legal requests, Microsoft 365's compliance features and auditing tools provide the necessary infrastructure to protect organizational data and meet regulatory standards.

This section will explore the various compliance features and auditing capabilities available within Microsoft 365, offering practical insights into how these tools can be implemented to strengthen an organization's compliance posture. From data classification and loss prevention to eDiscovery and audit log management, we'll examine the key components that make Microsoft 365 a powerful platform for maintaining compliance and ensuring data integrity in an increasingly complex regulatory environment.

Understanding compliance in Microsoft 365

Compliance in Microsoft 365 encompasses a range of tools and practices that are designed to help organizations adhere to legal, regulatory, and policy requirements. These requirements can vary significantly across industries and regions, making it essential for organizations to understand and implement the necessary compliance measures.

Microsoft 365's compliance features are integrated into its cloud services, providing a unified approach to managing data protection, privacy, and security. This enables organizations to classify and protect sensitive information, monitor and audit data usage, and ensure adherence to regulatory standards.

Regulatory landscape

Before diving into the specifics of Microsoft 365's compliance features, it's important to understand the broader regulatory landscape: various regulations and standards govern data protection and privacy, including GDPR in the European Union, HIPAA in the United States, and the **California Consumer Privacy Act** (**CCPA**). These regulations impose strict requirements on how organizations collect, store, process, and protect personal data.

Understanding these regulations is crucial for implementing effective compliance measures. Organizations must be able to identify which regulations apply to their operations and ensure that their compliance strategies address all relevant requirements. Failure to comply with these regulations can result in significant financial penalties and damage to an organization's reputation.

Let's look at each Microsoft 365 compliance feature that's available.

Data classification and sensitivity labels

Data classification is a foundational element of compliance in Microsoft 365. By classifying data according to its sensitivity, organizations can apply appropriate protection measures to ensure that sensitive information is handled securely.

Microsoft 365 provides built-in tools for data classification, including sensitivity labels. Sensitivity labels allow organizations to categorize data based on its sensitivity and apply specific policies to protect it. These labels can be customized to meet the organization's unique requirements and can be applied manually by users or automatically based on predefined rules.

Automating data classification

While manual classification is essential, automating data classification can significantly enhance compliance efforts. Microsoft 365 provides several tools for automating data classification, including machine learning models and predefined policies.

Machine learning models can analyze the content of documents and emails to identify sensitive information and apply the appropriate sensitivity labels automatically. These models can be trained to recognize patterns and keywords associated with different sensitivity levels, making them highly effective at identifying and classifying sensitive data.

In addition to machine learning models, Microsoft 365 includes predefined policies that organizations can use to automatically classify data. These policies are based on common regulatory requirements and industry standards, making them a valuable resource for organizations looking to enhance their compliance efforts. For example, a predefined policy might automatically classify any document containing credit card numbers as *Confidential* and apply the necessary protection measures.

Sensitivity labels

To implement sensitivity labels in Microsoft 365, organizations must first define their data classification framework. This framework should outline the different levels of sensitivity and the corresponding labels that will be used to classify data. Common sensitivity levels include public, internal, confidential, and highly confidential.

Once the classification framework is established, organizations can create sensitivity labels in the Microsoft 365 compliance center. These labels can be configured to apply various protection measures, such as encryption, access controls, and watermarking. For example, a *Confidential* label might encrypt the data and restrict access to authorized users only, while a *Public* label might allow unrestricted access.

After creating the sensitivity labels, organizations must educate their users on how to apply these labels to their data. This can be achieved through training sessions, documentation, and ongoing support. Users should understand the importance of data classification and how to use the sensitivity labels effectively.

Data loss prevention

Data loss prevention (DLP) is a critical compliance feature in Microsoft 365 that helps organizations prevent the unauthorized sharing and leakage of sensitive information. DLP policies enable organizations to monitor and control the flow of data, ensuring that sensitive information isn't exposed to unauthorized users or transmitted outside the organization.

To implement DLP policies in Microsoft 365, organizations must identify the types of sensitive information they need to protect. This might include personal data, financial information, intellectual property, and other confidential data. Once these data types are identified, organizations can create DLP policies to monitor and protect them.

In addition to predefined rules, organizations can create custom DLP policies to meet their specific requirements. These custom policies can be based on keywords, regular expressions, and other criteria that match the organization's unique compliance needs. For example, a custom DLP policy might flag any document containing proprietary research data and prevent it from being shared outside the organization.

Once these policies are in place, it's essential to monitor their effectiveness and respond to any incidents promptly. Microsoft 365 provides comprehensive reporting and alerting capabilities to help organizations track DLP incidents and take corrective actions.

DLP reports provide detailed information on policy matches, including the location of the incident, the type of sensitive information involved, and the user who triggered the policy. These reports can be accessed through the Microsoft 365 compliance center, allowing compliance officers and administrators to review incidents and identify trends.

In addition to reports, Microsoft 365 can generate alerts for high-severity DLP incidents. These alerts can be configured to notify specific individuals or groups, such as compliance officers or IT security teams, enabling them to respond quickly to potential data breaches. Responding to incidents involves investigating the cause of the policy match, assessing the impact, and taking appropriate actions to mitigate any risks. This might include notifying affected users, retraining employees on data handling practices, or adjusting DLP policies to improve their effectiveness.

Auditing and monitoring

Auditing and monitoring are essential components of compliance in Microsoft 365. These processes help organizations track user activities, detect suspicious behavior, and ensure adherence to compliance policies. Microsoft 365 provides a range of auditing and monitoring tools designed to give organizations visibility into their data and user actions.

Unified audit log

The **unified audit log** is a central repository for all audit logs that are generated within Microsoft 365. It provides a comprehensive view of user activities across various Microsoft 365 services, including Exchange Online, SharePoint Online, OneDrive for Business, and Microsoft Teams. The unified audit log enables organizations to track user actions, such as file accesses, email sends, and administrative changes, providing valuable insights for compliance and security purposes. To access the unified audit log, organizations can use the Microsoft 365 compliance center. The audit log can be searched using various criteria, such as date range, user, and activity type. This allows compliance officers and administrators to quickly find and review specific events. In addition to the unified audit log, Microsoft 365 offers advanced audit capabilities that provide more granular insights into user activities.

These capabilities include advanced search filters, longer retention periods, and the ability to capture additional events, such as mail flow and file permission changes.

Advanced audit capabilities are particularly useful for organizations with stringent compliance requirements, such as those in regulated industries. By leveraging these capabilities, organizations can ensure that they capture and retain all relevant audit data, enabling them to meet regulatory standards and conduct thorough investigations when necessary.

Monitoring user activity

Monitoring user activity is a crucial aspect of compliance in Microsoft 365. By keeping a close eye on user actions, organizations can detect and respond to potential security threats and compliance violations. Microsoft 365 provides several tools for monitoring user activity, including activity alerts, audit log search, and user activity reports.

Activity alerts enable organizations to receive real-time notifications of specific user actions. These alerts can be configured to trigger based on predefined criteria, such as changes to sensitive files, creation of new admin accounts, or unusual login patterns. By setting up activity alerts, organizations can quickly identify and respond to potentially suspicious behavior.

Audit log search allows organizations to perform detailed searches of the audit logs to investigate specific events. This tool provides a flexible search interface, enabling compliance officers to filter audit data based on various parameters, such as user, activity type, and date range. An audit log search is essential for conducting thorough investigations and identifying the root cause of compliance incidents.

User activity reports provide summarized information on user actions within Microsoft 365. These reports can be generated regularly and include details such as file accesses, email sends, and login attempts. User activity reports help organizations track user behavior over time, identify trends, and ensure compliance with internal policies.

Microsoft Purview Compliance Manager

Microsoft Purview Compliance Manager is a powerful tool within Microsoft 365 that helps organizations manage their compliance efforts. It provides a centralized dashboard for assessing compliance posture, managing compliance tasks, and tracking progress toward meeting regulatory requirements.

Compliance Manager enables organizations to assess their compliance posture by providing detailed assessments based on various regulatory standards and industry frameworks. These assessments include GDPR, HIPAA, ISO 27001, and more. Each assessment consists of a series of controls and actions that organizations must implement to achieve compliance.

To perform an assessment, organizations can select the relevant regulatory standard from the Compliance Manager dashboard. Compliance Manager then generates a list of controls and actions required to meet the standard, where each control includes detailed guidance on how to implement it, along with links to relevant documentation and resources.

Compliance Manager helps organizations manage their compliance tasks by providing a task management interface, allowing compliance officers to assign tasks to specific individuals or teams, track task progress, and set deadlines for completion. Each task is linked to a specific control within an assessment, ensuring that all compliance requirements are addressed.

Tracking compliance progress

Tracking progress toward compliance is a key feature of Compliance Manager. The tool provides a progress dashboard that displays the status of each assessment, including the number of completed tasks, pending tasks, and overall compliance score. This dashboard helps organizations monitor their compliance efforts and identify areas that require additional attention.

In addition to the progress dashboard, the Compliance Manager generates detailed reports that provide a comprehensive view of an organization's compliance posture. These reports include information on completed and pending tasks, identified risks, and recommendations for improving compliance. The reports can be shared with stakeholders, such as senior management or regulatory bodies, to demonstrate the organization's commitment to compliance.

eDiscovery and Content search

eDiscovery and Content search are essential tools for compliance and legal purposes in Microsoft 365. These tools enable organizations to search for, preserve, and export data in response to legal requests, investigations, and audits.

eDiscovery, or electronic discovery, is the process of identifying, collecting, and producing **electronically stored information** (**ESI**) in response to legal requests. In Microsoft 365, eDiscovery tools help organizations manage the eDiscovery process by providing a centralized platform for searching, preserving, and exporting data.

To implement eDiscovery in Microsoft 365, organizations must first set up an eDiscovery case in the compliance center. An eDiscovery case serves as a container for all the activities related to a specific legal request or investigation. Within an eDiscovery case, organizations can create and manage holds, searches, and exports.

When a legal request is received, organizations can use the eDiscovery tools to search for relevant data across various Microsoft 365 services, including Exchange Online, SharePoint Online, OneDrive for Business, and Microsoft Teams. The search results can then be reviewed and refined to identify the specific data that needs to be preserved or produced.

Preserving data with legal holds

Legal holds are an essential component of the eDiscovery process. A legal hold ensures that data related to a legal request is preserved and cannot be altered or deleted. In Microsoft 365, organizations can apply legal holds to mailboxes, sites, and other data sources to prevent data from being modified or purged during an investigation.

To apply a legal hold, organizations can create a hold within the eDiscovery case and specify the scope of the hold, including the data sources and date ranges. Once the hold is applied, Microsoft 365 automatically preserves the data in its original state, ensuring that it remains available for legal review. Once the relevant data has been identified and preserved, organizations can export the data for legal review. Microsoft 365 provides several options for exporting data, including exporting to PST files, CSV files, and native file formats. The exported data can then be shared with legal teams, external counsel, or regulatory bodies as needed.

Exporting data in Microsoft 365 is a straightforward process. Within the eDiscovery case, organizations can select the search results to be exported, choose the export format, and initiate the export. The exported data is then packaged and made available for download, ensuring that it can be easily transferred to the appropriate parties.

Using Content search for compliance

In addition to eDiscovery, Microsoft 365 includes the Content search tool, which allows organizations to perform large-scale searches across their entire environment. **Content search** is useful for compliance purposes, such as conducting internal investigations, responding to regulatory inquiries, or identifying potential compliance violations.

Content search provides a flexible search interface that allows organizations to define complex search queries based on keywords, metadata, and other criteria. The search results can be previewed, refined, and exported as needed. Due to this, Content search is an invaluable tool for organizations looking to maintain compliance and address potential risks proactively.

Information governance and retention

Information governance is a critical aspect of compliance in Microsoft 365 that involves managing the life cycle of information while ensuring that data is retained for the appropriate duration and that it is disposed of securely when it's no longer needed. Microsoft 365 provides a range of tools and policies to help organizations implement effective information governance and retention practices.

Implementing retention policies

Retention policies in Microsoft 365 allow organizations to specify how long data should be retained and when it should be deleted. These policies can be applied to various data sources, including email, documents, and chat messages. Retention policies help organizations meet regulatory requirements for data retention while ensuring that data is disposed of securely when it's no longer needed.

To implement retention policies, organizations can use the Microsoft 365 compliance center. Within the compliance center, organizations can create retention policies that define the retention period and the actions to be taken at the end of the retention period, such as deleting or archiving the data. These policies can be applied globally across the organization or target specific users, groups, or sites.

Managing records and legal holds

In addition to retention policies, Microsoft 365 provides tools for managing records and legal holds. Records management allows organizations to classify certain data as records, ensuring that it's retained and protected according to regulatory requirements. Legal holds, as mentioned earlier, ensure that data is preserved during legal proceedings or investigations.

To manage records in Microsoft 365, organizations can create and apply retention labels that classify data as a record. Once data is labeled as a record, it's protected from modification and deletion, ensuring that it remains available for compliance purposes.

Disposing of data securely

Disposing of data securely is a critical aspect of information governance. When data is no longer needed, organizations must ensure that it's deleted in a manner that complies with regulatory requirements and prevents unauthorized access. Microsoft 365 provides tools for secure data disposal, including the ability to automatically delete data at the end of its retention period.

To ensure secure disposal, organizations can configure their retention policies so that data is automatically deleted after a specified period. This ensures that data is removed from the environment when it's no longer needed, reducing the risk of data breaches and compliance violations.

Compliance features and auditing processes in Microsoft 365 are essential tools for organizations looking to meet regulatory requirements and ensure data integrity. By leveraging these features, organizations can classify and protect sensitive data, monitor and control data flow, audit user activities, and manage information governance effectively. This section has provided an in-depth exploration of the various compliance tools and processes available in Microsoft 365, offering practical guidance on how to implement them in real-world scenarios.

As we move forward, the next section will explore how to implement security measures in Microsoft 365, ensuring that an organization is not only compliant but also secure from potential threats.

Implementing security measures in Microsoft 365

Microsoft 365 provides a comprehensive suite of tools designed to safeguard data and enhance security. This section will walk us through implementing strong security measures in Microsoft 365, providing the crucial knowledge needed to safeguard an organization against potential threats and breaches.

Effective security measures in Microsoft 365 are crucial for several reasons:

- **Data protection**: Ensuring that sensitive information remains confidential and protected from unauthorized access

- **Regulatory compliance**: Meeting industry standards and regulatory requirements to avoid legal and financial penalties

- **Risk mitigation**: Reducing the likelihood of data breaches and cyberattacks, which can lead to significant reputational and financial damage

Multi-factor authentication

Multi-factor authentication (**MFA**) is a security mechanism that requires users to provide two or more verification factors to gain access to a resource, such as an application, online account, or VPN. MFA adds an extra layer of security, significantly reducing the risk of unauthorized access:

Figure 5.2 – MFA

Here are the steps for enabling MFA for users:

1. First, navigate to `https://admin.microsoft.com` and log in with your admin credentials:

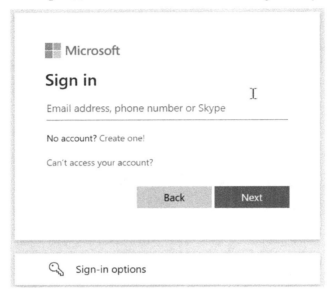

Figure 5.3 – Microsoft 365 login

2. **From** the left-hand navigation pane, click **Admin** to open the Microsoft 365 admin center:

Figure 5.4 – Microsoft 365 portal

3. Access the **Microsoft Entra** (formerly Azure AD) portal via the Microsoft 365 admin center:

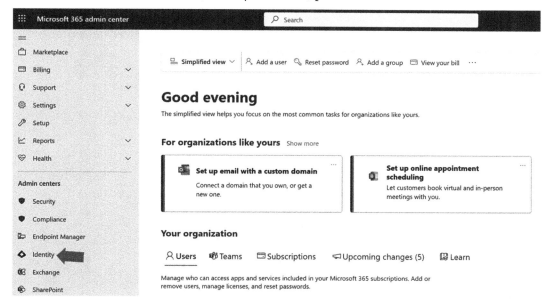

Figure 5.5 – Microsoft 365 admin center

4. Select **All users**, then **Per-user MFA**:

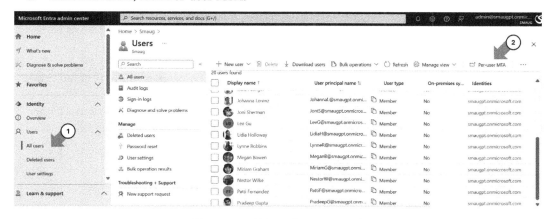

Figure 5.6 – Microsoft Entra portal

5. Select the relevant users and click **Enable**:

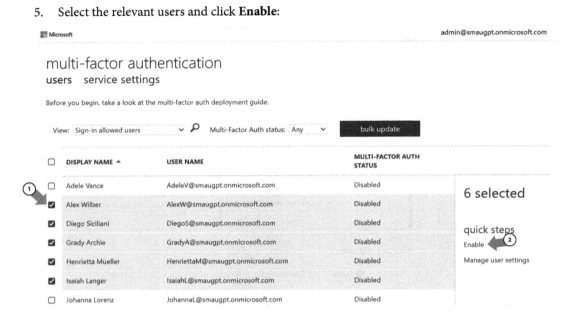

Figure 5.7 – MFA configuration

With that, you've implemented MFA, enhancing the security of your organization's resources by adding an extra layer of protection beyond passwords.

Role-based access control

Role-based access control is a method of restricting access to resources based on the roles of individual users within an organization. It allows administrators to assign specific roles to users or groups, each with a defined set of permissions, to ensure that users have only the access necessary to perform their job functions. This approach enhances security and compliance by minimizing the risk of unauthorized access to sensitive information or actions:

Figure 5.8 – Role-based access control

Here are the key components of role-based access control in Microsoft 365:

- **Roles**: Roles are sets of permissions that define what actions a user or group can perform. Microsoft 365 includes predefined roles, but custom roles can also be created to meet specific needs. The following are some common roles:

    - **Global Administrator**: Full access to all administrative features and data across Microsoft 365 services

    - **Exchange Administrator**: Manages the Exchange Online service

    - **SharePoint Administrator**: Manages the SharePoint Online service

    - **User Management Administrator**: Manages user accounts and groups

    - **Security Administrator**: Manages security-related features such as threat management and security reports

- **Role assignments**: These link a role to a user or group. When a role is assigned, the user or group gains the permissions associated with that role.

    Role assignments can be scoped to specific resources, such as a particular site in SharePoint, an Exchange mailbox, or an Azure resource group.

- **Role groups**: These are collections of roles that can be assigned to users or groups as a bundle. For example, in Exchange Online, we might have a role group for *Helpdesk* that includes roles such as **Mailbox Search** and **Message Tracking**.

Role groups simplify the management of permissions by allowing administrators to assign multiple roles simultaneously.

- **Custom roles**: While Microsoft 365 provides a range of built-in roles, administrators can create custom roles tailored to specific needs. This flexibility allows organizations to align access control more closely with their unique business processes.

- **Least privilege principle**: Role-based access control in Microsoft 365 supports the principle of least privilege, meaning users should only be granted the minimum level of access necessary to perform their job functions. This reduces the potential impact of security breaches or accidental data exposure.

Now, let's discuss the benefits of role-based access control in Microsoft 365:

- **Enhanced security**: By limiting access based on roles, role-based access control reduces the risk of unauthorized access to sensitive information

- **Simplified administration**: Administrators can efficiently manage permissions by assigning roles rather than configuring individual permissions for each user

- **Compliance and auditing**: Role-based access control helps organizations comply with regulatory requirements by enforcing strict access controls and providing audit trails of role assignments and changes

- **Scalability**: As organizations grow, role-based access control makes it easier to manage large numbers of users and resources without compromising security

To implement role-based access control, we need to follow these steps:

1. Define **Roles** and **Permissions**:

     I.   Identify and define various roles within the organization (for example, admin, manager, and employee).

     II.   Determine the permissions and access levels required for each role.

2. Assign **Roles** to users:

     I.   Go to the Microsoft 365 admin center.

     II.   Navigate to **Microsoft Entra** > **Roles and Administrators**.

     III. Assign the appropriate roles to users based on their job functions.

It's very important to review and update the roles regularly by conducting periodic reviews of roles and permissions to reflect changes in the organization or job functions.

Conditional Access policies

Conditional Access policies in Microsoft 365 are security measures that help organizations protect resources by applying specific access controls based on certain conditions. These policies are part of Microsoft Entra, the identity management service that underpins Microsoft 365:

Figure 5.9 – Conditional Access policies

The key concepts associated with Conditional Access policies are as follows:

- **Conditions**: Conditional Access policies are triggered based on conditions such as user identity, device state, location, and application being accessed. For example, we might want to enforce MFA if a user is trying to sign in from an unfamiliar location.

- **Access controls**: Once the conditions are met, the policy determines what kind of access control should be enforced. This could include requiring MFA, blocking access, or allowing access only on compliant devices.

- **Granular control**: Conditional Access allows for fine-tuned control over access to resources where we can define who can access what, under which conditions, and what actions are required for access.

- **Risk-based policies**: Conditional Access can also be integrated with Azure AD Identity Protection to enforce policies based on the risk level of the sign-in attempt. For example, if a sign-in attempt is deemed risky (for example, because it's from an unfamiliar IP address or with unusual behavior), stricter access controls can be applied.

Here are the steps for configuring Conditional Access policies:

1. Access the **Microsoft Entra** (formerly Azure AD) portal via the Microsoft 365 admin center:

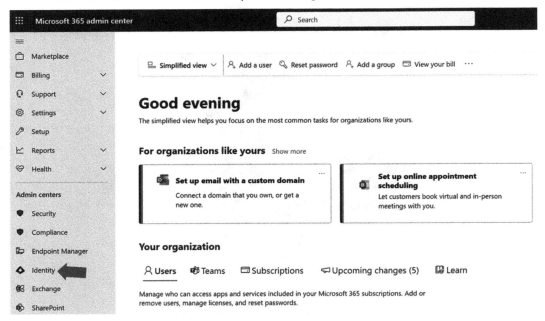

Figure 5.10 – Microsoft 365 admin center

2. Go to **Protection** > **Conditional Access**:

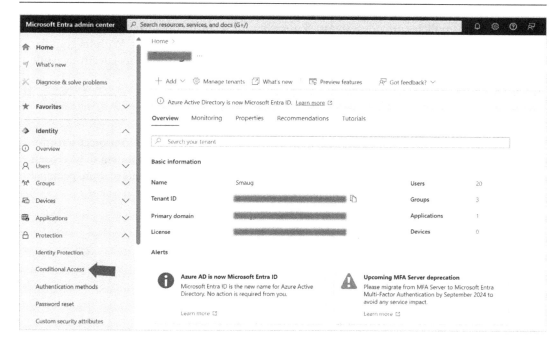

Figure 5.11 – Microsoft Entra admin center

Create policies that set up regulations to control access according to the needs and based on factors such as user location, device compliance, and risk level

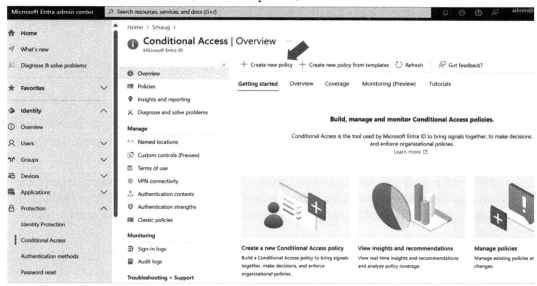

Figure 5.12 – Microsoft Entra admin center – Conditional Access options

Conditional Access policies provide a robust framework for securing organizational resources by implementing access controls that are tailored to specific conditions and risks. With its granular control and risk-based approach, organizations can safeguard their environments effectively while maintaining flexibility in how users access resources.

DLP

DLP in Microsoft 365 is a set of policies and tools designed to help organizations protect sensitive information and prevent accidental or intentional data leaks. It's a critical component of Microsoft 365's security framework that ensures that confidential data, such as financial information, personal data, or intellectual property, remains secure and compliant with regulatory requirements:

Figure 5.13 – DLP

Let's look at the key components of DLP in Microsoft 365:

- **Being able to identify sensitive information**:

    - DLP policies can identify and monitor sensitive information within emails, documents, and other data in Microsoft 365 services such as Exchange Online, SharePoint Online, OneDrive for Business, and Microsoft Teams.

    - Microsoft provides pre-configured templates for common sensitive information types, such as credit card numbers, Social Security numbers, health records, and more. These templates help organizations quickly set up DLP policies without needing to define every sensitive data type.

- **Policy enforcement**:

  - DLP policies allow organizations to create and enforce policies that dictate how sensitive information is handled. For example, a policy might prevent an email containing credit card information from being sent outside the organization.

  - Policies can be customized based on the organization's specific needs, such as setting thresholds (for example, how many instances of sensitive data trigger a policy), and defining actions (for example, blocking access, notifying users, or requiring justification).

- **Monitoring and reporting**:

  - DLP policies in Microsoft 365 include monitoring tools that track when and how sensitive information is used and shared within the organization

  - Administrators can receive alerts when a DLP policy is violated, providing visibility into potential data loss incidents

  - Comprehensive reporting features allow organizations to review and analyze how sensitive data is being handled and whether DLP policies are effective

- **Automated protection**:

  - DLP policies can automatically apply protections to sensitive data. For example, if a document containing sensitive information is uploaded to SharePoint Online, the system can automatically apply encryption or restrict sharing based on the policy

  - Automated actions can include blocking access to the content, notifying users about the policy violation, and providing guidance on how to comply with data protection rules

- **User education and awareness**:

  - It supports compliance with various regulations, such as GDPR and others. Organizations can configure policies so that they align with these regulations, helping to ensure that data handling practices meet legal and regulatory requirements.

  - Policies can also be tied into broader compliance frameworks within Microsoft 365 to provide a unified approach to data security and compliance.

- **Flexible scoping and targeting**: Policies can be scoped to specific users, groups, or departments, allowing for targeted protection where it's needed most. For example, different policies can be applied to finance departments versus marketing teams, reflecting the different types of sensitive data each might handle.

Now, let's focus on the various advantages of DLP.

Benefits of DLP in Microsoft 365

DLP in Microsoft 365 offers numerous benefits that help organizations protect sensitive information, comply with regulations, and reduce the risk of data breaches:

- **Protection of sensitive data** is one of the primary benefits of DLP. Policies automatically detect sensitive information such as credit card numbers, Social Security numbers, and personal health information across emails, documents, and other data stored or shared in Microsoft 365. By identifying and blocking the unauthorized sharing of sensitive information, DLP prevents accidental or malicious data leaks.

- **Regulatory compliance** is another key benefit. It helps organizations meet regulatory requirements such as GDPR, HIPAA, and PCI-DSS by enforcing data protection policies while also providing comprehensive auditing and reporting tools, making it easier for organizations to demonstrate compliance during audits.

- DLP also significantly **reduces risk by minimizing insider threats**. Policies help reduce the risk of insider threats by monitoring and controlling how sensitive information is accessed and shared by employees. Organizations gain better visibility into how data is used and shared, helping to identify potential risks before they become incidents.

- **User education and awareness** are enhanced through real-time alerts and notifications. Policies can notify users in real time when they are about to violate a policy, providing them with an opportunity to correct their actions. By guiding users on how to handle sensitive data correctly, DLP encourages adherence to best practices in data security.

- **Customizable DLP policies** help organizations create custom policies that align with their specific business needs, data types, and security requirements. Administrators can apply different policies to different departments, user groups, or data types, providing granular control over data protection.

- **Seamless integration** with Microsoft 365 is another significant advantage. It integrates seamlessly with other Microsoft 365 security and compliance tools, allowing for unified management across the entire environment. This integration ensures consistent protection across various Microsoft 365 services, including Exchange Online, SharePoint Online, OneDrive for Business, and Microsoft Teams.

- **Enhanced collaboration with security** is also a benefit of DLP. It ensures that collaboration and data sharing within the organization are done securely, without risking data exposure. As organizations increasingly adopt cloud services, DLP ensures that data remains protected in the cloud, especially in remote and hybrid work environments.

- **Real-time monitoring and incident response** are facilitated by DLP's continuous monitoring of data activities. This allows organizations to respond quickly to potential data breaches or policy violations. When a policy is violated, organizations can take immediate action, such as blocking access, notifying administrators, or logging the incident for further investigation.

- **Scalability** is another advantage as DLP is adaptable to business growth. As organizations grow and their data protection needs evolve, DLP can easily scale to meet new challenges without requiring significant additional investment or resources.

- **Cost efficiency** is achieved by reducing the risk of fines and lowering IT overhead. Preventing data breaches and ensuring compliance can help organizations avoid the substantial fines and penalties associated with data protection violations. Automation within DLP reduces the need for manual data monitoring and management, freeing up IT resources for other critical tasks.

Implementing DLP in Microsoft 365 provides organizations with a robust framework for safeguarding sensitive information, ensuring regulatory compliance, and mitigating data loss risks. With its comprehensive features and seamless integration into the Microsoft ecosystem, DLP empowers businesses to maintain security, streamline compliance, and enhance collaboration – all while minimizing potential breaches and reducing costs.

Implementing DLP policies

Follow these steps to configure a DLP policy:

1. From the left navigation pane, select **Compliance** to open the **Microsoft Purview** compliance portal:

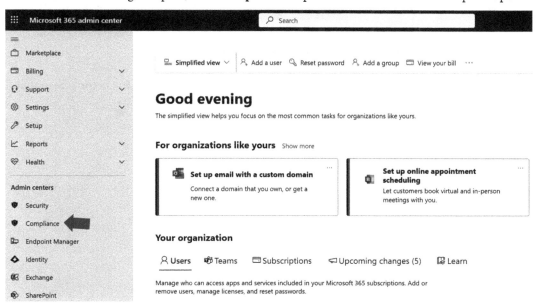

Figure 5.14 – Microsoft 365 admin center settings

> **Important note**
>
> **Microsoft Purview** is a cloud-based data governance and compliance solution that helps organizations manage and protect their data across various environments, ensuring regulatory compliance, data security, and effective data management.

Figure 5.15 – Microsoft Purview portal

2. Now, from the left-hand navigation pane, click **Policies** and select **DLP**. On the screen that opens, select the **Policies** tab and click **Create policy**:

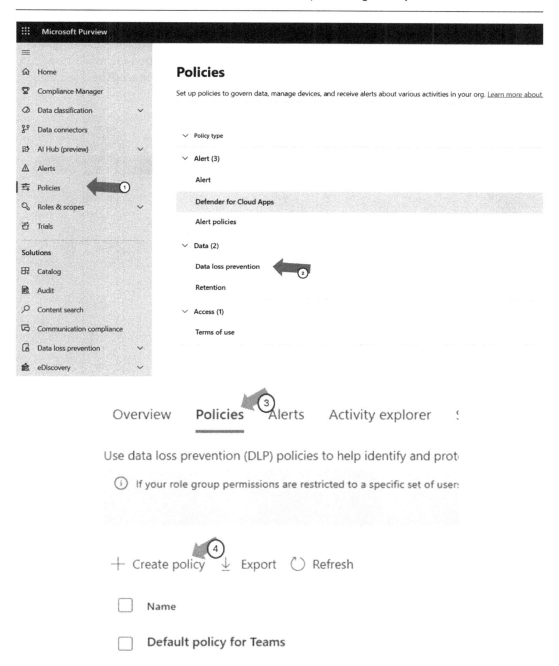

Figure 5.16 – Microsoft Purview – Policies settings

3. Follow the **DLP policy wizard** steps to create the policy.

    Through **predefined** or **custom templates**, choose the **type of information to protect** based on your specific needs. Microsoft provides templates for protecting common sensitive information types such as credit card numbers, Social Security numbers, and more.

    In this case, we'll establish a policy regarding the security of financial data.

4. Choose the type of information you wish to protect:

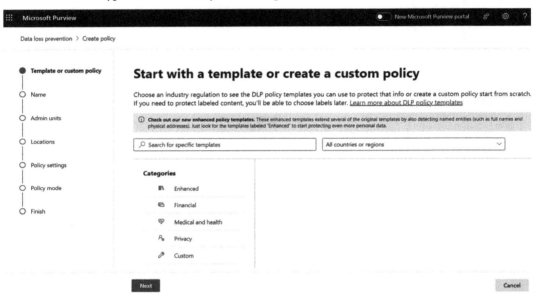

Figure 5.17 – Start with a template or create a custom policy

5.   Click **Next** to proceed to the **Name your policy** section, where you'll give the policy a name:

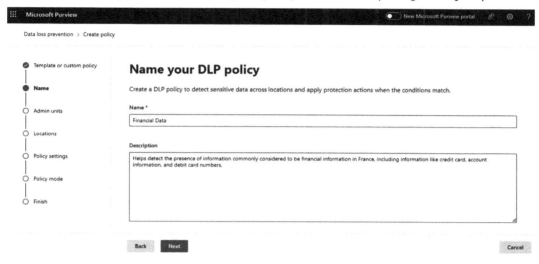

Figure 5.18 – Name your DLP policy

6.   Click **Next** and proceed to the **Assign Admin units** section.

In this instance, we wish to apply the policy to all users and groups:

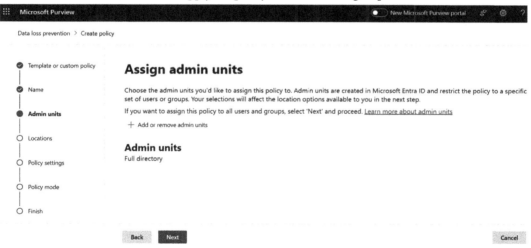

Figure 5.19 – Assign admin units

7. Click **Next** and proceed to the **Locations** section.

When applying a data classification or sensitivity labeling policy, we can choose where the policy will be enforced by selecting specific locations.

Keep in mind that at this time, policies that are applied to Power BI workspaces location aren't supported for these enhanced DLP templates:

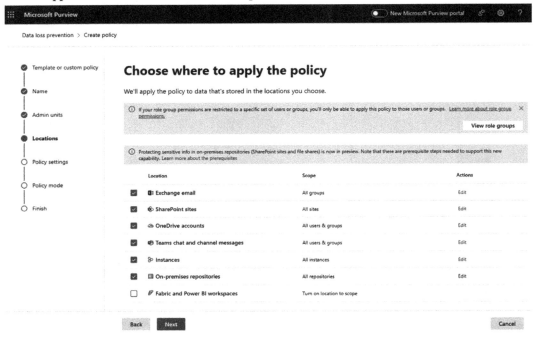

Figure 5.20 – Choose where to apply the policy

8. Click **Next** and proceed to the **Define Policy** section.

We can either use the default settings from the template or make our own rules to improve the policy more. In this instance, we aim to use the template's default settings:

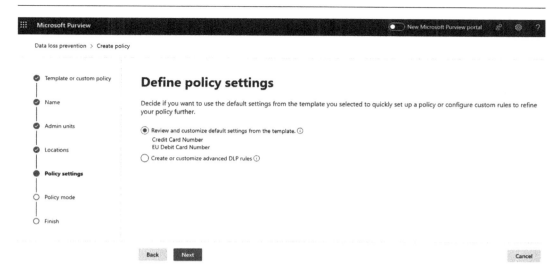

Figure 5.21 – Define policy settings

9. Click **Next** and proceed to the **Info to protect** section.

This policy will cover content that meets these criteria. Validate and edit them if needed. For example, we can change the criteria to find more sensitive information or content with a certain sensitivity:

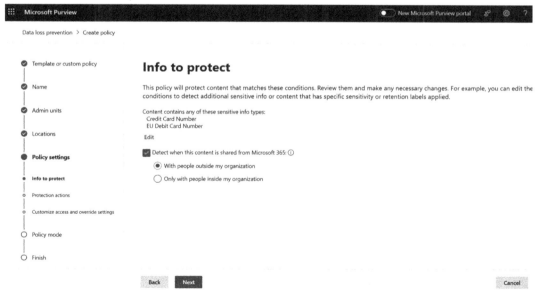

Figure 5.22 – Info to protect

10. Click **Next** and proceed to the **Protection actions** section.

Here, we can configure protection actions that are triggered when content matches the defined policy conditions. These actions help ensure that sensitive information is handled appropriately and that incidents are reported and managed effectively:

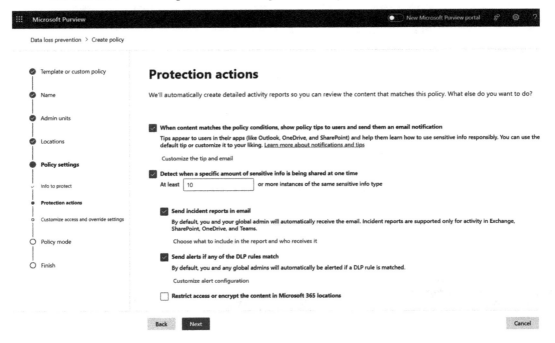

Figure 5.23 – Protection actions

11. Click **Next** and proceed to the **Customize access and override settings** section.

These settings allow administrators to configure access restrictions and override settings to protect sensitive content. By default, users are blocked from sending email and Teams chats that contain the type of content being protected. These configurations will help ensure that sensitive information is managed and shared securely, but only with authorized individuals:

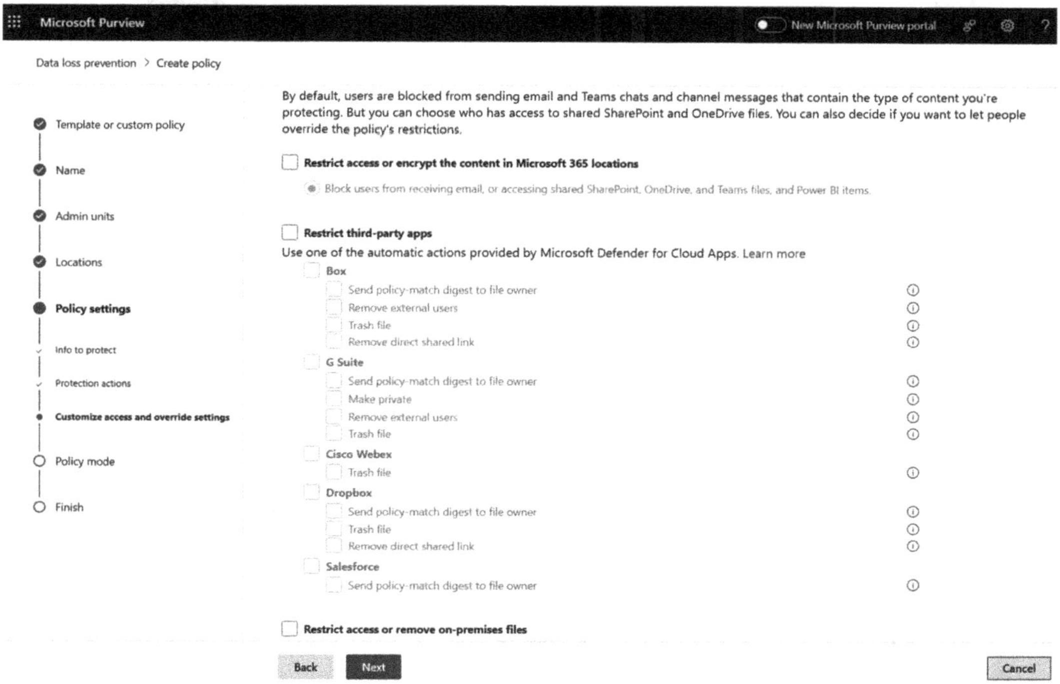

Figure 5.24 – Customize access and override settings

12. Click **Next** and proceed to the **Policy mode** section.

The **Policy mode** section allows administrators to choose how and when to activate a newly created or modified DLP policy. We can also use simulation mode to assess how the policy affects our data. This step is crucial for ensuring that the policy functions as intended without it immediately impacting users or workflows:

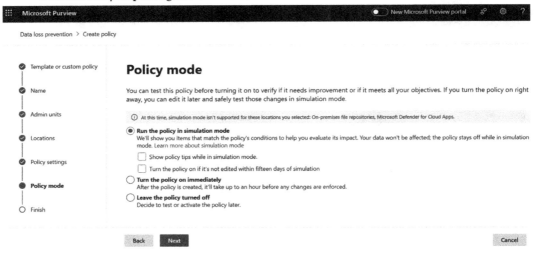

Figure 5.25 – Policy mode

13. Click **Next** and proceed to the **Review and Finish** section.

Keep in mind that after the policy is created, it will start applying to the selected locations. Review the settings on this page of the policy wizard and click **Submit** if everything is OK:

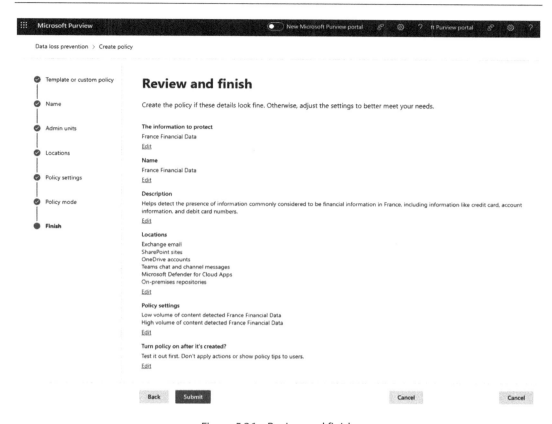

Figure 5.26 – Review and finish

By following these steps, we've successfully configured the Microsoft 365 tenant, helping us protect sensitive information and comply with data protection regulations. This ensures that the Microsoft 365 tenant is configured correctly and securely.

Adjust and revisit the settings as needed to accommodate any changes in the organization's requirements.

DLP in Microsoft 365 provides a robust framework for securing sensitive information, ensuring compliance, and fostering a culture of proactive data protection within the organization. By leveraging tools such as MFA, role-based access control, Conditional Access policies, and DLP, we can create a secure and resilient digital environment.

In the next section, we'll delve into data classification and sensitivity labels, which further enhance our ability to manage and protect an organization's most valuable data assets.

Data classification and sensitivity labels

In today's data-driven world, organizations are constantly handling vast amounts of information, much of which is sensitive and requires careful management to ensure security and compliance. Microsoft 365 offers robust tools for data classification and sensitivity labeling, enabling organizations to categorize and protect their data effectively:

Figure 5.27 – Data classification and sensitivity labels

This section delves into the intricacies of data classification and sensitivity labels within Microsoft 365, providing us with the knowledge and practical steps needed to safeguard an organization's critical information.

The importance of data classification

Data classification is the process of organizing data into categories that make it easy to retrieve, sort, and store for future use. It plays a crucial role in data management and protection, helping organizations do the following:

- Identify and prioritize data based on its sensitivity and importance
- Implement appropriate security measures to protect different types of data
- Ensure compliance with regulatory requirements and industry standards
- Improve data handling practices and reduce the risk of data breaches

By classifying data, organizations can create a structured approach to data security, ensuring that sensitive information receives the highest level of protection.

Understanding sensitivity labels

Sensitivity labels in Microsoft 365 are a key feature that allows organizations to classify and protect their data based on its sensitivity. These labels can be applied to emails, documents, and other types of data to enforce specific protection measures such as encryption, watermarking, and access restrictions.

Sensitivity labels help organizations do the following:

- Define clear rules for handling and protecting different types of data

- Automatically apply protections based on the sensitivity of the data.

- Track and monitor the use of sensitive data to prevent unauthorized access and misuse

- Provide users with guidance on how to handle data securely

By leveraging sensitivity labels, organizations can ensure that sensitive data is protected and handled consistently according to predefined policies.

Implementing data classification and sensitivity labels in Microsoft 365

To implement data classification and sensitivity labels in Microsoft 365, follow these steps:

1. **Define sensitivity labels**:

   - Start by identifying the different categories of data within the organization and determine the sensitivity levels for each category. Common sensitivity levels include **Public**, **Internal**, **Confidential**, and **Highly Confidential**.

   - Use the Microsoft 365 compliance center to create sensitivity labels that correspond to these categories. Each label should have a clear description and specify the protection measures to be applied.

2. **Publish sensitivity labels**:

   - Once the sensitivity labels have been defined, publish them so that they become available for users to apply. This can be done through label policies, which determine who can see and use the labels.

   - In the Microsoft 365 compliance center, create a label policy and select the sensitivity labels to include. Specify the users or groups that the policy applies to and configure any additional settings, such as requiring justification for label changes.

3. **Apply sensitivity labels to data:**

    -   Users can manually apply sensitivity labels to emails and documents based on the content's sensitivity. Microsoft 365 also offers automatic labeling based on predefined rules and conditions.

    -   Educate users on how to apply sensitivity labels and provide guidance on identifying sensitive information. This can be done through training sessions, documentation, and user guides.

4. **Monitor and manage sensitivity labels:**

    -   Use the Microsoft 365 compliance center to monitor the application of sensitivity labels and ensure compliance with data protection policies. The compliance center provides reports and dashboards that give insights into label usage and data protection status.

    -   Regularly review and update sensitivity labels and label policies to reflect changes in data sensitivity and organizational requirements.

By implementing data classification and sensitivity labels effectively within Microsoft 365, organizations can enhance their data protection strategies, ensure regulatory compliance, and empower users to handle sensitive information securely and efficiently.

Best practices for data classification and sensitivity labeling

To maximize the effectiveness of data classification and sensitivity labeling, consider the following best practices:

-   **Start with a data inventory**: Conduct a thorough inventory of the organization's data to identify what types of data we have, where it's stored, and how it's used. This will help us understand the sensitivity of the data and determine the appropriate classification levels.

-   **Involve stakeholders**: Engage key stakeholders, including data owners, security teams, and compliance officers, in the process of defining sensitivity labels and data classification policies. Their input and buy-in are essential for creating effective and practical policies.

-   **Keep it simple**: Avoid creating too many sensitivity labels or overly complex classification schemes. Keep the labels simple and intuitive to ensure that users can easily understand and apply them.

-   **Automate where possible**: Leverage Microsoft 365's automatic labeling capabilities to reduce the burden on users and ensure consistent application of sensitivity labels. Automatic labeling can be based on content inspection, metadata, and predefined rules.

-   **Educate and train users**: Provide comprehensive training and resources to help users understand the importance of data classification and how to apply sensitivity labels correctly. Ongoing education is crucial for maintaining awareness and adherence to data protection policies.

- **Monitor and review**: Regularly monitor the use of sensitivity labels and review the data classification policies to ensure they remain effective and relevant. Use the insights gained from monitoring to make necessary adjustments and improvements.

Incorporating these best practices into our data classification and sensitivity labeling strategy will help ensure that sensitive information is protected consistently and managed effectively across the organization, reducing risks while maintaining compliance with industry regulations.

Real-world scenario – implementing data classification and sensitivity labels

Consider a scenario where a financial services company needs to protect its sensitive customer data, including **personal identification information** (**PII**), financial records, and confidential business information. The company decided to implement data classification and sensitivity labeling in Microsoft 365 to achieve this goal:

Figure 5.28 – Real-world scenario

Here are the steps you'll need to implement:

1. **Define sensitivity labels**: The company identifies the following sensitivity levels:

   - **Public**: Data that can be freely shared without any restrictions

   - **Internal**: Data that's intended for internal use only and should not be shared externally

   - **Confidential**: Data that contains sensitive information and requires protection measures such as encryption and access restrictions

   - **Highly confidential**: Data that's extremely sensitive, such as PII and financial records, and requires the highest level of protection

2. **Publish sensitivity labels**: The company creates sensitivity labels in the Microsoft 365 compliance center for each of these levels and publishes them through label policies. The policies specify which users can access and apply the labels, ensuring that only authorized personnel can handle highly confidential data.

3. **Apply sensitivity labels to data**: Employees are trained on how to identify and classify sensitive data using the new sensitivity labels. They learn how to manually apply labels to emails and documents, as well as how to use automatic labeling features for consistent protection.

4. **Monitor and manage sensitivity labels**: The company uses the Microsoft 365 compliance center to monitor the application of sensitivity labels and generate reports on data protection status. Regular audits are conducted to ensure compliance with data protection policies and to identify any areas for improvement.

By following these steps, the financial services company successfully implements a robust data classification and sensitivity labeling system in Microsoft 365, protecting its sensitive data and ensuring compliance with regulatory requirements.

By effectively implementing data classification and sensitivity labels in Microsoft 365, organizations can ensure that their sensitive information is protected and managed consistently according to predefined policies, reducing the risk of data breaches and maintaining compliance with regulatory requirements.

Summary

In this chapter, we explored the vital role of data governance and compliance within Microsoft 365, emphasizing the importance of protecting sensitive data and adhering to regulatory standards. We discussed the comprehensive suite of compliance features available in Microsoft 365, including data classification, sensitivity labels, and auditing tools, which help organizations maintain data integrity and meet global and industry-specific regulations. These tools provide a robust framework for ensuring that sensitive information is protected and managed consistently according to best practices.

We also examined the implementation of essential security measures, such as MFA, role-based access control, and Conditional Access policies, which are critical for safeguarding an organization's data.

By mastering these tools and strategies, you'll be better prepared to protect an organization's sensitive data, ensure regulatory compliance, and maintain a secure digital environment.

In the next chapter, we'll delve into migration strategies, where we'll explore the best practices for transitioning to Microsoft 365, ensuring a seamless and efficient migration process.

6

Navigating the Microsoft 365 Migration Process

Migrating to Microsoft 365 is a pivotal process for organizations aiming to modernize their digital workplace. This chapter is dedicated to guiding you through the process of planning and executing a successful migration to Microsoft 365, helping you navigate the complexities and challenges that can arise during this process. We'll explore strategies that ensure a seamless transition, from planning to post-migration optimization, ensuring organizations can fully leverage the capabilities of the platform.

In this chapter, you'll gain practical insights and hands-on experience in implementing best practices for data migration, overcoming common challenges, and optimizing the environment post-migration. By the end of this chapter, you'll be equipped with the skills necessary to execute a smooth and effective migration to Microsoft 365, ensuring that the data remains secure, accessible, and integrated within the new platform. These lessons are crucial for minimizing disruption, maintaining data integrity, and maximizing the value of the Microsoft 365 investment.

In this chapter, we're going to cover the following main topics:

- Planning and executing a successful migration to Microsoft 365 with post-migration validation
- Overcoming common migration challenges

Throughout this chapter, you'll learn about the following aspects:

- How to implement best practices for data migration, ensuring data security, and evaluating costs
- The significance of meticulous planning and how it contributes to a successful migration
- Techniques for overcoming common migration challenges and optimizing the environment to ensure a smooth transition

This practical guide will provide you with the essential knowledge to plan, execute, and optimize a Microsoft 365 migration, ensuring that organizations can fully harness the power of this platform while maintaining data integrity and security throughout the process.

A strategic migration journey

The journey to Microsoft 365 represents a significant evolution in the way organizations manage and collaborate on their digital assets. SharePoint, as a foundational component of this ecosystem, has a rich history of facilitating document management, collaboration, and communication within organizations:

Figure 6.1 – Migrating SharePoint to Microsoft 365

Initially launched in 2001, SharePoint has undergone numerous transformations, moving from an on-premises solution to a cloud-based service. These changes have progressively expanded its capabilities, integrating it more deeply with other Microsoft services, ultimately culminating in its seamless integration into the Microsoft 365 suite.

The shift from traditional SharePoint environments to SharePoint Online as part of Microsoft 365 represents a broader trend toward cloud computing that emphasizes accessibility, scalability, and continuous updates.

Microsoft 365 creates a comprehensive cloud-based productivity platform, enhancing the functionalities of individual services such as SharePoint but also fostering a more unified and efficient digital workplace. The migration to Microsoft 365 involved transitioning from legacy systems, often deeply entrenched in organizational workflows, to this modern, cloud-based environment. The challenge lies in ensuring that the migration isn't just a technical transition but also a strategic move that enhances productivity and collaboration across the organization.

With SharePoint at its core, Microsoft 365 offers advanced tools for content management, data security, and team collaboration, making it a critical upgrade for organizations looking to stay competitive in the digital age.

Successfully migrating to Microsoft 365 requires careful planning and execution while considering both the technical and organizational impacts. Organizations must assess their current SharePoint environment, understanding the intricacies of their existing workflows, data structures, and user access controls. This assessment is crucial in mapping out a migration strategy that minimizes disruption while maximizing the benefits of Microsoft 365. The process involves selecting migration tools, ensuring data integrity, and implementing post-migration optimization to fully leverage the capabilities of the new platform.

By embracing the historical strengths of SharePoint and the innovative features of Microsoft 365, organizations can achieve a seamless migration that not only preserves but enhances their operational efficiency.

Migration phases

Migrating to Microsoft 365 requires meticulous planning, strategic execution, and continuous optimization to ensure a smooth transition from legacy systems to a modern cloud-based environment. The process involves several critical phases, each with its own set of tasks, considerations, and best practices:

Figure 6.2 – Migration phases

In the upcoming sections, we'll discuss the different phases that are required for a successful migration to Microsoft 365.

Pre-migration planning

Pre-migration planning is an essential and foundational phase in any IT migration project, especially when transitioning to a comprehensive and multifaceted platform such as Microsoft 365. This critical stage requires meticulous planning, where every detail is carefully considered to mitigate potential risks and avoid disruptions during the migration process.

It begins with an in-depth analysis of the existing IT infrastructure, understanding the current workflows, data management practices, and user needs to ensure that the transition will support and enhance organizational productivity.

Strategic decision-making is at the core of this phase as it involves identifying the key objectives of the migration, defining the scope, and setting realistic timelines that align with organizational goals.

This stage includes assessing the readiness of the organization, evaluating the impact on end users, and ensuring that adequate training and support mechanisms are in place. The goal of pre-migration planning is not just to facilitate a smooth transition, but to optimize the migration process, making it as seamless and efficient as possible while ensuring that the new platform will meet the evolving needs of the organization. By investing time and resources into thorough pre-migration planning, organizations can significantly reduce the risk of unforeseen challenges, minimize downtime, and ensure that the migration to Microsoft 365 is successful and aligned with their long-term strategic vision.

In the following subsections, we'll provide a detailed breakdown of the essential components of pre-migration planning.

Assessment and discovery

The foundation of a successful migration lies in a thorough understanding of the current environment. This step involves performing a detailed analysis of the existing IT infrastructure, data landscape, and user interactions:

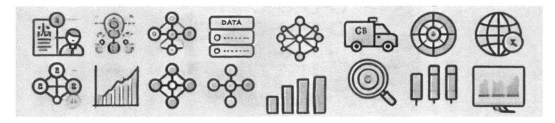

Figure 6.3 – Assessment and discovery

By comprehensively assessing these components, organizations can identify potential risks, dependencies, and areas that require optimization. This not only aids in minimizing disruptions during the migration but also ensures that the new environment is tailored to meet current and future business needs. This phase also allows innovation opportunities to be identified, enabling the organization to enhance efficiency and performance in the post-migration landscape.

Current environment analysis

The first step is to perform a comprehensive assessment of the existing IT infrastructure. This includes the following aspects:

- **SharePoint environments**: Identify all active SharePoint sites, document libraries, lists, and other content repositories. Evaluate the usage patterns, access controls, and any custom configurations or integrations that might affect the migration.

- **Email systems**: Assess the current email infrastructure, including servers, mailboxes, distribution groups, and any third-party email solutions. Consider the volume of data, the structure of email archives, and any existing rules or filters that need to be replicated in Microsoft 365.

- **File storage**: Catalog all existing file storage solutions, whether on-premises or cloud-based. This includes network drives, local server storage, third-party cloud storage (such as Google Drive or Dropbox), and user-specific storage locations. Understanding the structure, access permissions, and content of these storage solutions is critical for planning their migration.

- **Collaborative tools**: Identify any other collaborative tools currently in use, such as Slack, Zoom, Trello, or Asana. Determine how these tools are integrated with the existing systems and whether similar functionalities in Microsoft 365 will replace them.

Data inventory

A detailed inventory of all data is necessary for a smooth migration:

- **Data location**: Create a map of where all data is stored across different systems and platforms.

- **Data volume**: Estimate the total volume of data to be migrated. This helps in planning the logistics of data transfer, particularly in terms of time and bandwidth requirements.

- **Data type**: Classify the data by type – documents, spreadsheets, emails, databases, multimedia files, and so on. This classification helps in determining the best migration strategy for each data type.

- **Data sensitivity**: Identify data that's sensitive or subject to regulatory requirements. This includes **personally identifiable information** (**PII**), financial data, and intellectual property. Special considerations must be made to ensure this data is handled securely during migration.

User analysis

Understanding how users interact with the current systems is vital for ensuring a smooth transition:

- **User roles and access levels**: Identify different user groups and their respective roles. Determine the access levels they currently have and plan how these will be mapped to the new environment in Microsoft 365.

- **Usage patterns**: Analyze how users currently engage with the systems, including which features and tools are most frequently used. This can help prioritize which aspects of the system need to be migrated first and ensure minimal disruption to daily operations.

- **Provisioning and permissions**: Plan for user provisioning in the new system. This includes setting up accounts, assigning licenses, and ensuring that permissions are applied correctly based on the roles that have been identified.

Defining migration objectives

Defining clear objectives for the migration ensures that the project aligns with business goals and delivers tangible benefits:

Figure 6.4 – Migration objectives

In the following sections, we'll explore how to establish clear objectives and outline the essential guidelines to ensure alignment with organizational goals.

Business goals alignment

Align the migration with broader business objectives to maximize its impact:

- **Collaboration enhancement**: Identify how the migration can improve collaboration within the organization – for example, leveraging Microsoft Teams for communication, SharePoint for document management, and OneDrive for personal storage.

- **Security improvement**: Utilize Microsoft 365's advanced security features to enhance the organization's overall security posture. This could include **multi-factor authentication** (**MFA**), advanced threat protection, and **data loss prevention** (**DLP**).

- **Cost reduction**: Analyze how moving to Microsoft 365 could reduce costs by consolidating services, eliminating redundant systems, and reducing on-premises infrastructure.

Scope and scale

Defining the scope and scale of the migration helps in planning and resource allocation:

- **Systems and applications**: Determine which systems and applications will be included in the migration. This might include email, SharePoint, OneDrive, Teams, and other Microsoft 365 services.

- **Data prioritization**: Decide which data will be moved and in what order. For instance, critical business data might be prioritized, while less important data could be archived or deferred to a later phase.

- **Phased migration approach**: Consider a phased approach to migration, where different components (for example, email first, followed by SharePoint and Teams) are migrated in stages. This approach can reduce risk and allow for better management of resources.

Risk assessment and mitigation

Identifying potential risks and developing mitigation strategies is essential to prevent disruptions during migration:

Figure 6.5 – Risk assessment and mitigation

The upcoming sections will cover how to recognize potential risks and define mitigation strategies.

Identifying risks

The following common risks are associated with migration:

- **Data loss**: The possibility of losing data during transfer, especially if proper backups are not maintained

- **Downtime**: System downtime during migration can affect business operations, leading to potential revenue loss and productivity issues

- **User resistance**: Users may resist adopting the new system, particularly if it changes their workflows or if they are not properly trained

Mitigation strategies

You can develop various strategies to mitigate these risks:

- **Comprehensive backups**: Ensure that all data is backed up before migration begins. Consider multiple backup locations, including offsite or cloud-based storage.

- **Pilot testing**: Conduct pilot migrations with a small group of users to identify potential issues and refine the migration process before scaling up.

- **User training and support**: Provide thorough training and ongoing support to users to help them adapt to the new system. Consider setting up a helpdesk or support team specifically for the migration period.

Compliance and security

Ensure that the migration process complies with all relevant regulations and maintains high security standards:

- **Data encryption**: Encrypt sensitive data during the migration process to protect it from unauthorized access

- **Access control review**: Regularly review and update access controls to ensure that only authorized personnel can access sensitive data during and after migration

- **Ongoing compliance checks**: Implement continuous monitoring and compliance checks throughout the migration to ensure adherence to industry regulations and internal policies

Budget and timeline planning

A well-defined budget and timeline are critical for managing the migration effectively and ensuring that it stays on track:

Figure 6.6 – Budget and timeline planning

The following sections will cover the budget and timeline you need to consider in detail.

Cost estimation

Estimate all costs associated with the migration to avoid budget overruns:

- **Licensing**: Calculate the cost of Microsoft 365 licenses based on the number of users and the services they require

- **Migration tools**: Consider the cost of any third-party migration tools or software that might be needed to facilitate the process

- **Consulting services**: If external consultants or specialized services are needed, include their fees in the budget

- **Potential downtime**: Estimate the potential cost of downtime during the migration, including lost productivity and potential revenue loss

Timeline development

Develop a detailed timeline that accounts for all aspects of the migration:

- **Key milestones**: Identify major milestones, such as the completion of the assessment phase, the pilot migration, and the final cutover.

- **Dependencies**: Map out any dependencies that could affect the timeline, such as the availability of resources, completion of preparatory tasks, or approval processes.

- **Detailed project plan**: Create a comprehensive project plan that outlines all tasks, assigns responsibilities, and sets clear deadlines. This plan should be reviewed and updated regularly to reflect progress and address any issues that arise.

Migration preparation

Migration preparation is the phase where the groundwork that was laid during the pre-migration planning is transformed into actionable steps that will ensure a smooth and successful migration to Microsoft 365.

This stage involves finalizing migration strategies, preparing systems and data, setting up user training, and conducting comprehensive testing. This section provides a detailed guide to the key activities involved in migration preparation.

Review migration strategy

After thorough planning, the migration strategy needs to be reviewed and re-evaluated. This strategy will serve as the blueprint for the entire migration process:

Figure 6.7 – Finalizing the migration strategy

In the following sections, we'll outline the steps for reviewing and refining the migration strategy.

Selecting the migration approach

Choose the most suitable migration approach based on the organization's needs and the complexity of the existing environment:

- **Cutover migration**: This is suitable for small to medium-sized organizations where all users and data are migrated at once. This approach is quick but requires downtime during the migration.

- **Staged migration**: This is ideal for larger organizations, where the migration is done in phases. Different systems or groups of users are migrated at different times, minimizing disruption.

- **Hybrid migration**: This approach is for organizations that need to maintain some on-premises infrastructure while migrating to Microsoft 365. It allows for a gradual migration and co-existence between on-premises and cloud systems.

Migration tools and services

Identify and finalize the tools and services required for migration:

- **Third-party tools**: Evaluate and select third-party tools that can facilitate data transfer, manage user accounts, or ensure data integrity during the migration

- **Microsoft-native tools**: Consider using Microsoft's native tools such as the SharePoint Migration Tool, Azure Migrate, or FastTrack for specific migration tasks

- **Consulting services**: If external expertise is needed, finalize contracts with consultants or migration service providers

Data segmentation and prioritization

Determine how data will be segmented and prioritized for migration:

- **Critical data first**: Plan to migrate the most critical and frequently used data first to ensure that essential operations can continue with minimal disruption.

- **Archive legacy data**: Decide on a strategy for handling legacy data that may not need to be migrated immediately. This could involve archiving or storing it in a less expensive storage solution.

- **Data transformation**: If necessary, prepare data for transformation during migration, ensuring it meets the requirements of the new platform in terms of format, structure, and compatibility.

System and data preparation

Preparing systems and data for migration is a critical step that involves cleaning, securing, and organizing the assets that will be moved:

Figure 6.8 – System and data preparation

The next few sections will outline the steps needed to clean, secure, and organize systems and data to ensure a smooth and efficient migration process.

System readiness

Ensure that all systems are ready for migration:

- **Infrastructure upgrades**: Perform any necessary upgrades to the existing infrastructure to support the migration. This could include increasing bandwidth, upgrading servers, or ensuring that current systems meet the minimum requirements for migration.

- **Software updates**: Ensure that all software is up to date. This includes both the systems that are being migrated and the systems that will remain in use during and after the migration.

- **Backup systems**: Set up and verify backup systems to ensure that all data is backed up securely before migration begins. This backup should be stored in a separate location to mitigate the risk of data loss.

Data cleanup and organization

Clean and organize data to ensure a smooth migration:

- **Duplicate data removal**: Identify and remove duplicate data to reduce the volume of data that needs to be migrated and to improve data quality.

- **Obsolete data purge**: Identify and archive or delete obsolete data that's no longer needed. This helps to streamline the migration process and reduce clutter in the new system.

- **Data structuring**: Organize data in a way that aligns with the structure of the target system in Microsoft 365. This might involve reorganizing folders, tagging data, or restructuring databases to ensure compatibility.

Security and compliance preparation

Ensure that all security and compliance measures are in place:

- **Data encryption**: Encrypt sensitive data before migration to protect it from unauthorized access during the transfer process

- **Access controls**: Review and update access controls to ensure that only authorized personnel can access the systems and data during the migration

- **Compliance checklists**: Prepare compliance checklists to ensure that all regulatory requirements are met throughout the migration process, particularly for data handling and user privacy

User training and communication

User preparedness is essential for a successful migration. Proper training and communication help minimize disruption and ensure a smooth transition:

Figure 6.9 – User training and communication

The following sections will focus on strategies for effective user training and clear communication to facilitate a smooth migration.

User training programs

Develop and implement training programs for users:

- **Role-based training**: Tailor training sessions based on user roles. For example, administrators may need in-depth training on managing Microsoft 365, while end users may only need to understand the basics of using the new system.

- **Hands-on workshops**: Conduct hands-on workshops to give users practical experience with Microsoft 365 before the migration. This helps to build familiarity and confidence in the new system.

- **Self-help resources**: Provide access to self-help resources such as video tutorials, user manuals, and FAQs that users can refer to during and after the migration.

Communication plan

Develop a clear communication plan to keep all stakeholders informed:

- **Migration timeline**: Share the migration timeline with all users, including key milestones and any expected downtime.

- **Regular updates**: Provide regular updates on the progress of the migration and any changes to the plan. This helps to manage expectations and reduce uncertainty.

- **Support channels**: Establish clear support channels that users can access during the migration. This could include a dedicated helpdesk, chat support, or a hotline.

Tests

Testing is a crucial part of migration preparation. It ensures that the migration process will work as expected and that all systems will function correctly in the new environment:

Figure 6.10 – Testing the new environment

The following sections will provide the necessary steps to validate that the migration process functions as intended and that all systems operate seamlessly in the new environment.

Pilot testing

Conduct pilot tests to validate the migration process:

- **Small-scale migration**: Perform a small-scale migration with a limited set of data and a small group of users. This allows us to identify and address potential issues before the full migration.

- **User acceptance testing (UAT)**: Engage users in the testing process to ensure that the migrated systems meet their needs and expectations. Gather feedback from UAT and make necessary adjustments.

- **System performance testing**: Test the performance of the systems in Microsoft 365 to ensure that they meet the required standards for speed, reliability, and scalability.

Disaster recovery testing

Test disaster recovery procedures to ensure data integrity and availability:

- **Backup validation**: Verify that all backups are complete and accessible. Test the restoration process to ensure that data can be recovered quickly in the event of a failure.

- **Failover testing**: Test failover systems to ensure that critical operations can continue with minimal disruption in the event of a system outage during migration.

- **Security testing**: Conduct security tests to ensure that all data is protected during migration, including penetration testing and vulnerability scanning.

Final review

Before proceeding with the full migration, conduct a final review and make a go/no-go decision:

Figure 6.11 – Final review

The next few sections will guide us through performing a final review so that we can make an informed decision.

Conclusive evaluation

A thorough and final assessment must be conducted to verify that all objectives and requirements of a project or initiative have been successfully achieved.

First, you must review all aspects of the migration preparation:

- **Readiness checklist**: Go through a readiness checklist to ensure that all systems, data, users, and processes are fully prepared for migration
- **Stakeholder approval**: Obtain approval from key stakeholders, including IT leadership, compliance officers, and business unit leaders, to proceed with the migration

Go/no-go decision

Make a final go/no-go decision based on the readiness assessment:

- **Go decision**: If all systems are ready, users are trained, and the testing has been successful, proceed with the full migration
- **No-go decision**: If some outstanding issues or risks haven't been adequately addressed, delay the migration until these are resolved

Migration

The migration phase is where the actual transition from the current environment to Microsoft 365 takes place. This phase is critical as it involves moving data, configuring systems, and ensuring that all users can access and use the new platform with minimal disruption:

Figure 6.12 – Migration

This section provides a comprehensive guide to the key activities involved in the migration phase.

Execution

With preparation complete, the migration process begins. This phase involves following the strategy that has been meticulously planned and ensuring that all steps are executed correctly.

Data migration

Data migration is the core component of this phase. It involves transferring data from the current environment to Microsoft 365:

- **Data transfer**: Begin the data transfer process according to the migration plan. Depending on the migration strategy (cutover, staged, or hybrid), this could involve transferring all data at once or in phases.

- **Monitoring the transfer**: Continuously monitor the data transfer process to ensure that it's proceeding as planned. Use migration tools and dashboards to track progress, identify any bottlenecks, and resolve issues as they arise.

- **Verifying data integrity**: Once the data has been transferred, verify that all data has been migrated accurately. This involves checking data completeness, ensuring that no data was lost or corrupted during the transfer, and validating that the data is accessible in the new environment.

System configuration

Once data has been migrated, systems need to be configured in Microsoft 365 to ensure they function correctly:

- **Service configuration**: Configure the various Microsoft 365 services, such as Exchange Online, SharePoint Online, OneDrive for Business, and Teams. This includes setting up email routing, configuring SharePoint sites, and ensuring that file storage is allocated correctly.

- **Permissions and access control**: Set up user permissions and access controls based on the pre-defined roles and requirements. Ensure that all users have the correct level of access to the resources they need and that sensitive data is protected.

- **Customizations and integrations**: Apply any necessary customizations to Microsoft 365 to match the functionality of the previous environment. Integrate third-party tools and applications as needed, ensuring they work seamlessly with Microsoft 365.

User provisioning

Ensure that all users are set up and ready to use Microsoft 365:

- **Account creation**: Provision user accounts in Microsoft 365, ensuring that each user has the appropriate licenses assigned. Set up user profiles, including email addresses, OneDrive storage, and Teams membership.

- **Profile migration**: If applicable, migrate user profiles from the old environment to Microsoft 365. This includes migrating email settings, signatures, and user preferences.

- **Access and authentication**: Ensure that users can log in to Microsoft 365 using their existing credentials. Set up MFA for enhanced security if it hasn't been implemented already.

Testing and validation

Testing during the migration phase is crucial to ensure that everything is functioning as expected before the final cutover:

Figure 6.13 – Testing and validation

In the following sections, we'll outline the steps and best practices you must follow to ensure thorough testing during the migration phase. This will help you verify that everything operates as expected before the final cutover.

Post-migration testing

Conduct thorough testing of all migrated systems and data:

- **Functional testing**: Verify that all key functions of the migrated systems work as intended. This includes checking email flow in Exchange Online, file access in OneDrive and SharePoint, and communication in Teams.

- **Performance testing**: Test the performance of the migrated systems to ensure they meet the required standards for speed and reliability. Identify and address any performance issues that could affect user experience.

- **Data validation**: Double-check that all data has been migrated correctly. This involves spot-checking files, emails, and other critical data types to ensure they are intact and accessible.

UAT

Involve end users in testing to ensure the system meets their needs:

- **User feedback**: Gather feedback from a representative group of users on the functionality and usability of the migrated systems. This can help you identify any issues that weren't caught during earlier testing phases.

- **Issue resolution**: Address any problems or bugs that were identified during UAT. This may involve reconfiguring certain settings, correcting data discrepancies, or providing additional user support.

- **Final approval**: Once UAT is complete and all issues have been resolved, obtain final approval from key stakeholders to proceed with the full rollout.

Cutover and go-live

The cutover to the new environment is the point where the organization fully transitions to Microsoft 365:

Figure 6.14 – Cutover and go-live

The next few sections will outline the steps and best practices needed to achieve a successful cutover to the new Microsoft 365 environment.

Final cutover planning

Ensure that the final cutover is carefully planned and communicated:

- **Cutover timing**: Choose a cutover time that minimizes disruption to the organization. This is often done during off-peak hours, such as overnight or over the weekend.

- **Communication**: Communicate the cutover plan to all users well in advance. Provide clear instructions on what to expect during the cutover, including any expected downtime and how to get help if needed.

- **Backup verification**: Before the cutover, verify that all backups are complete and accessible. This is a critical safety net in case anything goes wrong during the final transition.

Go-live execution

Execute the final cutover to Microsoft 365:

- **System switch**: Switch users from the old environment to Microsoft 365. This may involve updating DNS records, redirecting email traffic, and ensuring that users can access their data and applications in the new environment.

- **User support**: Provide immediate support to users during the go-live phase. Set up a dedicated helpdesk or support team to assist with any issues that arise during the transition.

- **Monitoring**: Closely monitor the systems and user activity during the initial hours of going live. Be prepared to address any issues quickly to minimize disruption.

Post-go-live support

Provide ongoing support after the cutover to ensure a smooth transition:

- **Helpdesk availability**: Keep the helpdesk or support team available for an extended period after going live to assist users with any problems or questions.

- **User feedback collection**: Continue to collect user feedback to identify any issues that weren't immediately apparent. Use this feedback to make further improvements to the system.

- **System stabilization**: Monitor the performance and stability of the migrated systems over the first few days or weeks. Address any emerging issues promptly to ensure the system remains stable.

Post-migration activities

After the migration is complete and the system is live, there are several important post-migration activities you must perform to ensure long-term success:

Figure 6.15 – Post-migration activities

In the upcoming sections, we'll cover the essential steps related to post-migration activities.

Documentation and knowledge transfer

Ensure all migration activities are thoroughly documented:

- **Migration documentation**: Create detailed documentation of the migration process, including steps taken, issues encountered, and how they were resolved. This documentation will be invaluable for future reference and any similar projects.

- **Knowledge transfer**: Conduct knowledge transfer sessions with the internal IT team to ensure they're fully equipped to manage and maintain the new environment.

Decommissioning legacy systems

Once the migration has been confirmed as successful, decommission legacy systems:

- **Data archiving**: Archive any data that wasn't migrated but still needs to be retained for compliance or historical reasons

- **System shutdown**: Gradually shut down legacy systems, ensuring that all dependencies are resolved, and no critical operations are disrupted

- **Resource reallocation**: Reallocate any resources that were dedicated to the legacy systems, such as server space or IT personnel, to more productive tasks

Optimization and continuous improvement

Optimize the new environment and plan for continuous improvement:

- **Performance tuning**: Optimize the performance of Microsoft 365 services based on initial user feedback and system performance data. This might include adjusting resource allocation, optimizing network settings, or refining system configurations.

- **User training and adoption**: Continue to provide training and resources to help users fully adopt and leverage the new tools and features available in Microsoft 365. Encourage ongoing learning and exploration of advanced capabilities.

- **Feedback loops**: Establish feedback loops with users and IT staff to continually assess the effectiveness of the migration and adjust as needed. This helps to ensure that the organization continues to benefit from the new environment over time.

In this section, we explored the essential phases and strategic considerations for a successful migration to Microsoft 365. Understanding these elements is crucial as it ensures that organizations not only transition smoothly but will also fully leverage the benefits of Microsoft 365, enhancing productivity and collaboration. The knowledge you've gained here lays the groundwork for identifying and overcoming potential challenges, which are vital for a successful migration.

As we move forward, we'll delve into the specific migration challenges we may encounter and strategies to address them to help ensure a resilient and efficient transition.

Challenges faced in migration

Migrating to Microsoft 365 is a significant step for any organization that promises enhanced collaboration, improved security, and greater productivity. However, the migration process isn't without its challenges. These can range from technical issues and data migration complexities to user adoption hurdles and security concerns:

Figure 6.16 – Myriad challenges

This section will explore the common challenges organizations face during the migration to Microsoft 365 and provide practical solutions to overcome them.

We'll also include a real-world scenario to illustrate how these challenges manifest and how they can be managed effectively.

Data migration complexity

Challenge: Migrating data from legacy systems to Microsoft 365 can be a complex and time-consuming task. Organizations often have vast amounts of data spread across different platforms, including on-premises servers, cloud storage solutions, and various databases.

The diversity in data types, structures, and formats further complicates the migration process. Moreover, ensuring data integrity and preventing data loss during the migration is a significant concern.

Solution: Address data migration complexities through the following:

- **Data inventory and classification**: Begin by creating a detailed inventory of all data across the organization. Classify data by type (for example, documents, emails, and databases) and prioritize it based on business needs.

- **Use of migration tools**: Leverage specialized migration tools such as the Microsoft SharePoint Migration Tool, Azure Migrate, or third-party solutions such as ShareGate or BitTitan. These tools can automate the migration process, handle different data types, and ensure data integrity.

- **Phased migration**: Consider adopting a phased migration approach, where critical data is migrated first, followed by less essential data. This reduces the risk of disruptions and allows for easier management of the migration process.

- **Data validation**: After migration, perform thorough data validation to ensure all data has been accurately transferred and is accessible in Microsoft 365.

User adoption and resistance

Challenge: One of the most significant challenges in any IT migration project is ensuring that end users adopt the new system. Users may resist change due to unfamiliarity with the new platform, fear of losing data or functionality, or simply because they're comfortable with the old system. Without proper adoption, the benefits of Microsoft 365 can't be fully realized.

Solution: Do the following to overcome user adoption challenges:

- **Comprehensive training programs**: Develop role-based training programs that cater to the needs of different user groups. Offer hands-on workshops, self-paced learning modules, and ongoing support to help users familiarize themselves with Microsoft 365.

- **Early involvement**: Involve key users early in the migration process. By engaging them in planning and pilot testing, we can gather valuable feedback, address concerns, and create a sense of ownership.

- **Communication**: Establish a clear communication plan to keep users informed about the migration timeline, the benefits of Microsoft 365, and how it will enhance their day-to-day work. Highlight success stories and quick wins to build positive momentum.

- **Post-migration support**: Provide a helpdesk or dedicated support team to assist users during and after the migration. Address issues quickly to minimize frustration and build confidence in the new system.

Compatibility issues with legacy applications

Challenge: Many organizations rely on legacy applications that may not be fully compatible with Microsoft 365. These applications could include custom-built software, third-party tools, or outdated versions of standard software that don't integrate well with the cloud-based Microsoft 365 environment.

Solution: To address compatibility issues, do the following:

- **Conduct an application inventory and assessment**: Conduct a thorough inventory of all applications in use across the organization. Assess their compatibility with Microsoft 365 and identify those that require updates or replacements.

- **Upgrade or replace legacy applications**: Where possible, upgrade legacy applications to versions that are compatible with Microsoft 365. If an upgrade isn't feasible, consider replacing the application with a modern, cloud-compatible solution.

- **Use compatibility layers**: In some cases, compatibility layers or virtualization solutions can be used to run legacy applications in the new environment. This approach can be a temporary solution while a more permanent replacement is being developed.

- **Perform pilot testing**: Before full migration, conduct pilot testing with the most critical applications to ensure they function correctly in the Microsoft 365 environment. This allows for early identification and resolution of compatibility issues.

Security and compliance concerns

Challenge: Migrating to Microsoft 365 involves moving sensitive organizational data to the cloud, which may raise concerns about data security and compliance with regulatory requirements. Organizations must ensure that the migration process doesn't expose them to security risks or result in non-compliance with data protection laws.

Solution: You can mitigate security and compliance risks in various ways:

- **Data encryption**: Ensure that all sensitive data is encrypted both during the migration and in the Microsoft 365 environment. Microsoft 365 offers built-in encryption features that can be configured to meet specific security requirements.

- **Access control**: Implement strict access controls to ensure that only authorized personnel can access sensitive data during and after the migration. Use MFA to enhance security.

- **Compliance configuration**: Microsoft 365 includes tools such as Compliance Manager and DLP, which help organizations meet regulatory requirements. Configure these tools so that they align with the organization's compliance policies.

- **Regular security audits**: Conduct regular security audits and compliance checks throughout the migration process to ensure adherence to industry standards and internal policies.

Managing downtime and business continuity

Challenge: During the migration to Microsoft 365, there may be periods of downtime or reduced functionality, which can disrupt business operations. Ensuring business continuity during this transition is critical, especially for organizations that rely on constant access to their data and communication systems.

Solution: Here are some ways you can manage downtime and ensure business continuity:

- **Phased migration**: A phased migration approach can minimize downtime by allowing different parts of the organization to migrate at different times. This ensures that critical operations can continue while the migration is underway.

- **Off-peak migration**: Schedule the most disruptive parts of the migration, such as data transfer or system cutover, during off-peak hours (for example, overnight or during weekends) to reduce the impact on daily operations.

- **Backup systems**: Ensure that all data is backed up before migration begins and that backup systems are in place to restore data quickly in case of a failure.

- **Contingency plans**: Develop contingency plans for critical business functions. These plans should outline steps to take if the migration encounters issues that cause unexpected downtime.

Network bandwidth and latency issues

Challenge: Migrating large volumes of data to Microsoft 365 can strain an organization's network, leading to bandwidth limitations and latency issues. These problems can slow down the migration process and affect the performance of Microsoft 365 services after migration.

Solution: There are various ways you can address network bandwidth and latency challenges:

- **Network assessment**: Conduct a thorough assessment of the organization's current network infrastructure. Identify potential bottlenecks and determine whether upgrades are needed to support the migration.

- **Bandwidth management**: Implement bandwidth management techniques, such as **Quality of Service (QoS)** settings, to prioritize critical migration traffic and minimize the impact on other network activities.

- **Staggered data transfer**: Instead of migrating all data at once, consider staggering the data transfer over time. This approach reduces the load on the network and helps maintain performance.

- **Content delivery networks (CDNs)**: After migration, use CDNs to cache content closer to users. This reduces latency and improves access speeds for Microsoft 365 services.

Customizing and configuring Microsoft 365

Challenge: Organizations often have specific needs that require custom configurations or customizations within Microsoft 365. The challenge lies in replicating the functionality of customized legacy systems while leveraging the advanced features of the platform.

Solution: You can do the following to manage customization and configuration effectively:

- **Identify custom requirements**: Before migration, identify the custom features and configurations that are critical to the organization's operations. Determine whether these can be replicated in Microsoft 365 or if alternative solutions are needed.

- **Leverage Microsoft 365 capabilities**: Where possible, use built-in Microsoft 365 features to replace custom solutions. For example, SharePoint Online, Microsoft Teams, and Power Platform offer extensive customization options that can fulfill many business needs.

- **Perform custom development**: If specific customizations are required, consider developing custom solutions using Microsoft 365's APIs and development tools. This can include custom workflows, forms, or integrations with other systems.

- **Test and validate**: Thoroughly test all customizations and configurations in a non-production environment before rolling them out to the entire organization. This ensures that they work as expected and don't introduce new issues.

Licensing and cost management

Challenge: Managing 365 licenses and ensuring that the organization isn't overspending on unused features or licenses can be challenging. It's important to strike the right balance between providing users with the tools they need and managing costs effectively.

Solution: There are various ways you can manage licensing and costs:

- **License optimization**: Conduct an audit of current user needs and match them to the appropriate Microsoft 365 licenses. Microsoft offers various license types (for example, E1, E3, and E5) with different levels of features, allowing organizations to optimize costs by assigning the right license to each user.

- **License management tools**: Use Microsoft's licensing management tools to monitor license usage and ensure that the organization isn't paying for unused licenses. Regularly review license allocations and make adjustments as needed.

- **Bundle services**: Consider bundling services where possible to take advantage of cost savings. For example, Microsoft 365 bundles that include Teams, SharePoint, and OneDrive can be more cost-effective than purchasing these services separately.

- **Budget forecasting**: Develop a budget forecast for Microsoft 365 licensing costs while considering expected growth in users and any additional features that may be needed in the future.

Integrating Microsoft 365 with existing systems

Challenge: Organizations often need to integrate Microsoft 365 with existing on-premises systems or other cloud-based services. These integrations can be complex, especially if the systems weren't originally designed to work together.

Solution: Here are some ways you can address integration challenges:

- **Integration planning**: Develop a detailed integration plan that identifies all systems that need to be integrated with Microsoft 365. Determine the specific integration points and how data will flow between systems.

- **Use integration tools**: Leverage integration tools such as Microsoft Power Automate, Azure Logic Apps, or third-party solutions to facilitate seamless integration between Microsoft 365 and other systems.

- **Custom APIs**: If necessary, develop custom APIs to enable communication between Microsoft 365 and legacy systems. Ensure these APIs are secure and scalable to handle future growth.

- **Test integrations**: Test all integrations thoroughly in a non-production environment to identify and resolve issues before they impact users. Monitor integrations post-migration to ensure ongoing reliability.

Post-migration optimization and continuous improvement

Challenge: Even after a successful migration, organizations may struggle to fully optimize their use of Microsoft 365 and continuously improve their digital workplace. Without ongoing optimization, the organization may not fully realize the benefits of Microsoft 365.

Solution: To ensure post-migration optimization and continuous improvement, you can implement the following aspects:

- **Regular performance reviews**: Conduct regular reviews of Microsoft 365 performance and usage to identify areas for improvement. This includes monitoring user activity, system performance, and security metrics.

- **User feedback**: Continuously gather feedback from users to understand their experiences with Microsoft 365. Use this feedback to adjust, provide additional training, or introduce new features.

- **Feature adoption**: Encourage users to adopt new Microsoft 365 features as they're released. Provide training and resources to help users understand how these features can enhance their productivity.

- **Continuous learning**: Foster a culture of continuous learning within the organization by offering ongoing training opportunities and resources. This helps users stay up to date with the latest Microsoft 365 capabilities and best practices.

Real-world scenario 1 – migrating a mid-sized manufacturing company to Microsoft 365

Background: A mid-sized manufacturing company with 500 employees decided to migrate from their on-premises Exchange server and SharePoint environment to Microsoft 365. The company had been using these legacy systems for over a decade and faced several challenges, including data migration complexity, user adoption issues, and ensuring business continuity during the migration:

Figure 6.17 – Real-world scenario 1

Let's understand the challenges that were faced by this company and the solutions it adopted.

The company encountered the following challenges:

- **Data migration complexity**: The company had over 5 TB of data stored in various locations, including on-premises servers, network drives, and individual user devices. Ensuring that all data was migrated without loss was a significant concern.

- **User adoption and resistance**: Many employees were accustomed to the legacy systems and were resistant to change, fearing that the new system would disrupt their workflows.

- **Compatibility issues**: Some of the company's critical applications were custom-built and not fully compatible with Microsoft 365.

- **Ensuring business continuity**: The company couldn't afford significant downtime during the migration as this would impact production schedules and customer deliveries.

The following solutions were implemented:

- **Phased data migration**: The company opted for a phased migration approach, starting with non-critical data and gradually moving to more essential data. They used third-party migration tools to automate the process and ensure data integrity.

- **Comprehensive training and communication**: A detailed training program was carried out, including hands-on workshops and online tutorials. Key users were involved in pilot testing, which helped address concerns and build confidence in the new system.

- **Application upgrades and compatibility layers**: The company upgraded several legacy applications to versions compatible with Microsoft 365. For those that couldn't be upgraded, they used virtualization to run the applications in the new environment temporarily.

- **Off-peak migration and contingency planning**: The migration was scheduled during weekends to minimize disruption. Backup systems were tested and verified before the migration to ensure data could be quickly restored in case of issues.

Outcome: The migration was completed successfully with minimal downtime. The company achieved a seamless transition to Microsoft 365, enhancing collaboration and productivity. The phased approach, combined with thorough training and careful planning, helped mitigate the challenges and ensured that the migration aligned with the company's business goals.

Real-world scenario 2 – migrating a medium-sized financial services company to Microsoft 365

Background: A medium-sized financial services company with 1,000 employees decided to migrate from its on-premises Exchange server, legacy file storage systems, and a variety of third-party collaboration tools to Microsoft 365. The company's primary goal was to streamline its IT infrastructure, enhance collaboration across departments, and improve data security in response to increasingly stringent regulatory requirements:

Figure 6.18 – Real-world scenario 2

Let's understand the challenges that were faced by this company and the solutions it adopted.

The company encountered the following challenges:

- **Data security and compliance concerns**: Given the nature of the financial services industry, the company was particularly concerned about maintaining compliance with regulatory requirements such as GDPR and PCI-DSS during and after the migration.

- **User adoption resistance**: Many employees were accustomed to using a variety of legacy tools for email, file storage, and collaboration. There was significant resistance to adopting the new, unified Microsoft 365 platform, particularly among senior staff.

- **Complexity of data migration**: The company had over 10 TB of critical financial data stored across various legacy systems, including on-premises servers, network drives, and third-party cloud services. Ensuring data integrity and security during the migration was a top priority.

- **Integration with legacy applications**: The company relied on several custom-built financial applications that weren't immediately compatible with Microsoft 365, particularly with SharePoint and Exchange Online.

The following solutions were implemented:

- **Rigorous compliance planning**: The company engaged a team of compliance experts to map out a migration strategy that ensured adherence to all relevant regulations. This included implementing data encryption, strict access controls, and detailed audit trails throughout the migration process.

- **Comprehensive training and early user involvement**: To address user resistance, the company launched a comprehensive training program, offering personalized training sessions for different departments and roles. Senior staff were involved early in the process, particularly in pilot testing, to gain their buy-in and to act as champions for the new system.

- **Phased data migration with enhanced security measures**: The company opted for a phased migration approach, starting with non-critical data. They utilized BitTitan's MigrationWiz tool to automate the data migration process, ensuring that sensitive data was encrypted and that the migration progress was monitored continuously for any anomalies.

- **Application compatibility solutions**: The IT team worked closely with the application development team to upgrade key legacy applications to versions compatible with Microsoft 365. Where upgrades weren't possible, they implemented virtualization solutions to allow these applications to function in the new environment temporarily.

Outcome: The migration was completed successfully within 6 months, with minimal disruption to business operations. The company achieved its goals of enhancing collaboration, improving data security, and ensuring compliance with industry regulations. The phased approach, combined with rigorous training and strategic planning, resulted in high user adoption rates and a smooth transition to the new system.

Real-world scenario 3 – migrating a large multinational corporation to Microsoft 365

Background: A large multinational corporation with over 50,000 employees across multiple continents decided to migrate its entire IT infrastructure, including email, document management, and collaboration tools, to Microsoft 365. The company's goals were to standardize its IT environment across all global offices, reduce IT costs, and improve global collaboration and communication:

Figure 6.19 – Real-world scenario 3

Let's understand the challenges that were faced by this company and the solutions it adopted.

The company encountered the following challenges:

- **Global scale and coordination**: Coordinating a migration of this scale across multiple time zones and regions posed significant logistical challenges. Ensuring that the migration was executed simultaneously and seamlessly across all offices was critical to avoid disruptions in global operations.

- **Managing network bandwidth and latency**: The company's extensive global presence meant that network bandwidth and latency issues were a major concern, particularly during data migration and when ensuring the performance of Microsoft 365 services post-migration.

- **Customization and localization needs**: The company had heavily customized its legacy systems to meet the specific needs of different regions. Migrating these customizations to Microsoft 365 while maintaining consistency and standardization across the organization was a complex task.

- **Ensuring business continuity**: Given the size and global reach of the company, any significant downtime during the migration could have resulted in substantial financial losses and disruption to critical business processes.

The following solutions were implemented:

- **Centralized project management with regional coordination**: The company established a centralized **project management office (PMO)** to oversee the entire migration process. Regional IT teams were formed to coordinate and execute the migration in their respective regions, ensuring that local needs were addressed while maintaining overall consistency.

- **Network optimization and bandwidth management**: The company conducted a thorough network assessment and implemented QoS settings to prioritize critical migration traffic. They also used Azure's ExpressRoute to establish private connections between their on-premises infrastructure and Microsoft's cloud, reducing latency and improving performance.

- **Custom development and localization**: To address the diverse needs of different regions, the IT team developed custom solutions using Microsoft 365's APIs and Power Platform. These solutions allowed for localized customizations while maintaining the overall standardization required by the corporate headquarters.

- **Phased rollout with contingency planning**: The migration was executed in a phased manner, starting with smaller, less critical offices before the company moved on to larger regional hubs. The company implemented robust contingency plans, including maintaining parallel systems during the migration and ensuring that data was backed up at every stage.

Outcome: The migration to Microsoft 365 was completed over a year, with each phase meticulously planned and executed to minimize disruption. The company successfully standardized its IT environment, reducing overall IT costs and significantly improving global collaboration. The use of custom solutions and careful planning ensured that the specific needs of different regions were met, leading to a smooth and efficient transition.

These real-world scenarios highlight the importance of strategic planning, user involvement, and the use of appropriate tools and techniques in overcoming the challenges associated with migrating to Microsoft 365. By addressing these challenges proactively, organizations can ensure a smooth and successful transition to a modern digital workplace.

In this section, we explored the challenges organizations face during their migration to Microsoft 365, ranging from data migration complexities and user adoption resistance to security concerns and compatibility issues. Understanding these challenges is crucial for any organization looking to make a seamless transition to Microsoft 365 as it allows for proactive planning and mitigation strategies. As we've seen, addressing these challenges effectively can prevent disruptions and ensure a successful migration that aligns with business goals.

Summary

In this chapter, we delved into the essential strategies and best practices for migrating to Microsoft 365, emphasizing the importance of meticulous planning, effective data migration, and overcoming common challenges such as user adoption resistance, security concerns, and integration with legacy systems. We also explored real-world scenarios that demonstrated how organizations of various sizes successfully navigated these challenges, reinforcing the critical need for strategic planning, stakeholder involvement, and the use of specialized tools.

The skills and insights you've gained here will ensure a smooth and efficient transition to Microsoft 365, allowing organizations to fully leverage the platform's capabilities while maintaining data integrity and security. These lessons are vital in minimizing disruption, ensuring business continuity, and maximizing the value of the investment in Microsoft 365.

In the next chapter, we'll explore real-world case studies, sharing practical lessons and best practices for implementing Microsoft 365 and SharePoint across industries. We'll also highlight new features and trends, helping optimize the platform and stay ahead in the evolving Microsoft 365 landscape.

Part 4:
Solving Real-World Challenges and Shaping the Future

We step out of the theoretical and dive straight into how businesses across various industries are actually using Microsoft 365 and SharePoint to tackle their everyday challenges. It's not just about what these tools can do; it's about what they are doing for organizations in the real world. You will get to see how teams, from healthcare to tech start-ups, are streamlining their processes, boosting collaboration, and staying ahead of the competition using these platforms.

But we don't stop there. Looking ahead, we'll explore the trends shaping the future of Microsoft 365 and SharePoint. It's all about staying one step ahead and understanding what's coming next so you can future-proof your operations.

This part contains the following chapter:

- *Chapter 7, Real-World Case Studies and Future Trends*

7

Real-World Case Studies and Future Trends

In this chapter, we'll delve into real-world case studies to uncover the practical lessons learned and best practices that can be applied across different industries when implementing Microsoft 365 and Microsoft SharePoint Online. This chapter reflects on what has worked successfully in various sectors and highlights upcoming features and trends in the evolving landscape of Microsoft 365 and Microsoft SharePoint.

You'll learn how to extract valuable insights from real-world examples and implement best practices tailored to specific business needs. Additionally, you'll gain insight into the future advancements within Microsoft 365, ensuring you're equipped to stay ahead of industry trends and innovations. The knowledge you'll gain here will provide you with a competitive edge, helping you to optimize your platform use while preparing for what's next.

In this chapter, we're going to cover the following main topics:

- Lessons learned and best practices from diverse industries
- Exploring upcoming features in Microsoft 365 and Microsoft SharePoint

By completing this chapter, you'll be able to do the following:

- Analyze real-world case studies
- Extract key lessons for any organization
- Implement future-proof strategies that align with the latest advancements in Microsoft 365 and Microsoft SharePoint

By the time you've completed this chapter, you'll be thoroughly prepared to navigate complex challenges that arise when integrating Microsoft 365 and SharePoint across diverse industries. With a deep understanding of how real-world case studies provide actionable insights, you'll be able to apply tailored best practices to meet an organization's unique needs. Armed with this knowledge, you'll be able to not only streamline operations but also elevate productivity across every level of different organizations.

Moreover, you'll be empowered to stay ahead of the curve, leveraging upcoming features in Microsoft 365 and SharePoint to maintain a competitive edge in an ever-evolving digital landscape. Whether it's improving team collaboration, ensuring data security, or optimizing workflows through advanced AI tools, the skills and strategies you'll gain here will allow you to harness the full potential of Microsoft 365, positioning an organization's business for long-term success in an increasingly digital-first world.

Lessons learned and best practices from various industries

Picture a doctor accessing patient records securely from a mobile device or a tech team collaborating in real time to meet a product deadline. Across industries, Microsoft 365 is transforming the way organizations operate, offering solutions for unique challenges – from ensuring data security and compliance in healthcare and finance to boosting agility and collaboration in tech and retail.

Let's explore how businesses across different sectors are using Microsoft 365 to streamline operations, foster innovation, and stay compliant. Here, we'll discover practical insights and best practices that demonstrate the platform's versatility – whether it's automating workflows, enabling remote work, or enhancing collaboration.

Are you ready to see how Microsoft 365 can make business more efficient?

Figure 7.1 – Microsoft 365's adaptability, coupled with its suite of tools,
enables organizations to address their specific needs

In sectors such as manufacturing, retail, and energy, the need for real-time communication, supply chain management, and operational automation is critical. Microsoft 365's integration capabilities with third-party tools, automation workflows, and mobile accessibility help organizations optimize their processes, reduce human error, and make data-driven decisions faster.

Meanwhile, industries such as education, non-profits, and hospitality leverage Microsoft 365 to enhance collaboration, streamline administrative tasks, and improve customer or stakeholder engagement. Tools such as Microsoft Teams, Microsoft SharePoint, and Power BI play a pivotal role in these industries by enabling virtual learning, centralizing information sharing, and offering real-time analytics.

Throughout this chapter, we'll explore 10 diverse industries, each with its own set of challenges, to highlight the key lessons learned and best practices gleaned from real-world Microsoft 365 implementations. By examining these sectors, we can uncover valuable insights into how different organizations have customized Microsoft 365 capabilities to meet their unique needs, ensuring enhanced productivity, compliance, and innovation across their operations.

Whether it's automating workflows, securing sensitive data, enabling remote work, or fostering collaboration, the implementation of Microsoft 365 offers organizations the flexibility and power to adapt to their evolving industry demands.

Healthcare – ensuring data security, compliance, and streamlined patient care

Healthcare organizations must manage highly sensitive data, including patient medical records:

Figure 7.2 – Microsoft 365 helps healthcare organizations ensure data
security, compliance, and streamlined patient care

They face stringent regulatory requirements such as the **Health Insurance Portability and Accountability Act (HIPAA)** and **General Data Protection Regulation (GDPR)**, which demand a robust approach to data security and compliance. Microsoft 365 offers many features that can help healthcare institutions meet these requirements when they're implemented correctly.

Lessons learned

Here are some key lessons learned that highlight best practices for data security, compliance, and operational efficiency:

- **Granular role-based access controls**: Healthcare institutions must customize access based on job roles (for example, doctors, nurses, and administrative staff) to prevent unauthorized access to patient data

- **End-to-end data encryption**: Both in-transit and at-rest encryption must be utilized to safeguard sensitive data from external threats

- **Compliance-driven retention**: Automated data retention schedules ensure compliance with healthcare data retention policies, minimizing legal risks

- **Centralized patient portals**: Microsoft SharePoint's collaboration features enable the creation of centralized portals for medical records, accessible to both patients and healthcare professionals

- **Streamlined emergency response**: Real-time collaboration tools in Microsoft 365, such as Microsoft Teams, can aid in faster communication during emergencies

- **Data loss prevention (DLP)**: DLP policies prevent accidental or unauthorized sharing of sensitive health information via email or external drives

- **Two-factor authentication**: Implementing **multi-factor authentication (MFA)** strengthens security by requiring multiple verification steps

- **Device security**: Only allowing access from secure, authorized devices minimizes the risk of data breaches

- **Mobile collaboration**: Secure mobile access allows healthcare professionals to update and retrieve patient records on the go without compromising security

- **Audit trails**: Enforcing regular audits of user activity ensures that unauthorized access attempts are identified and addressed swiftly

Now, let's turn to the best practices that organizations in this industry can adopt to maximize the benefits of Microsoft 365.

Best practices

Here are the best practices to follow:

- **Conditional access based on location**: Limit access to health records to specific secure networks, such as hospital systems, and block access from untrusted locations

- **Automated compliance audits**: Set up automated compliance check systems in Microsoft 365 to regularly monitor for regulatory adherence

- **Advanced threat protection**: Leverage advanced threat protection to detect and respond to potential cyberattacks before they breach the system

- **Encrypt emails**: Secure emails through Microsoft 365 encryption tools to prevent sensitive information from being accessed during transmission

- **Integrate telemedicine**: Integrate Microsoft Teams with telemedicine platforms such as *Teladoc Health*, *Amwell*, *Doxy.me*, and *eVisit* to provide secure video consultations and document sharing

- **Document version control**: Use Microsoft SharePoint's versioning tools to keep track of patient record changes, ensuring accurate medical histories

- **Mobile access with conditional security**: Enable secure mobile device access with stringent security settings, such as MFA, conditional access policies, mobile application management, and device compliance checks, to enhance care flexibility

- **Training programs for compliance**: Conduct regular staff training on HIPAA and GDPR compliance using built-in Microsoft 365 learning tools

- **Automated data retention policies**: Automate the retention and deletion of medical data in line with legal and regulatory timelines

- **Use eDiscovery for legal cases**: Quickly locate documents for legal audits using Microsoft 365's eDiscovery feature

- **Cross-departmental collaboration**: Use Microsoft Teams for communication between medical departments to streamline patient handoffs

- **Patient portals in Microsoft SharePoint**: Create patient access portals where they can access their medical records and appointments securely

In this section, we explored key lessons learned and best practices for implementing Microsoft 365 in healthcare while focusing on data security, compliance, and operational efficiency.

We discussed how tools such as granular role-based access controls, end-to-end encryption, centralized patient portals, and mobile collaboration are essential in safeguarding sensitive patient information and enhancing the quality of care.

Additionally, adopting best practices such as conditional access, automated compliance audits, and the integration of telemedicine platforms with Microsoft Teams enables healthcare organizations to meet regulatory requirements while optimizing patient services.

Education – fostering remote learning, collaboration, and student engagement

Educational institutions rely on collaboration and seamless communication between students, teachers, and administrators:

Figure 7.3 – Microsoft 365 fosters remote learning, collaboration, and student engagement

With the rise of remote learning, Microsoft 365 and Microsoft SharePoint have become essential tools for creating virtual classrooms, streamlining administrative processes, and fostering inclusive learning environments.

Lessons learned

Here are some key lessons learned that highlight best practices for data security, compliance, and operational efficiency:

- **Centralized learning hubs**: Combining Microsoft Teams and Microsoft SharePoint creates centralized virtual learning hubs for remote students and educators
- **Collaboration beyond classrooms**: Students and teachers use OneNote and Microsoft Teams to collaborate on assignments and projects in real time

- **Scalability**: Microsoft 365's scalability allowed educational institutions to quickly expand virtual classrooms during crises such as COVID-19

- **Content accessibility**: Immersive Reader and live captions in Microsoft Teams have made educational content more accessible to students with disabilities

- **Customized learning paths**: Microsoft SharePoint can be used to create personalized learning experiences based on individual student's progress

- **Paperless administrative tasks**: Automating grade submission, attendance, and course scheduling reduces administrative burden

- **Parent-teacher collaboration**: Microsoft SharePoint can enable better collaboration between parents and teachers, allowing them to share assignments, reports, and progress updates

- **Remote learning engagement**: Microsoft Whiteboard and other tools help maintain student engagement in virtual settings

- **Integration of third-party learning tools**: Microsoft 365 integrates seamlessly with third-party apps, enhancing the virtual classroom experience

- **Mobile learning access**: Students can access learning materials on mobile devices, enabling flexible learning

Now, let's turn to the best practices that organizations in this industry can adopt to maximize the benefits of Microsoft 365.

Best practices

Here are the best practices to follow:

- **Microsoft Teams for virtual classrooms**: Implement Microsoft Teams to conduct virtual lessons, break-out sessions, and group projects.

- **Digital notebooks with OneNote**: Encourage students to use OneNote so that they can organize their notes and homework.

- **Automate grading systems**: Use Microsoft SharePoint workflows to automate assignment collection and grading.

- **Collaboration with parents**: Set up Microsoft SharePoint portals for parents to track their child's performance and communicate with teachers.

- **Enable accessibility tools**: Provide Immersive Reader and live captions to ensure all students, including those with disabilities, can engage with content.

- **Train educators on technology**: Establish early and ongoing training for teachers on Microsoft 365's features to ensure they use the platform to its fullest potential.

- **Streamline course registration**: Automate course registration and scheduling workflows using Power Automate and Microsoft SharePoint.

- **Create assignment libraries**: Use Microsoft SharePoint to store reusable resources and assignments for students and teachers.

- **Digital field trips**: Use Microsoft Team's video conferencing features to organize virtual field trips and guest lectures.

- **Use analytics to track student progress**: Leverage Power BI to create dashboards that monitor student progress and identify areas for improvement.

- **Hybrid learning models**: Establish systems that blend in-person and online learning seamlessly, ensuring flexibility. Use Microsoft Teams for virtual classrooms, OneNote for collaborative notetaking, and Microsoft SharePoint for organizing resources, allowing students to engage in both in-person and online learning environments seamlessly.

- **Student-led collaboration spaces**: Use Microsoft Teams to allow students to collaborate independently outside of class hours.

In this section, we explored how Microsoft 365 and its suite of tools, which includes Microsoft Teams, OneNote, and SharePoint, have empowered educational institutions to foster remote learning, streamline collaboration, and enhance student engagement.

The lessons learned, such as creating centralized learning hubs, enabling real-time collaboration, and leveraging scalable, accessible tools, demonstrate how these platforms can adapt to the unique needs of students, educators, and administrators alike.

By applying best practices such as automating administrative tasks, integrating accessibility tools, and implementing hybrid learning models, educational institutions can significantly enhance learning outcomes while reducing operational burdens.

Finance – enhancing governance, data security, and regulatory compliance

The finance sector operates in a highly regulated environment, requiring strict data security, governance, and compliance measures:

Figure 7.4 – Microsoft 365 enhances governance, data security,
and regulatory compliance for the finance sector

Microsoft 365 can address these needs by offering data governance tools, secure access controls, and compliance automation.

Lessons learned

Here are some key lessons learned that highlight best practices for data security, compliance, and operational efficiency:

- **Strict data classification policies**: Financial organizations must classify all data based on sensitivity and assign appropriate protection levels

- **Data encryption mandates**: In the finance sector, regulatory compliance requires encrypting both stored and transmitted data

- **Automated retention labels**: Microsoft 365's retention labels enable financial institutions to automate data retention and deletion, ensuring compliance with regulations such as GDPR and SOX

- **Enhanced legal hold capabilities**: Microsoft SharePoint's eDiscovery and legal hold features simplify responding to audits and investigations

- **Real-time fraud monitoring**: Finance companies can use advanced threat analytics in Microsoft 365 to monitor suspicious activities in real time

- **Identity and access management**: The use of Microsoft Entra ID for identity and access management enhances security by enabling strict user authentication and access control

- **Compliance certifications**: Leveraging Microsoft 365's built-in compliance certifications (for example, ISO and SOC) streamlines regulatory audits

- **Internal collaboration audits**: Regular internal audits are crucial to ensure data security policies are followed

- **MFA**: Enforcing MFA across all financial applications ensures a higher security standard

- **Robust DLP**: Configure DLP policies to prevent sensitive data from being shared outside the organization enhances data security

Now, let's turn to the best practices that organizations in this industry can adopt to maximize the benefits of Microsoft 365.

Best practices

Here are the best practices to follow:

- **Data governance framework**: Implement a comprehensive data governance framework using Microsoft 365's compliance features

- **Advanced threat protection**: Use advanced threat protection to defend against phishing attacks and malware

- **Automated retention policies**: Automate data retention for financial records to ensure compliance

- **Use eDiscovery for regulatory compliance**: Leverage the eDiscovery tool to retrieve documents for legal or regulatory audits quickly

- **Real-time fraud detection**: Set up real-time alerts for suspicious activity using Microsoft 365's security monitoring tools

- **Identity-based access control**: Use Microsoft Entra ID to implement identity-based access control, ensuring only authorized users access sensitive financial data

- **Role-based access to sensitive data**: Ensure that only those in specific roles (for example, compliance officers, and auditors) have access to high-sensitivity data

- **Automated audit trails**: Set up automated audit trails in Microsoft 365 to track changes and data access

- **Secure document sharing**: Use Microsoft 365's secure file-sharing capabilities to share sensitive financial documents

- **Risk management dashboards**: Use Power BI to monitor financial performance, compliance risks, and operational data

- **Mobile device security**: Ensure that all mobile access to financial data is through secure and authorized devices

- **Backup and recovery systems**: Implement backup and recovery systems within Microsoft 365 to safeguard critical financial data

In this section, we explored the critical lessons learned and best practices for enhancing governance, data security, and regulatory compliance in the finance sector using Microsoft 365.

We learned how financial organizations can safeguard sensitive data, streamline compliance processes, and improve operational efficiency through the implementation of strict data classification policies, encryption mandates, and automated retention systems.

Additionally, we covered essential best practices, such as establishing a robust data governance framework, implementing advanced threat protection, and leveraging tools such as eDiscovery and Power BI to support regulatory compliance and risk management.

Manufacturing – optimizing supply chain operations and production efficiency

Manufacturers need to streamline operations across multiple locations, manage supply chains, and collaborate with external partners:

Figure 7.5 – Microsoft 365 in manufacturing optimizes supply chain operations and production efficiency

Microsoft 365 facilitates collaboration, automates workflows, and enables real-time data monitoring, helping manufacturers boost efficiency and reduce costs.

Lessons learned

Here are some key lessons learned that highlight best practices for data security, compliance, and operational efficiency:

- **Real-time supply chain monitoring**: Microsoft SharePoint portals enable manufacturers to monitor their supply chains in real time, reducing bottlenecks

- **Collaboration with suppliers**: Manufacturers create Microsoft SharePoint collaboration portals where suppliers can update inventories, track orders, and manage deliveries

- **Data-driven decision-making**: Integration with Power BI allows manufacturers to create dashboards that track production efficiency, helping with real-time decision-making

- **Workflow automation for efficiency**: Automating repetitive tasks such as inventory updates and quality control checks reduces human error

- **Cross-location collaboration**: Microsoft Teams enable seamless communication between manufacturing facilities in different regions

- **Predictive maintenance**: Using Power Automate, manufacturers can create workflows to schedule maintenance before equipment failures occur

- **Safety compliance**: Manufacturing organizations can track safety compliance documentation using Microsoft SharePoint's document management features

- **Secure file sharing**: Microsoft SharePoint allows manufacturers to share product designs and confidential information with external partners securely

- **Centralized knowledge base**: Microsoft SharePoint serves as a centralized repository for technical documents, training materials, and standard operating procedures

- **Vendor performance tracking**: Manufacturers track vendor performance using Microsoft SharePoint's custom list features to monitor timely deliveries, quality, and responsiveness

Now, let's turn to the best practices that organizations in this industry can adopt to maximize the benefits of Microsoft 365.

Best practices

Here are the best practices to follow:

- **Automated workflow for order processing**: Use Power Automate to streamline order processing, reducing delays

- **Supplier portals in Microsoft SharePoint**: Create supplier-specific portals to manage orders, invoices, and deliveries in real time

- **Predictive analytics with Power BI**: Implement predictive analytics dashboards using Power BI to optimize production lines

- **Quality control automation**: Automate quality control workflows using Microsoft SharePoint to minimize defects

- **Equipment maintenance alerts**: Set up automated alerts for scheduled maintenance to prevent downtime

- **Collaborative design spaces**: Use Microsoft SharePoint to create secure spaces for sharing and collaborating on design prototypes

- **Vendor performance dashboards**: Leverage Power BI to track vendor performance and adjust supply chain strategies accordingly

- **Real-time inventory management**: Automate inventory tracking and stock level alerts to avoid overstocking or stockouts

- **Compliance documentation tracking**: Use Microsoft SharePoint to ensure all compliance and safety documents are up-to-date and easily accessible

- **Custom Microsoft SharePoint lists for supply chain activities**: Use custom lists in Microsoft SharePoint to monitor the progress of supply chain activities, including delivery timelines and bottlenecks

- **Cross-departmental communication**: Use Microsoft Teams to facilitate communication across various departments, including procurement, production, and logistics

- **Secure file sharing with contractors**: Ensure all designs and confidential documents shared with contractors use secure file-sharing protocols in Microsoft 365

In this section, we explored the key lessons learned and best practices for leveraging Microsoft 365 to optimize supply chain operations and production efficiency in the manufacturing sector.

By implementing real-time monitoring, automating workflows, enhancing collaboration with suppliers, and utilizing data-driven decision-making tools such as Power BI, manufacturers can significantly boost their operational efficiency, reduce bottlenecks, and improve overall productivity.

Technology – innovating with agile development and collaboration tools

Technology companies often focus on innovation, requiring platforms that enable rapid collaboration, agile project management, and seamless integration with development tools:

Figure 7.6 – Innovating with agile development and collaboration tools

Microsoft 365 and Microsoft SharePoint help tech companies streamline development cycles, improve cross-functional collaboration, and protect intellectual property.

Lessons learned

Here are some key lessons learned that highlight best practices for data security, compliance, and operational efficiency:

- **Agile project management**: Microsoft 365 integrates with tools such as Azure DevOps, enabling agile development practices such as sprint planning and backlog tracking

- **Version control in Microsoft SharePoint**: Tech companies benefit from Microsoft SharePoint's version control, ensuring technical documents are always up to date

- **Collaboration across Microsoft Teams**: Microsoft Teams enables real-time collaboration between engineers, designers, and product managers during product development

- **Data security for intellectual property**: Tech companies implement stringent access controls to protect intellectual property, including patents and code repositories

- **Innovation hubs**: Microsoft SharePoint serves as an innovation hub, where employees can share new ideas, research, and best practices

- **Third-party integrations**: Seamlessly integrating third-party development tools such as GitHub with Microsoft 365 enhances productivity

- **Cloud-based development environments**: The integration of Microsoft 365 with cloud development platforms allows for remote software development and testing

- **Collaboration with clients**: Microsoft SharePoint portals provide secure spaces for collaborating with clients on projects, enabling them to track progress and provide feedback

- **Continuous learning and documentation**: Microsoft SharePoint is used for knowledge sharing and continuous learning within organizations, housing technical documentation and best practices

- **Automated security audits**: Automated security audits help ensure compliance with industry standards, protecting sensitive development environments from cyber threats

Now, let's turn to the best practices that organizations in this industry can adopt to maximize the benefits of Microsoft 365.

Best practices

Here are the best practices to follow:

- **Agile project management in Microsoft Teams**: Integrate Microsoft Teams with Azure DevOps to facilitate daily scrums, sprint reviews, and sprint planning meetings

- **Cross-functional collaboration**: Set up dedicated Microsoft Teams channels for product development, bringing together engineers, designers, and product managers

- **IP protection with conditional access**: Implement conditional access policies to ensure only authorized team members have access to sensitive intellectual property

- **Automated development pipelines**: Use Power Automate to automate development tasks such as code compilation and testing

- **Continuous learning portals**: Use Microsoft SharePoint to create internal knowledge-sharing hubs, enabling employees to learn new skills and best practices

- **Custom dashboards for development metrics**: Leverage Power BI to track key software development metrics such as sprint velocity, bug resolution rates, and deployment frequency

- **Secure client collaboration portals**: Create client-specific Microsoft SharePoint portals to collaborate on product development and project progress securely

- **IP protection with MFA**: Ensure MFA is in place for all team members handling sensitive intellectual property

- **Automated bug tracking**: Use Power Automate to streamline bug tracking and reporting, linking it with Microsoft Teams for real-time updates

- **DLP for source code**: Configure DLP policies to prevent unauthorized sharing of source code or proprietary data

In this section, we explored key lessons and best practices for technology companies using Microsoft 365 to drive innovation, enhance collaboration, and safeguard intellectual property.

From agile project management to securing sensitive development environments, we've highlighted how Microsoft 365's tools such as Teams, SharePoint, and Power Automate can streamline workflows and ensure compliance with industry standards.

Retail – enhancing customer experience, operations, and data-driven decisions

Retail companies require effective collaboration tools to manage store operations, supply chains, and customer engagement:

Figure 7.7 – Microsoft 365 enhances customer experience, operations, and data-driven decisions in retail

Microsoft 365 and Microsoft SharePoint offer retailers real-time inventory management, customer data protection, and collaborative platforms for marketing and operations.

Lessons learned

Here are some key lessons learned that highlight best practices for data security, compliance, and operational efficiency:

- **Centralized store operations management**: Retail companies use Microsoft SharePoint to centralize store operations, including inventory management, staffing, and customer support

- **Marketing campaign collaboration**: Microsoft Teams enables marketing teams to collaborate on product launches and promotions in real time

- **Real-time inventory tracking**: Microsoft SharePoint portals enable real-time tracking of inventory across multiple locations, reducing stockouts and overstocking

- **Data-driven marketing**: Integrating Power BI with customer data platforms helps retailers make data-driven decisions for personalized marketing campaigns

- **Customer data security**: Retailers must ensure that customer data is encrypted and protected through role-based access controls

- **Automated loyalty program management**: Microsoft 365 automates the management of customer loyalty programs, ensuring accurate tracking of customer rewards

- **Cross-channel marketing**: Retailers use Microsoft 365 to manage cross-channel marketing campaigns, ensuring consistent messaging across digital and in-store channels

- **Mobile-friendly store collaboration**: Retail employees can use mobile devices to access training materials, update inventories, and communicate with teams in real time

- **Customer feedback loops**: Microsoft SharePoint portals allow for centralized collection and analysis of customer feedback, which can drive improvements in services and products

- **Streamlined vendor collaboration**: Retailers use Microsoft SharePoint to manage vendor relationships and ensure timely product deliveries

Now, let's turn to the best practices that organizations in this industry can adopt to maximize the benefits of Microsoft 365.

Best practices

Here are the best practices to follow:

- **Store operation portals in Microsoft SharePoint**: Create store-specific portals to manage day-to-day operations, inventory, and staffing efficiently

- **Automated inventory management**: Use Power Automate to trigger restock orders based on real-time inventory data from Microsoft SharePoint

- **Cross-channel collaboration in Microsoft Teams**: Use Microsoft Teams to collaborate on marketing campaigns, ensuring that in-store and online promotions are synchronized

- **Customer data protection with DLP**: Implement strict DLP policies to safeguard customer data and prevent unauthorized sharing

- **Real-time sales analytics with Power BI**: Integrate Power BI to analyze real-time sales data, enabling faster decisions on promotions and product placements

- **Centralized customer feedback portals**: Use Microsoft SharePoint to gather customer feedback across channels, helping retailers respond to customer needs quickly

- **Vendor performance dashboards**: Monitor vendor performance using Power BI dashboards, ensuring timely deliveries and product quality

- **Mobile-friendly employee access**: Ensure retail employees have access to Microsoft SharePoint on mobile devices, enabling efficient store management

- **Training materials in Microsoft SharePoint**: Store all retail training materials in Microsoft SharePoint, providing easy access to onboarding and training content for employees

- **Collaborative marketing platforms**: Create dedicated Microsoft SharePoint spaces for marketing teams to collaborate on promotions, ensuring seamless execution

- **Loyalty program automation**: Automate the management of customer loyalty programs, ensuring that customers receive rewards based on their purchase history

- **Store inventory alerts**: Set up automated alerts for low-stock items, enabling store managers to reorder products before they run out

In this section, we explored how Microsoft 365 enhances retail operations by improving customer experience, streamlining supply chain management, and enabling data-driven decision-making.

Key lessons learned include the importance of centralized store operations, real-time inventory tracking, and customer data protection. We also highlighted best practices such as creating store-specific portals, automating loyalty programs, and using Power BI for sales analytics.

Legal – streamlining case management, compliance, and collaboration

Legal firms require robust tools for case management, document collaboration, and compliance with industry regulations:

Figure 7.8 – Microsoft 365 streamlines case management, compliance, and collaboration in the legal sector

Microsoft 365 and Microsoft SharePoint help legal teams manage documents securely, ensure compliance, and collaborate effectively on legal matters.

Lessons learned

Here are some key lessons learned that highlight best practices for data security, compliance, and operational efficiency:

- **Centralized case management**: Legal firms use Microsoft SharePoint to centralize case files and streamline access for attorneys and support staff

- **Document version control**: Microsoft SharePoint's version control ensures that legal documents remain accurate, with a clear record of changes

- **Secure document collaboration**: Legal teams benefit from secure document collaboration features in Microsoft 365, allowing them to work on cases without risking data breaches

- **Automated document workflows**: Power Automate allows legal firms to automate document approvals and review processes, speeding up case management

- **Legal hold for compliance**: Microsoft 365's legal hold capabilities ensure that documents are preserved for regulatory audits and legal proceedings

- **eDiscovery for litigation**: Microsoft 365's eDiscovery tool helps legal teams quickly locate relevant case documents for litigation

- **Client collaboration portals**: Legal teams create Microsoft SharePoint portals for clients to access case updates securely and collaborate with attorneys

- **Compliance monitoring**: Legal firms use Microsoft Purview and Power BI to monitor compliance with industry regulations such as GDPR

- **Encrypted communication**: Microsoft 365's email encryption features ensure that sensitive legal communications remain secure

- **Internal knowledge sharing**: Legal teams use Microsoft SharePoint to store and share internal knowledge, best practices, and case law

Now, let's turn to the best practices that organizations in this industry can adopt to maximize the benefits of Microsoft 365.

Best practices

Here are the best practices to follow:

- **Case management in Microsoft SharePoint**: Create case-specific portals in Microsoft SharePoint, centralizing all relevant documents and communications

- **Automated document review workflows**: Use Power Automate to streamline document review and approval workflows, reducing delays in case management

- **Legal hold for case preservation**: Implement Microsoft SharePoint's legal hold feature to ensure that relevant documents are preserved for legal proceedings

- **eDiscovery for legal investigations**: Use Microsoft 365's eDiscovery tool to quickly locate documents during legal investigations or audits

- **Secure client portals**: Create client-specific portals to share case updates and documents with clients securely

- **Version control for legal documents**: Ensure that all legal documents in Microsoft SharePoint have version control enabled to maintain accuracy

- **Automated compliance audits**: Set up automated compliance monitoring in Microsoft Purview and Power BI to ensure adherence to industry regulations

- **Email encryption for legal communication**: Encrypt all legal communications sent via email using Microsoft 365's encryption tools

- **Knowledge-sharing platforms**: Create internal knowledge-sharing portals where legal teams can collaborate on case law, best practices, and research

- **Cross-team collaboration in Microsoft Teams**: Use Microsoft Teams to enable seamless collaboration between attorneys, paralegals, and clients on legal matters

- **Client billing automation**: Automate client billing workflows using Power Automate, ensuring accurate and timely invoicing

- **Compliance dashboards in Power BI**: Use Power BI to monitor key compliance metrics and ensure that legal teams stay on top of regulatory requirements

In this section, we explored how legal firms can streamline case management, ensure compliance, and enhance collaboration using Microsoft 365 and SharePoint.

We learned about the importance of centralized case management, document version control, and secure collaboration, as well as how automation tools such as Power Automate and eDiscovery can speed up legal processes and improve efficiency.

These tools not only help legal teams stay compliant with industry regulations but also ensure the security and accuracy of sensitive legal documents.

Energy – enhancing field operations, compliance, and environmental monitoring

Energy companies operate in highly regulated environments where efficient field operations, data management, and environmental compliance are critical:

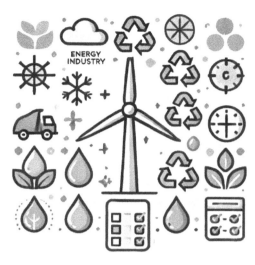

Figure 7.9 – Microsoft 365 enhances field operations, compliance, and environmental monitoring in energy companies

Microsoft 365 and Microsoft SharePoint provide tools for managing compliance, improving collaboration, and monitoring **key performance indicators (KPIs)** in real time.

Lessons learned

Here are some key lessons learned that highlight best practices for data security, compliance, and operational efficiency:

- **Field operations management**: Microsoft SharePoint allows energy companies to manage field operations by providing real-time updates and access to key documents
- **Environmental compliance tracking**: Microsoft SharePoint can store and manage compliance documentation related to environmental regulations
- **Collaboration with contractors**: Energy companies use Microsoft Teams and Microsoft SharePoint to collaborate with external contractors on on-site management and project updates
- **Energy consumption monitoring**: Integration with Power BI allows companies to monitor energy consumption and environmental impacts in real time
- **Data security for field operations**: Microsoft 365's security features ensure that sensitive operational data from the field is protected against breaches
- **Automated compliance audits**: Power Automate can be used to schedule regular compliance audits, ensuring adherence to industry regulations
- **Mobile access for field workers**: Field workers can use mobile devices to access Microsoft SharePoint for real-time updates on project status and environmental regulations

- **Emergency response coordination**: Microsoft Teams enables faster coordination during emergency response situations, ensuring communication between field workers and headquarters

- **Document version control for compliance**: Ensuring accurate version control of compliance documents is critical to meeting regulatory standards

- **Automated data collection**: Field data can be collected and automatically uploaded to Microsoft SharePoint for real-time monitoring and analysis

Now, let's turn to the best practices that organizations in this industry can adopt to maximize the benefits of Microsoft 365.

Best practices

Here are the best practices to follow:

- **Field operation portals in Microsoft SharePoint**: Set up field-operation-specific portals to manage workflows, project documentation, and real-time updates

- **Automated compliance tracking**: Automate compliance tracking workflows to ensure timely submission of regulatory documents

- **Environmental impact monitoring**: Use Power BI to monitor energy consumption and environmental impact in real time

- **Secure mobile access for field workers**: Provide field workers with secure mobile access to Microsoft SharePoint, ensuring they have the information they need

- **Collaboration with external contractors**: Create Microsoft SharePoint portals for external contractors to collaborate on projects and share updates

- **Version control for compliance documents**: Implement version control in Microsoft SharePoint to ensure that all compliance-related documents are up to date and accurate

- **Emergency response with Microsoft Teams**: Use Microsoft Teams to set up emergency response groups for faster communication during crises

- **Real-time data collection**: Automate the collection of field data using Microsoft SharePoint, allowing for real-time analysis of KPIs

- **Energy performance dashboards**: Leverage Power BI to create dashboards that monitor energy production, consumption, and operational efficiency

- **Automated document approval workflows**: Use Power Automate to streamline document approval processes for compliance and safety protocols

- **Mobile-friendly access for compliance monitoring**: Enable mobile access for compliance officers to track and monitor regulatory adherence from the field

- **Data encryption for field operations**: Ensure that all field data transmitted through mobile devices is encrypted to maintain security

In this section, we explored how Microsoft 365 enhances field operations, compliance, and environmental monitoring in the energy sector.

The key lessons learned include how tools such as Microsoft SharePoint, Teams, and Power BI streamline field operations, ensure compliance, and provide real-time insights into energy consumption and environmental impact.

By understanding these practices, energy companies can safeguard data, improve operational efficiency, and respond quickly in critical situations.

Hospitality – streamlining guest services, collaboration, and operations

Hospitality organizations require guest services, staff collaboration, and operational processes to be managed efficiently so that they can provide top-tier customer experiences:

Figure 7.10 – Microsoft 365 streamlines guest services, collaboration,
and operations in the hospitality sector

Microsoft 365 and Microsoft SharePoint offer solutions that enhance guest experience, streamline operations, and improve collaboration across departments.

Lessons learned

Here are some key lessons learned that highlight best practices for data security, compliance, and operational efficiency:

- **Centralized guest management**: Microsoft SharePoint portals allow hospitality companies to centralize guest records and service requests, improving customer service

- **Staff collaboration tools**: Microsoft Teams enables real-time communication between staff across departments, improving the coordination of guest services

- **Data security for guest information**: Microsoft 365 ensures that guest information is stored securely and protected from unauthorized access

- **Automated booking systems**: Hospitality organizations automate booking workflows, ensuring that guest reservations and room assignments are handled efficiently

- **Mobile access for guest services**: Staff can use mobile devices to access guest requests and service information, improving response times

- **Real-time analytics for guest satisfaction**: Integration with Power BI allows companies to monitor guest satisfaction and service performance in real time

- **Document management for training**: Microsoft SharePoint is used to store and manage training materials for staff, ensuring consistency in service quality

- **Compliance with data protection laws**: Microsoft 365's compliance features help hospitality companies meet data protection regulations such as GDPR

- **Automated billing workflows**: Power Automate allows hospitality companies to automate guest billing and payment processes, ensuring accuracy

- **Cross-location collaboration**: Microsoft SharePoint portals enable collaboration between hotel locations, streamlining operations and resource sharing

Now, let's turn to the best practices that organizations in this industry can adopt to maximize the benefits of Microsoft 365.

Best practices

Here are the best practices to follow:

- **Guest service portals in Microsoft SharePoint**: Create centralized guest service portals to manage requests, reservations, and service updates

- **Automated booking and room assignments**: Automate booking workflows using Power Automate to ensure efficient room assignments and guest check-ins

- **Real-time guest satisfaction dashboards**: Use Power BI to monitor guest satisfaction scores and respond to service issues in real time

- **Mobile access for staff**: Enable staff to access guest information and service requests via mobile devices, improving response times

- **Cross-department collaboration in Microsoft Teams**: Use Microsoft Teams to improve communication and collaboration between housekeeping, front desk, and maintenance staff

- **Automated billing and payments**: Automate guest billing workflows to ensure accurate and timely billing processes

- **Guest data protection with DLP**: Implement DLP policies to protect sensitive guest data from unauthorized access

- **Training materials in Microsoft SharePoint**: Store all staff training materials in Microsoft SharePoint, ensuring consistent onboarding and ongoing training

- **Centralized document management**: Use Microsoft SharePoint to manage operational documents, including service protocols, training guides, and guest management procedures

- **Collaboration across hotel locations**: Set up Microsoft SharePoint portals to facilitate collaboration between different hotel locations

- **Automated guest feedback collection**: Automate guest feedback collection processes, ensuring timely analyses and responses to service improvements

- **Mobile-first staff access**: Provide mobile-friendly access to Microsoft SharePoint, ensuring that staff can respond to guest requests and collaborate efficiently

In this section, we explored the key lessons learned and best practices for implementing Microsoft 365 in the hospitality industry and focused on improving guest services, streamlining staff collaboration, and ensuring data security.

By leveraging tools such as Microsoft SharePoint for centralized guest management and training, Power Automate for automating booking and billing workflows, and Power BI for real-time guest satisfaction tracking, hospitality organizations can enhance operational efficiency and deliver superior customer experiences.

Non-profit – enhancing donor engagement, volunteer management, and operations

Non-profit organizations rely on collaboration, volunteer management, and donor engagement to achieve their goals:

Figure 7.11 – Microsoft 365 enhances donor engagement, volunteer management, and operations in non-profit organizations

Microsoft 365 and Microsoft SharePoint help streamline these processes, enabling better engagement with stakeholders and more efficient management of operations.

Lessons learned

Here are some key lessons learned that highlighted best practices for data security, compliance, and operational efficiency:

- **Donor management portals**: Non-profits use Microsoft SharePoint to manage donor information, track donations, and communicate with supporters

- **Volunteer collaboration**: Microsoft Teams facilitates collaboration between volunteers and staff, ensuring clear communication and coordination during events and campaigns

- **Secure data for donors and volunteers**: Microsoft 365 ensures that sensitive donor and volunteer data is stored securely and protected

- **Automated donation tracking**: Power Automate helps non-profits track donations and generate reports automatically, reducing administrative burden

- **Event management collaboration**: Microsoft SharePoint portals enable better collaboration between teams working on fundraising events and campaigns

- **Mobile access for volunteers**: Volunteers can access information about events, schedules, and responsibilities through mobile devices

- **Centralized knowledge sharing**: Non-profits can use Microsoft SharePoint to store and share best practices, campaign strategies, and training materials

- **Grant management workflows**: Power Automate can streamline grant application and reporting processes, ensuring compliance with funding requirements

- **Real-time donor engagement analytics**: Integration with Power BI allows non-profits to monitor donor engagement in real time and adjust strategies accordingly

- **Compliance with donor privacy laws**: Microsoft 365's compliance features help non-profits meet data protection regulations related to donor information

Now, let's turn to the best practices that organizations in this industry can adopt to maximize the benefits of Microsoft 365.

Best practices

Here are the best practices to follow:

- **Donor management portals in Microsoft SharePoint**: Use Microsoft SharePoint to create centralized donor management portals, enabling better tracking of donations and communication with supporters

- **Automated donation tracking**: Automate donation tracking workflows to reduce the manual effort required to manage donor contributions

- **Volunteer collaboration in Microsoft Teams**: Use Microsoft Teams to facilitate communication and collaboration between volunteers, ensuring they have the information they need for events and campaigns

- **Mobile access for volunteers**: Provide mobile access to Microsoft SharePoint, enabling volunteers to check schedules, tasks, and event information

- **Automated grant application processes**: Streamline the grant application process using Power Automate, ensuring timely submissions and compliance with funding requirements

- **Centralized knowledge sharing for campaigns**: Use Microsoft SharePoint to store and share best practices for campaigns and events, enabling collaboration across teams

- **Real-time donor engagement dashboards**: Use Power BI to monitor donor engagement metrics, allowing non-profits to adjust strategies based on real-time insights

- **Automated compliance audits**: Automate compliance tracking for donor privacy regulations, ensuring that all donor data is handled securely and in compliance with legal requirements

- **Event management collaboration**: Create Microsoft SharePoint portals for event management, allowing teams to collaborate on planning, execution, and follow-up

- **Automated volunteer onboarding**: Automate the onboarding process for volunteers using Power Automate, reducing the time required to get new volunteers up to speed

- **Donor privacy protection with DLP**: Implement strict DLP policies to protect sensitive donor information and ensure compliance with privacy laws

- **Volunteer performance tracking**: Use Microsoft SharePoint to track volunteer contributions and performance, helping non-profits recognize and reward top performers

In this section, we explored how Microsoft 365 enhances donor engagement, volunteer management, and operational efficiency in the non-profit sector. Through real-world examples, we've seen the power of tools such as Microsoft SharePoint for managing donor relationships, Power Automate for streamlining workflows, and Microsoft Teams for improving volunteer collaboration. These lessons learned and best practices demonstrate the importance of secure data management, compliance, and the ability to automate critical processes.

Microsoft 365 provides a flexible and scalable platform for organizations across diverse industries. By understanding the lessons learned and applying best practices from real-world implementations, organizations can tailor these tools to meet their unique needs, whether they're focused on compliance, collaboration, data security, or operational efficiency.

As industries continue to evolve, Microsoft 365 will remain vital in driving innovation, enhancing productivity, and ensuring seamless operations across sectors.

Throughout this section, we've explored the lessons learned and best practices from various industries implementing Microsoft 365, highlighting how organizations can leverage its adaptability to address specific industry challenges.

Understanding these insights is important as it shows how Microsoft 365 can be tailored to optimize collaboration, ensure compliance, and enhance operational efficiency across sectors.

These lessons set the stage for the next section, where we'll delve deeper into understanding future trends and exploring upcoming features in Microsoft 365 and Microsoft SharePoint. This will help organizations stay ahead of the curve by anticipating changes and leveraging new tools to drive even greater innovation and productivity in their operations.

Emerging trends and upcoming features in Microsoft 365 and Microsoft SharePoint

Staying ahead of technological advancements is crucial for businesses to remain competitive and efficient. Microsoft 365 and Microsoft SharePoint have been pivotal in supporting organizations' collaborative efforts, providing a dynamic and secure environment for team communication, document management, and workflow automation:

Figure 7.12 – Emerging trends and upcoming features in Microsoft 365 and SharePoint

The latest innovations introduced by Microsoft, particularly Microsoft SharePoint Premium and AI-driven tools such as Microsoft Copilot, are reshaping how businesses operate.

Let's explore the emerging trends and features in Microsoft 365 and SharePoint while focusing on AI capabilities and how companies need to adapt to these advancements for long-term success.

SharePoint Premium – a new standard for enterprise collaboration

SharePoint Premium is the latest evolution of the widely used Microsoft SharePoint platform that's designed to meet the growing demands of modern enterprises:

Figure 7.13 – SharePoint Premium

This enhanced version of Microsoft SharePoint builds upon the robust collaboration and document management features of the standard offering, introducing new capabilities tailored to large organizations.

Here are some of the key features of SharePoint Premium:

- **Advanced security and compliance**: SharePoint Premium provides more granular controls and enhanced DLP features. This is especially important for industries with strict regulatory requirements, such as healthcare and finance.

- **Extended integration**: While Microsoft SharePoint has always been integrated with Microsoft 365, the Premium version offers deeper, more seamless connections to other tools, such as Microsoft Teams, Outlook, and OneDrive. This level of integration ensures that employees can access all the necessary tools from a single, streamlined interface.

- **Customizable workflows**: SharePoint Premium empowers companies with highly customizable workflows, enabling businesses to create bespoke solutions tailored to their unique processes and challenges. This flexibility accelerates business operations and optimizes performance across departments.

- **Enhanced user experience**: The user interface of SharePoint Premium is designed for efficiency, offering a more intuitive experience that simplifies content creation, sharing, and management.

As more enterprises move toward hybrid work environments, SharePoint Premium has emerged as a critical platform for ensuring business continuity. Companies should invest in this new tool to stay competitive and maintain a collaborative culture across distributed teams.

Artificial intelligence and machine learning – transforming business operations

Artificial intelligence (**AI**) and **machine learning** (**ML**) are revolutionizing the way organizations work:

Figure 7.14 – AI and ML

In Microsoft 365 and SharePoint, AI-driven features are designed to automate repetitive tasks, streamline workflows, and provide insights that enhance decision-making processes. These features are as follows:

- **Automated content management**: AI capabilities within Microsoft SharePoint allow organizations to automatically tag, classify, and manage content based on predefined rules. This reduces the time employees spend on administrative tasks, allowing them to focus on more strategic work.

- **Predictive insights**: With ML algorithms, Microsoft 365 provides insights into user behavior, document usage patterns, and overall productivity trends. These insights help organizations identify areas where processes can be optimized.

- **Natural language processing**: AI-powered chatbots and virtual assistants within Microsoft 365 offer real-time support, enabling employees to quickly find the information they need without needing to navigate complex systems.

- **AI-powered search**: The enhanced search functionality in Microsoft SharePoint uses AI to deliver more accurate and context-relevant search results, helping employees find the right information quickly and efficiently.

The integration of AI in Microsoft 365 and Microsoft SharePoint represents a fundamental shift in how businesses approach their day-to-day operations. It automates manual processes, reduces human error, and empowers employees to make data-driven decisions.

Companies that invest in AI-driven tools will experience increased productivity, enhanced user satisfaction, and better overall performance.

Microsoft Copilot – revolutionizing knowledge work

One of the most exciting innovations in Microsoft 365 is **Microsoft Copilot**.

This AI-powered assistant is designed to support knowledge workers by automating tasks, suggesting content, and providing real-time recommendations based on user activity:

Figure 7.15 – Microsoft Copilot

Microsoft Copilot is integrated across the entire Microsoft 365 ecosystem and offers the following features, among others:

- **Task automation**: Copilot can automate a wide range of tasks, from scheduling meetings to generating reports, allowing users to save time and focus on higher-value activities.

- **Smart recommendations**: Based on the context of ongoing work, Copilot offers suggestions to help users complete tasks more efficiently. For instance, if a user is drafting a document, Copilot may recommend templates and relevant data, or even assist with writing.

- **Real-time collaboration**: Copilot enhances team collaboration by suggesting relevant documents, messages, and contacts during meetings or discussions. This feature ensures that team members have access to the right resources without having to search for them manually.

By integrating Microsoft Copilot into their daily workflows, companies can significantly improve the productivity and efficiency of their workforce. Copilot represents the future of knowledge work, where AI seamlessly augments human capabilities, enabling faster and more informed decision-making.

The role of AI in enhancing data security and compliance

In today's business environment, data security and compliance are top concerns:

Figure 7.16 – AI in enhancing data security and compliance

The introduction of AI capabilities in Microsoft 365 and Microsoft SharePoint plays a pivotal role in addressing the following challenges:

- **AI-driven threat detection**: AI algorithms can detect abnormal activity or potential security threats in real time, allowing organizations to respond swiftly to any vulnerabilities. This is crucial for preventing data breaches and ensuring the integrity of sensitive information.

- **Automated compliance monitoring**: Microsoft 365 uses AI to automatically monitor compliance with industry regulations. This reduces the burden on IT teams and ensures that companies remain compliant without having to perform manual audits.

- **Data classification and protection**: AI enables advanced data classification, allowing organizations to automatically identify and protect sensitive information. SharePoint Premium takes this further with enhanced DLP features, providing an added layer of protection for confidential documents.

As organizations face increasing pressure to comply with regulations such as GDPR, AI-driven security and compliance tools are essential. Businesses that fail to invest in these technologies risk not only regulatory penalties but also damage to their reputation.

Preparing for the future of work

The introduction of SharePoint Premium, AI capabilities, and tools such as Microsoft Copilot signals a new era in the way organizations operate:

Figure 7.17 – The future of work

These advancements are not just about improving productivity; they represent a fundamental shift in how work is performed and how employees engage with technology.

To stay competitive, companies need to embrace this new way of working by doing the following:

- **Investing in training and development**: As AI-driven tools become more prevalent, employees will need training to use them effectively. Organizations must invest in upskilling their workforce to ensure they can fully leverage these technologies.

- **Adopting a cloud-first strategy**: The cloud is the backbone of Microsoft 365 and SharePoint, and companies that prioritize cloud adoption will be better positioned to take advantage of future innovations.

- **Embracing flexibility**: The future of work is flexible, with hybrid work environments becoming the norm. Microsoft SharePoint and Microsoft 365 offer the tools needed to support remote and in-office collaboration, allowing businesses to remain agile and responsive to change.

- **Focusing on data-driven decision-making**: AI tools within Microsoft 365 provide valuable insights that can inform decision-making processes. Organizations must embrace data-driven strategies to remain competitive in an increasingly complex business landscape.

Microsoft 365 and Microsoft SharePoint are at the forefront of technological innovation, with emerging trends such as AI, Microsoft Copilot, and SharePoint Premium revolutionizing how businesses operate. These tools provide organizations with the capabilities they need to improve productivity, enhance collaboration, and ensure data security and compliance.

However, the successful adoption of these technologies requires a proactive approach. Companies must invest in training, embrace flexible working models, and develop a cloud-first mindset to prepare for the future of work. By doing so, businesses can position themselves to thrive in a rapidly evolving digital landscape.

In this section, we delved into the transformative trends within Microsoft 365 and SharePoint, focusing on the pivotal role of AI-driven tools such as Microsoft Copilot and the advanced capabilities of SharePoint Premium. These innovations aren't just technological enhancements; they represent a significant shift in how businesses manage collaboration, data, and workflows. By automating routine tasks, optimizing content management, and improving data security, these tools empower organizations to operate more efficiently and stay competitive in an ever-evolving marketplace.

Understanding these advancements is essential for any business looking to thrive in today's fast-paced digital environment. Integrating AI and ML into daily workflows simplifies complex tasks, allowing employees to focus on higher-value activities, while enhanced security features ensure data integrity and compliance. As companies increasingly adopt hybrid work models, the seamless collaboration capabilities of Microsoft 365 and Microsoft SharePoint become even more critical.

Summary

In this chapter, we explored real-world case studies across various industries to demonstrate how organizations have successfully implemented Microsoft 365 and Microsoft SharePoint solutions to address unique challenges. From enhancing data security in healthcare to optimizing supply chain efficiency in manufacturing, we covered a wide range of lessons learned and best practices that have led to significant improvements in productivity, compliance, and collaboration. Additionally, we delved into future trends, such as AI-powered tools such as Microsoft Copilot and SharePoint Premium, which are revolutionizing the way businesses operate by automating workflows, enhancing decision-making, and improving data security.

These lessons are critical for helping businesses remain competitive in a rapidly evolving digital landscape. By applying these insights, organizations can tailor Microsoft 365 to meet their specific needs, whether they aim to strengthen security, streamline operations, or foster greater collaboration. The skills you acquired in this chapter provide a strong foundation for harnessing the full potential of Microsoft 365 and SharePoint, preparing businesses to adapt to emerging technologies and future trends.

In the next chapter, we'll build upon all lessons learned through all previous chapters, offering a step-by-step guide to effectively deploying Microsoft 365 and Microsoft SharePoint within an organization. We'll cover practical implementation strategies, ensuring that you can put the knowledge you've gained so far into action to drive tangible results within any business.

Part 5: Wrapping Up

Now, it's time to put all the pieces together. This part is where the magic happens, where strategy meets execution, and where you begin turning ideas into real, functional solutions. We're diving into both high-level planning and the nuts and bolts of implementation, so by the end of these chapters, you'll have everything you need to confidently roll out Microsoft 365 and SharePoint solutions that make a difference for your organization.

This part contains the following chapters:

- *Chapter 8, Implementing Microsoft 365 and SharePoint Solutions – Strategic Blueprints*
- *Chapter 9, Implementing Microsoft 365 and SharePoint Solutions – Implementation Playbooks*

8

Implementing Microsoft 365 and SharePoint Solutions – Strategic Blueprints

In this chapter, we'll explore the key strategies for building a sustainable and effective Microsoft 365 and SharePoint environment. We'll cover everything from high-level planning and governance to change management and collaboration models, all with the added benefit of using **artificial intelligence (AI)** tools such as Microsoft 365 Copilot to enhance your digital workspace.

You'll learn how to create a phased implementation roadmap that aligns with your organization's goals, ensuring a smooth rollout of Microsoft 365 features over time. This roadmap will help you set priorities, establish milestones, and use AI insights to make better decisions.

We'll also dive into governance and compliance strategies, showing you how AI can help automate data governance, manage compliance risks, and control access dynamically. These practices are crucial for keeping your environment secure and compliant as your organization grows.

On top of that, we'll cover change management techniques that will help drive user adoption and keep people engaged with Microsoft 365. By leveraging AI, you'll be able to personalize user experiences, automate routine tasks, and make transitions easier for your team.

By the end of this chapter, you will be equipped to implement a holistic strategy that aligns Microsoft 365 solutions with your business objectives, ensures robust governance, and leverages AI to elevate productivity and collaboration.

In this chapter, we're going to cover the following main topics:

- Aligning governance, compliance, and AI with change management
- Using AI to drive adoption and build a long-term collaboration model
- Developing a phased strategy for Microsoft 365 implementation with AI integration

This chapter is your strategic guide to mastering Microsoft 365 and SharePoint with a forward-thinking approach.

Revolutionizing the digital workspace with AI and strategic planning

Welcome to a world where the digital workspace isn't just a set of tools but an evolving ecosystem. Microsoft 365 and SharePoint have changed the way organizations collaborate, but let's face it, there's more to this story.

It's not just about the software we use; it's about how we plan, govern, manage change, and, most importantly, leverage AI to push the boundaries of what's possible.

Figure 8.1 – AI digital workspace

AI is no longer a futuristic concept, it's now a crucial player in the digital workspace. When we think about AI, perhaps the first thing that comes to mind is automation: the ability to handle repetitive tasks without a hitch. However, AI in Microsoft 365 and SharePoint goes beyond just performing tasks; it's about enhancing productivity, simplifying complex processes, and providing insights that were once buried deep in heaps of data.

Imagine a workday where AI becomes the personal assistant, guiding through meetings, summarizing documents, and offering suggestions on how to optimize workflows. That's what Microsoft 365 Copilot does: it transforms raw data into actionable insights. But as exciting as AI is, it's important to remember that it's not just plug-and-play. We need a strategy, a plan that acknowledges both the opportunities and the responsibilities that come with such powerful technology.

AI, when strategically implemented, can revolutionize collaboration within organizations: think of it as having a team member who never gets tired, doesn't miss deadlines, and constantly learns and adapts to the working style. From identifying trends in data to assisting in decision-making, AI tools provide an edge. Yet, while this paints a promising picture, integrating AI into the digital workspace requires more than enthusiasm; it demands careful planning, a robust governance framework, and a willingness to embrace change.

So, why does governance matter when we talk about AI and collaboration? In simple terms, it's about control. It's ensuring that as we open the floodgates to AI and enhance collaboration, we're doing so with the right guardrails in place. AI thrives on data, and with tools such as Microsoft 365 Copilot digging deep into the workspace, identifying sensitive information, and automating tasks, we need to be clear about who has access to what and how this data is being used.

A well-governed environment sets boundaries, not to restrict innovation but to guide it in the right direction. For instance, deploying AI without considering compliance or privacy issues could lead to unexpected risks. When employees use Copilot to draft documents or analyze sensitive data, proper governance ensures that information stays secure, complies with regulations, and is utilized ethically. Governance, therefore, isn't the enemy of progress; it's the guardian of sustainable innovation.

Introducing AI tools into a digital workspace is a transformative process that affects how people work. The magic lies not in the technology itself but in how smoothly people adapt to it where change management becomes the bridge that connects the technical aspects of AI implementation with the human side of the organization.

We can't just drop a new AI tool into the mix and expect everyone to jump on board, there will be questions, resistance, and a learning curve: a structured approach to change management ensures that users understand the benefits of AI, see how it fits into their daily routines, and feel confident in using it. The right communication strategy, coupled with training and support, is key to a successful transition. When people see AI not as a threat to their roles but as a means to enhance their capabilities, that's when the real magic happens.

Collaboration models enriched by AI

Now, let's talk about **collaboration**. At its core, collaboration is about people coming together to achieve common goals. However, AI can elevate this dynamic to a whole new level where Microsoft 365 and SharePoint are designed to facilitate teamwork, and AI acts as the catalyst that makes collaboration not only possible but effortless.

Figure 8.2 – AI collaboration models

By understanding the context of conversations, suggesting relevant documents, and automating routine tasks, AI redefines how teams interact within the digital workspace.

Still, AI-enhanced collaboration doesn't mean doing away with human input. It's about providing tools that augment human decision-making and creativity. By defining clear collaboration models within the Microsoft 365 environment, we can use AI to break down silos, encourage knowledge sharing, and streamline communication.

In this exploration, we'll go through the essentials of creating a digital workspace where AI and human creativity work in tandem, covering how to design a Microsoft 365 and SharePoint environment that isn't just technically sound but also flexible, secure, and prepared for the future.

With the right mix of planning, governance, change management, and AI-enriched collaboration, our digital workspace won't just survive, it will thrive.

Crafting a phased strategy for Microsoft 365 implementation with AI integration

Embarking on a Microsoft 365 implementation journey with a focus on AI integration, particularly with tools such as Microsoft 365 Copilot, requires careful planning and strategic execution.

The following is a phased strategy that outlines how to successfully implement Microsoft 365 and progressively incorporate AI to revolutionize a digital workspace.

Phase 1 – Foundation – laying the groundwork for Microsoft 365 and AI integration

This phase focuses on engaging key stakeholders to clearly define the vision, goals, and expected outcomes of the implementation, ensuring alignment with the organization's strategic objectives. Through comprehensive workshops and consultations with business leaders, IT teams, and compliance specialists, the foundation is set for establishing the necessary technical and governance frameworks to support the transition.

These early efforts are essential in addressing potential pain points, understanding user needs, and aligning technology goals with organizational priorities.

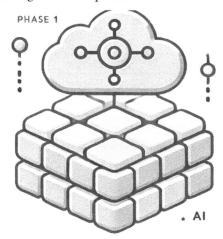

Figure 8.3 – Microsoft 365/AI groundwork

In addition to stakeholder engagement, this phase includes a thorough assessment of the current technical environment, identifying infrastructure gaps, and preparing a detailed roadmap for migration to the Microsoft cloud.

Ensuring the organization's readiness for Microsoft 365 deployment and AI integration, including proper governance policies for data security and AI usage, is paramount to the success of subsequent implementation phases. By the end of this phase, the groundwork will be laid, allowing the organization to move forward confidently with the integration of Microsoft 365 and AI capabilities such as Copilot.

Stakeholder engagement and goal definition

Objective: Engage key stakeholders across the organization to define the vision and goals for Microsoft 365 implementation and AI integration.

Actions to be taken:

- Conduct workshops with business leaders, IT, compliance teams, and end users to understand their needs and pain points.

Timeline	Stakeholders	Output
Weeks 1–2	Project manager, IT team	A comprehensive list of needs, requirements, and potential challenges

- Define clear objectives for Microsoft 365 usage, such as improving collaboration, streamlining workflows, and leveraging AI for enhanced productivity.

    Task: Collaborate with stakeholders to define objectives, focusing on improving collaboration, streamlining workflows, and leveraging AI tools such as Copilot.

Timeline	Stakeholders	Output
Weeks 3–4	Project manager, business analysts	Documented objectives and expected outcomes for Microsoft 365 implementation

- Create a strategic roadmap outlining the desired outcomes from Microsoft 365 and AI tools such as Copilot.

    Task: Develop a strategic roadmap outlining short-term and long-term goals for Microsoft 365 and Copilot implementation.

Timeline	Stakeholders	Output
Weeks 5–6	Governance committee, IT team	A finalized strategic roadmap that aligns with the organization's vision for Microsoft 365 and AI integration

To ensure the successful integration of Microsoft 365 and AI tools such as Copilot, it is crucial that these defined goals, strategies, and stakeholder insights form the foundation of a carefully structured implementation plan.

Technical readiness assessment

Objective: Evaluate the current technical environment to ensure compatibility and readiness for Microsoft 365 deployment and AI integration.

Actions to be taken:

- Conduct a thorough assessment of current IT infrastructure, network capabilities, and security policies.

Timeline	Stakeholders	Output
Weeks 2–3	IT team, data governance team	An assessment report detailing the current infrastructure status, network capabilities, and security posture

- Identify potential areas that require upgrades, such as network bandwidth or security configurations, to support Microsoft 365 and AI operations.

Timeline	Stakeholders	Output
Weeks 4–5	IT team, network engineers	A list of required upgrades and an action plan to address infrastructure gaps

- Develop a migration strategy for data, including SharePoint content, email, and files, to the Microsoft cloud.

Timeline	Stakeholders	Output
Weeks 6–7	Data governance team, IT team	A detailed data migration strategy, including steps, timelines, and teams

After completing the technical readiness assessment and addressing any necessary upgrades, the organization will be well-positioned to begin a smooth transition toward the full deployment of Microsoft 365 and AI capabilities.

Governance framework establishment

Objective: Define governance policies to manage data, permissions, compliance, and AI usage within Microsoft 365.

Actions to be taken:

- Create a governance committee that will oversee the implementation and ongoing management of Microsoft 365 and AI tools.

Timeline	Stakeholders	Output
Week 1	Senior management, project manager	Formation of a governance committee with defined roles and responsibilities

- Establish policies for data security, privacy, and compliance to meet organizational and regulatory standards.

Timeline	Stakeholders	Output
Weeks 2–4	Governance committee, compliance team	A comprehensive set of policies that ensure data security, privacy, and regulatory compliance

- Develop guidelines for using AI tools, setting boundaries on how and where Copilot can be employed, and defining data access controls.

Timeline	Stakeholders	Output
Weeks 4–5	Governance committee, AI specialists	Documented guidelines for AI usage, including access controls and boundaries for Copilot use within the organization

The establishment of a solid governance framework will not only ensure that the integration of Microsoft 365 and AI tools such as Copilot is secure and compliant but will also set the foundation for sustainable and responsible growth, fostering alignment across all the teams involved. With clear roles, policies, and guidelines in place, organizations can confidently navigate the complexities of data management and AI usage.

Milestones for Phase 1 completion

Monitoring the following milestones is crucial to ensure the timely completion of Phase 1:

- **Week 2**: Stakeholder workshops completed and requirements assessment finalized
- **Week 4**: Objectives for Microsoft 365 usage defined and IT infrastructure assessment completed
- **Week 5**: Governance committee established and data security and compliance policies developed
- **Week 6**: Strategic roadmap for Microsoft 365 and AI created and guidelines for AI tool usage finalized
- **Week 7**: Technical readiness assessment and data migration strategy completed

By the end of this phase, the groundwork for Microsoft 365 and AI integration, particularly Copilot, will be well-established, ensuring the organization is prepared for the subsequent deployment and implementation phases.

Here's a timeline for this phase:

PHASE 1 - TASKS	W1	W2	W3	W4	W5	W6	W7
Stakeholder engagement and goal definition							
Define objectives for Microsoft 365 usage							
Create a strategic roadmap for M365 and AI							
Assess existing IT infrastructure							
Identify required upgrades							
Develop a migration strategy for data							
Form governance committee							
Establish data security and compliance policies							
Develop AI usage guidelines							

Figure 8.4 – Phase 1 timeline

Now that we've explored the foundational functional steps for implementing Microsoft 365 and AI integration, we should have a solid understanding of the importance of engaging stakeholders, assessing technical readiness, and setting up proper governance frameworks.

This ensures that all critical elements are aligned with organizational goals and prepares organization infrastructure to handle the demands of advanced tools such as Microsoft 365 and Copilot. By establishing clear objectives and policies, we've laid the groundwork for a smooth transition.

Phase 2 – Deployment – implementing core Microsoft 365 services

The second phase of the Microsoft 365 deployment plan is dedicated to a methodical and organized implementation of key Microsoft 365 services throughout the company, guaranteeing a smooth transition for every user. It is designed to begin with a pilot implementation, where a small group of users will be introduced to essential tools such as Exchange Online, OneDrive, SharePoint Online, and Teams.

Feedback from this pilot group will help fine-tune the deployment strategy, ensuring that any potential issues are addressed before scaling up across the organization. The pilot phase also includes comprehensive user training, designed to familiarize the team with collaboration, document storage, and communication capabilities.

Figure 8.5 – Microsoft 365 core services

As the phased rollout continues, emphasis is placed on gradual adoption, department by department, based on each group's technical readiness and business needs.

Alongside the deployment of core services, robust training and support systems will be implemented to empower users and ensure that they are proficient in using Microsoft 365 tools.

The groundwork for future AI integration will be established by preparing the necessary infrastructure and deploying compliance tools to support data-driven decision-making and the eventual integration of advanced AI capabilities such as Microsoft 365 Copilot.

Pilot implementation with core Microsoft 365 tools

Objective: Begin with a phased rollout of key Microsoft 365 services to a select group of users for initial feedback and adjustments.

Actions to be taken:

- Deploy core services such as Exchange Online, OneDrive, SharePoint Online, and Teams to a pilot group.

Timeline	Stakeholders	Output
Weeks 1–2	IT team, project manager	Successful setup of core Microsoft 365 services for a small group of users; initial configuration of communication, storage, and collaboration features

- Encourage pilot users to explore collaboration features, document storage, and communication tools, while providing training on best practices.

Timeline	Stakeholders	Output
Weeks 3–4	IT support team, training coordinator	Completion of user training sessions; feedback collection on collaboration tools, document storage, and communication processes

- Collect feedback from pilot users to identify any issues or gaps and use this data to refine the overall deployment strategy.

Timeline	Stakeholders	Output
Week 5	User support team, business analysts	Feedback report highlighting user experiences, challenges, and suggestions; refined deployment plan for wider rollout

To ensure a smooth transition and optimize the overall adoption of Microsoft 365 services, it is crucial to use the insights gained from the pilot phase. By analyzing user feedback and addressing any identified gaps, the organization can make informed adjustments, paving the way for a more effective and seamless broader deployment.

Gradual rollout across the organization

Objective: Expand the deployment of Microsoft 365 services organization-wide, ensuring a smooth transition for all users.

Actions to be taken:

- Roll out Microsoft 365 services in phases, starting with departments most ready for adoption based on technical readiness and business needs.

Timeline	Stakeholders	Output
Weeks 6–8	IT team, project manager	Phased deployment plan; Microsoft 365 services deployed to initial departments, with incremental onboarding for other departments

- Provide comprehensive training sessions focusing on specific Microsoft 365 tools relevant to each department's work processes.

Timeline	Stakeholders	Output
Weeks 9–12	Training coordinator, department heads	Training completion reports; increased user proficiency in Microsoft 365 tools such as Teams, OneDrive, and SharePoint

- Establish a support system, including help desks and knowledge bases, to assist users during the transition.

Timeline	Stakeholders	Output
Weeks 13–14	IT support team, knowledge management team	Fully operational support system; knowledge base articles and FAQs available to assist users

By following this structured approach, the organization can ensure a smooth and effective adoption of Microsoft 365 services, minimizing disruption while maximizing user engagement and proficiency across all departments.

AI infrastructure preparation

Objective: Set up the necessary infrastructure and data governance to prepare for AI integration within Microsoft 365.

Actions to be taken:

- Integrate Microsoft Purview and other compliance tools to manage and monitor data usage across Microsoft 365 services.

Timeline	Stakeholders	Output
Weeks 15–16	Data governance team, IT security team	Integration of compliance tools; data monitoring system in place for secure and compliant data handling

- Review and classify data to identify sensitive information and set up appropriate access controls in preparation for Copilot usage.

Timeline	Stakeholders	Output
Weeks 17–18	Data governance team, IT team	Data classification and access control policies; secure environment for Copilot integration

- Deploy Power Platform tools to facilitate data-driven decision-making and readiness for more advanced AI capabilities.

Timeline	Stakeholders	Output
Weeks 19–20	Power Platform team, business analysts	Deployed Power Platform tools

To ensure a seamless and secure integration of AI within Microsoft 365, these foundational steps will establish a robust infrastructure, laying the groundwork for future advancements and more effective data-driven decision-making across the organization.

Milestones for Phase 2 completion

Monitoring the following milestones is crucial to ensure the timely completion of Phase 2:

- **Week 5**: Completion of the pilot implementation; feedback collection and strategy refinement
- **Week 14**: Gradual rollout across the organization completed; support system established and operational
- **Week 20**: AI infrastructure preparation completed; compliance tools integrated, data classified, and Power Platform tools deployed

Here's a timeline for this phase:

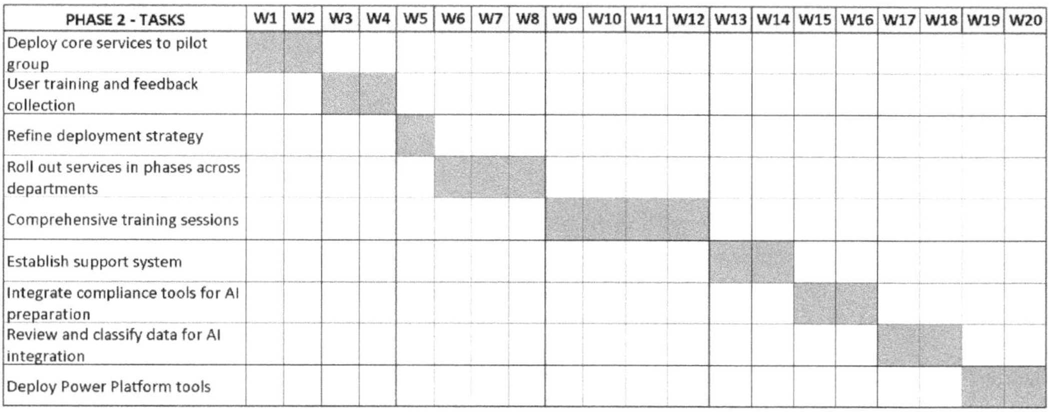

PHASE 2 - TASKS	W1	W2	W3	W4	W5	W6	W7	W8	W9	W10	W11	W12	W13	W14	W15	W16	W17	W18	W19	W20
Deploy core services to pilot group	X	X																		
User training and feedback collection			X	X																
Refine deployment strategy					X															
Roll out services in phases across departments						X	X													
Comprehensive training sessions									X	X	X									
Establish support system													X							
Integrate compliance tools for AI preparation																X				
Review and classify data for AI integration																		X		
Deploy Power Platform tools																				X

Figure 8.6 – Phase 2 timeline

By the end of Phase 2, Microsoft 365 core services will be fully deployed and functional across the organization, customized to suit the specific needs of each department.

A comprehensive support system, including user training and a robust knowledge base, will be established to assist employees throughout and beyond the transition.

Additionally, the necessary infrastructure for AI integration, including compliance tools and data governance frameworks, will be in place, setting the foundation for deploying advanced AI tools such as Microsoft 365 Copilot in the upcoming phases.

Phase 3 – AI integration – incorporating Copilot into the digital workspace

The objective of this phase is to seamlessly introduce Copilot into the organizational workflow, allowing us to explore its potential while ensuring that the teams adapt to the new capabilities. By starting with a targeted rollout to specific departments, we'll be able to carefully assess its effectiveness, gather valuable user feedback, and make any necessary adjustments before full-scale deployment.

Figure 8.7 – Microsoft 365 Copilot

This phase will not only focus on integrating AI into daily tasks but also on providing tailored training to ensure teams are comfortable leveraging Copilot's advanced features. From drafting documents and summarizing meetings to optimizing workflows and generating actionable insights, Copilot promises to transform how we work.

By gathering insights and measuring its impact, we will refine our approach, ensuring that the AI-driven enhancements align with the overall goals and empower the teams in the long run.

Initial rollout of Microsoft 365 Copilot

Objective: Introduce Copilot to a controlled environment to test its effectiveness and gauge user adaptation.

Actions to be taken:

- Begin by deploying Copilot to a specific team or department where AI-driven productivity gains are most beneficial, such as the marketing or finance team.

Timeline	Stakeholders	Output
Weeks 1–2	IT team, AI implementation team	Initial deployment of Copilot within the selected department (e.g., marketing or finance) with configuration and access control in place

- Provide targeted training on how to use Copilot, focusing on functions such as drafting documents, summarizing meetings, and generating insights from data.

Timeline	Stakeholders	Output
Weeks 3–4	User support team, training coordinator	Completion of targeted training sessions focusing on Copilot's key functions, such as document drafting, meeting summarization, and data insights
Ongoing from Week 5	AI implementation team, business analysts	Feedback reports collected from initial users, highlighting Copilot's usage patterns, effectiveness, and areas requiring improvement or adjustments

To ensure a smooth transition and the optimal use of Microsoft 365 Copilot, these steps will lay the groundwork for a measured and effective rollout, enabling teams to fully harness AI-driven features while allowing for feedback-driven refinements in the process.

AI-driven workflow optimization

Objective: Use Copilot to streamline workflows, reduce repetitive tasks, and improve decision-making processes.

Actions to be taken:

- Integrate Copilot into everyday tasks such as email drafting, meeting scheduling, and data analysis, demonstrating how AI can enhance efficiency.

Timeline	Stakeholders	Output
Weeks 6–8	IT team, workflow optimization specialists	Successful integration of Copilot into daily activities, such as email drafting, meeting scheduling, and data analysis, to enhance productivity

- Encourage teams to use Copilot's natural language capabilities to query data and generate reports, enhancing data accessibility and insights.

Timeline	Stakeholders	Output
Weeks 9–10	User support team, business analysts	Increased utilization of Copilot's natural language features for querying data and generating reports, with a recorded uptick in data accessibility and insights

- Implement automated approval workflows in Microsoft Teams and SharePoint, using Copilot to recommend actions based on historical data and patterns.

Timeline	Stakeholders	Output
Weeks 11–12	IT team, AI implementation team	Automated workflows established, allowing Copilot to provide action recommendations based on historical data, streamlining approvals in Microsoft Teams and SharePoint

By following these steps, organizations can begin to seamlessly incorporate Copilot into their daily operations, driving efficiency and improving decision-making. These efforts will not only enhance productivity but also lay the groundwork for a more intelligent, data-driven workflow.

AI impact and user adoption assessment

Objective: Evaluate the impact of AI integration on productivity and refine the strategy based on user feedback and performance data.

Actions to be taken:

- Conduct surveys and feedback sessions to understand user experiences and challenges with Copilot.

Timeline	Stakeholders	Output
Weeks 13–14	Business analysts, user support team	Completion of surveys and feedback sessions, providing qualitative insights into user experiences, challenges, and the overall effectiveness of Copilot

- Analyze metrics such as task completion times, collaboration effectiveness, and user engagement to measure Copilot's impact.

Timeline	Stakeholders	Output
Week 15	Data analysts, AI implementation team	Analysis report detailing key performance metrics such as task completion times, collaboration effectiveness, and user engagement levels post-Copilot integration

- Use insights gathered to adjust AI deployment, provide additional training, or refine governance policies as necessary.

Timeline	Stakeholders	Output
Week 16	AI implementation team, governance committee	Adjustments made to Copilot's deployment, including additional training sessions or policy refinements to enhance user adoption and data governance

To ensure the ongoing success and relevance of Copilot in your organization, it is crucial to continuously monitor its integration, collect feedback, and adapt based on real-world data. By aligning the deployment with user needs and performance metrics, the AI can be refined to deliver maximum value while addressing any challenges that arise.

Milestones for Phase 3 completion

Monitoring the following milestones is crucial to ensure the timely completion of Phase 3:

- **Weeks 1–2**: Initial deployment of Copilot to a selected team or department
- **Weeks 3–4**: Completion of Copilot training sessions for targeted users
- **Weeks 6–8**: Integration of Copilot into everyday tasks to streamline workflows
- **Weeks 9–10**: Enhanced use of Copilot's natural language capabilities for data queries
- **Weeks 11–12**: Implementation of automated workflows using Copilot in Microsoft Teams and SharePoint
- **Weeks 13–14**: Completion of surveys and feedback sessions to assess AI impact
- **Week 15**: Analysis of performance metrics to measure the effectiveness of Copilot
- **Week 16**: Final adjustments to Copilot deployment, ensuring readiness for full-scale integration

Upon completing Phase 3, Copilot will be successfully integrated into everyday workflows within the organization, streamlining routine tasks and providing insightful data analysis. The initial rollout will have enabled teams to adapt to AI-enhanced processes, while targeted training will have built confidence in using Copilot's advanced functionalities.

Here's a timeline for this phase:

PHASE 3 - TASKS	W1	W2	W3	W4	W5	W6	W7	W8	W9	W10	W11	W12	W13	W14	W15	W16
Initial deployment of Copilot to a selected department	▨	▨														
Completion of Copilot training sessions for targeted users			▨													
Feedback reports					Ongoing from Week 5					▨						
Integration of Copilot into everyday tasks to streamline workflows							▨									
Enhanced use of Copilot's natural language capabilities for data queries										▨						
Implementation of automated workflows using Copilot in MS Teams & SharePoint											▨					
Completion of surveys and feedback sessions to assess AI impact													▨			
Analysis of performance metrics to measure effectiveness of Copilot															▨	
Final adjustments to Copilot deployment																▨

Figure 8.8 – Phase 3 timeline

A thorough assessment of AI's impact will offer crucial feedback to refine and optimize the deployment further, paving the way for a more efficient, collaborative, and data-driven digital workspace in the subsequent phases of the Microsoft 365 implementation journey.

Phase 4 – Optimization – expanding AI capabilities and enhancing the Microsoft 365 environment

Optimization marks a crucial stage in the journey of integrating and expanding AI capabilities and enhancing the Microsoft 365 environment. This phase aims to build on the foundational work laid out in the earlier stages, ensuring that Copilot is not only seamlessly woven into everyday workflows but also customized to meet the specific needs of various departments. By doing so, the organization will leverage the full potential of Copilot, driving efficiency, collaboration, and data-driven decision-making across all levels.

Figure 8.9 – AI capabilities and enhancement

The primary objective of this phase is to enable Copilot for all teams, with tailored configurations that align with departmental requirements such as sales insights, customer support analysis, and project management assistance. This customization will involve close collaboration between the IT team and departmental leads, ensuring that settings are adjusted to optimize performance and deliver actionable insights.

Through this targeted approach, the organization will unlock new capabilities, further fostering a culture of innovation and continuous improvement.

Full-scale Copilot integration and customization

Objective: Expand Copilot integration across all relevant departments and tailor its functionalities to suit specific business needs.

Actions to be taken:

- Enable Copilot for all teams, adjusting settings to align with departmental requirements, such as sales insights, customer support analysis, or project management assistance.

Timeline	Stakeholders	Output
Weeks 1–2	IT team, departmental leads	Custom Copilot configurations for different departments (e.g., sales insights, customer support analysis)

- Integrate Copilot with Power Automate to create customized workflows, automating routine processes such as generating invoices or scheduling follow-up emails.

Timeline	Stakeholders	Output
Weeks 2–4	IT team, process automation specialists	Automated workflows using Copilot and Power Automate, such as invoice generation and email scheduling

- Develop internal Copilot plugins to address unique organizational needs, such as extracting specific insights from proprietary data sources.

Timeline	Stakeholders	Output
Weeks 3–6	AI specialists, software development team	Custom Copilot plugins designed to extract specific insights from proprietary data sources

To ensure a smooth transition and maximize the value Copilot can bring, the following steps outline a strategic approach to full-scale integration, customization, and automation across departments, enabling tailored solutions that enhance productivity and streamline workflows.

Leverage advanced AI tools

Objective: Incorporate other AI tools available within the Microsoft ecosystem to further enhance productivity and collaboration.

Actions to be taken:

- Introduce AI features in Power Apps to automate data entry and provide predictive analytics for various business scenarios.

Timeline	Stakeholders	Output
Weeks 2–5	Power Apps development team, data analysts	Automated data entry solutions and predictive analytics dashboards for business scenarios

- Use Azure AI Services to integrate speech-to-text, language translation, and image recognition capabilities into Microsoft 365 workflows.

Timeline	Stakeholders	Output
Weeks 4–7	AI specialists, IT security team	Integration of speech-to-text, language translation, and image recognition in Microsoft 365 workflows

- Set up AI-driven virtual agents in Microsoft Teams using custom Copilots to handle common queries and support requests.

Timeline	Stakeholders	Output
Weeks 5–8	IT team, customer support team	AI-powered virtual agents in Microsoft Teams to handle common queries and support requests

By strategically leveraging AI capabilities across various Microsoft platforms, organizations can significantly streamline operations, improve decision-making processes, and drive greater efficiency in day-to-day workflows.

Continuous improvement and governance refinement

Objective: Establish a cycle of continuous evaluation and improvement for AI usage, ensuring alignment with business objectives.

Actions to be taken:

- Regularly review AI performance, focusing on metrics such as productivity gains, user satisfaction, and data security compliance.

Timeline	Stakeholders	Output
Ongoing, with monthly reviews	AI governance committee, business analysts	Reports on productivity gains, user satisfaction, and data security compliance

- Update governance policies to adapt to evolving AI capabilities, ensuring data privacy, ethical use, and compliance with industry standards.

Timeline	Stakeholders	Output
Week 8 and then quarterly	Governance committee, IT security team	Updated governance policies that adapt to evolving AI capabilities, ensuring data privacy and ethical use

- Keep users informed of new features and best practices, promoting an ongoing culture of learning and innovation.

Timeline	Stakeholders	Output
Ongoing, with monthly training sessions	Training and development team, IT team	User engagement programs, regular newsletters, and updated knowledge bases

To ensure the long-term success of AI initiatives such as Copilot, these steps foster not only the effective use of the technology but also an adaptable governance framework that evolves alongside the organization's needs and industry standards.

Milestones for Phase 4 completion

Monitoring the following milestones is crucial to ensure the timely completion of Phase 4:

- **Week 4**: Copilot fully integrated and customized for core departments
- **Week 6**: Internal plugins for Copilot developed and tested

- **Week 7**: Azure Cognitive Services features are incorporated into Microsoft 365 workflows
- **Week 8**: AI-driven virtual agents are active in Microsoft Teams
- **Ongoing**: Continuous evaluation of AI performance and governance policy updates

By the end of this phase, the organization will have a fully integrated AI ecosystem within Microsoft 365, tailored to suit specific departmental needs. Copilot's functionalities will be optimized to enhance workflow automation, data analysis, and customer support. Advanced AI tools will be seamlessly embedded into daily operations, providing predictive analytics, natural language processing, and virtual assistance. Additionally, a robust governance structure will be in place to ensure ethical and compliant use of AI, supported by a cycle of continuous improvement.

Here's a timeline for this phase:

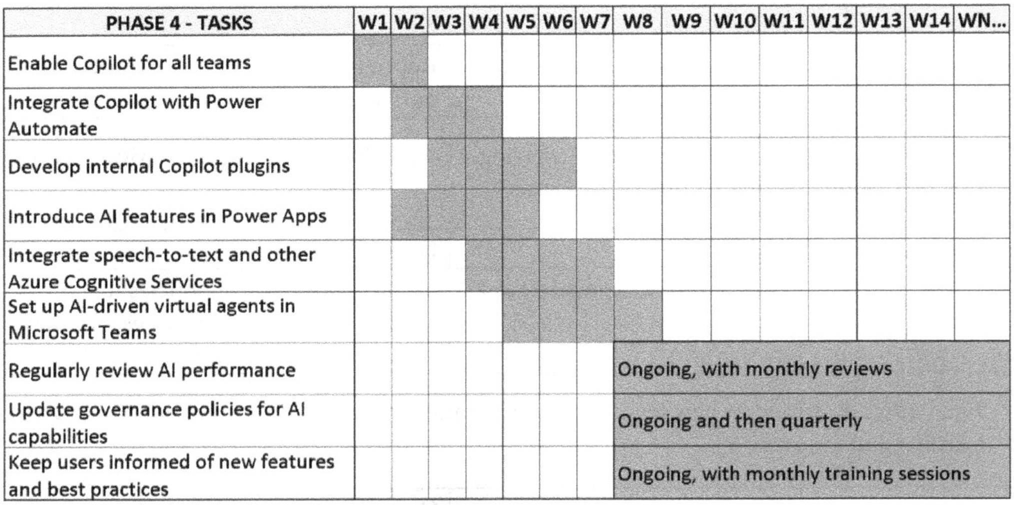

PHASE 4 - TASKS	W1	W2	W3	W4	W5	W6	W7	W8	W9	W10	W11	W12	W13	W14	WN...
Enable Copilot for all teams	█														
Integrate Copilot with Power Automate		█	█												
Develop internal Copilot plugins		█													
Introduce AI features in Power Apps			█	█											
Integrate speech-to-text and other Azure Cognitive Services					█	█	█								
Set up AI-driven virtual agents in Microsoft Teams						█	█	█							
Regularly review AI performance								Ongoing, with monthly reviews							
Update governance policies for AI capabilities								Ongoing and then quarterly							
Keep users informed of new features and best practices								Ongoing, with monthly training sessions							

Figure 8.10 – Phase 4 timeline

This phase not only empowers teams with intelligent tools but also fosters an innovative culture of AI adoption within the organization.

Phase 5 – Future-proofing – evolving the Microsoft 365 and AI strategy

In this phase, the focus shifts to future-proofing our Microsoft 365 environment by evolving the AI strategy and ensuring the team stays ahead of the curve.

It's all about keeping the organization up to date on the latest AI advancements while fostering a culture of continuous learning and innovation. Regular training sessions will be key to introducing new features such as Copilot and other AI tools, making sure the team is not just aware but confident in using these technologies.

By creating an AI-friendly workplace where employees are encouraged to explore AI's potential and share their successes, we help drive long-term engagement and adoption. Staying ahead of emerging technologies is just as important.

Figure 8.11 – AI capabilities and enhancement

This phase emphasizes the need for the continuous monitoring of Microsoft's roadmap, adjusting the strategy to incorporate the latest AI features that align with business objectives.

By regularly assessing new AI technologies and integrating them into workflows, we'll ensure that the organization remains competitive and ready for future growth.

With a structured approach to upskilling and adopting new tools, this phase will position a team to fully leverage AI's potential, keeping the digital workspace at the cutting edge of innovation.

AI awareness and upskilling

Objective: Keep the organization updated on AI advancements and ensure users continue to maximize Microsoft 365 tools.

Actions to be taken:

- Conduct regular training sessions to introduce new Copilot features and other AI tools.

Timeline	Stakeholders	Output
Start in Week 1 and continue quarterly. Initial full-day training in Week 2, followed by monthly refresher sessions.	Training and development team. AI specialists for conducting hands-on workshops.	A well-informed workforce with up-to-date knowledge of new AI features. Increased confidence and proficiency in using AI tools.

- Foster an AI-friendly culture by encouraging employees to explore AI's potential in their daily work and share success stories.

Timeline	Stakeholders	Output
From Week 3 onward, establish an internal AI community forum. Once every two months "AI in Practice" sessions starting in Week 5.	HR and communication teams to manage culture initiatives. AI Champions within each department to lead discussions.	Active engagement in internal AI forums and knowledge-sharing sessions. A collaborative space for employees to share use cases and success stories.

To ensure the long-term success of AI initiatives within the organization, a continuous focus on upskilling and creating an environment that fosters AI adoption is essential. By providing structured learning opportunities and encouraging open collaboration, the organization can fully harness the potential of AI tools such as Copilot, driving both individual and collective growth.

Adaptation to emerging technologies

Objective: Stay ahead of technological changes by adopting new Microsoft 365 and AI functionalities.

Actions to be taken:

- Monitor Microsoft's roadmap for updates on Microsoft 365 and AI tools, adapting the internal strategy as needed.

Timeline	Stakeholders	Output
Continuous monitoring beginning in Week 1, with monthly reviews.	IT team and governance committee to track Microsoft updates.	Up-to-date strategic roadmap aligned with the latest Microsoft 365 and AI features.
Quarterly strategy meetings starting in Week 6 to align with Microsoft's roadmap updates.	AI specialists to evaluate potential impacts.	Improved organizational readiness for new technology rollouts.

- Evaluate emerging AI technologies, integrating them into the Microsoft 365 environment where they align with business objectives.

Timeline	Stakeholders	Output
Initial assessment of current AI tools in Week 4.	AI implementation team for conducting evaluations.	Reports detailing the suitability and potential impact of emerging AI technologies.
Ongoing evaluations quarterly, starting in Week 8.	Business analysts to identify areas where new AI integrations can optimize workflows.	Pilot integration of selected AI tools within key business processes.

By maintaining a proactive approach to technology adoption and continuously evaluating new advancements, the organization ensures that it remains agile and well-prepared to leverage the latest innovations within the Microsoft 365 ecosystem.

Milestones for Phase 5 completion

Monitoring the following milestones is crucial to ensure the timely completion of Phase 5:

- **Week 1**: Kick off Phase 5 with an internal announcement and setup of the training schedule
- **Week 2**: Conduct the first comprehensive training session on new AI features
- **Week 3**: Launch an internal AI community forum for knowledge-sharing
- **Week 5**: Initiate bi-monthly "AI in Practice" sessions for employees
- **Week 6**: Conduct the first quarterly strategy meeting to align with Microsoft's roadmap

- **Week 8**: Begin quarterly evaluations of emerging AI technologies for potential integration
- **Week 12**: Review progress, gather feedback, and plan the next steps for ongoing AI awareness and technology adaptation

By the end of this phase, the organization will be well-versed in the latest AI tools within Microsoft 365, and a culture of AI exploration and knowledge-sharing will be firmly established. Employees will feel empowered to integrate AI into their daily tasks, leveraging Copilot and other AI-driven functionalities to boost productivity and collaboration.

Here's a timeline for this phase:

PHASE 5 - TASKS	W1	W2	W3	W4	W5	W6	W7	W8	W9	W10	W11	W12	W13	W14	WN...
Kickoff Phase 5 with an internal announcement and setup of the training schedule.															
Conduct the first comprehensive training session on new AI features.	Start and continue quarterly. Initial full-day training in **Week 2**, followed by monthly refresher sessions.														
Launch internal AI community forum for knowledge sharing.			From this point forward, establish an internal AI community forum. Once every two months, 'AI in Practice' sessions starting **Week 5.**												
Initiate bi-monthly "AI in Practice" sessions for employees.	Continuous monitoring with monthly reviews. Quarterly strategy meetings starting **Week 6** to align with Microsoft's roadmap updates.														
Conduct the first quarterly strategy meeting to align with Microsoft's roadmap.					Initial assessment of current AI tools . Ongoing evaluations quarterly, starting **Week 8.**										
Begin quarterly evaluations of emerging AI technologies for potential integration.								Begin quarterly evaluations of emerging AI technologies for potential integration.							
Review progress, gather feedback, and plan next steps for ongoing AI awareness and technology adaptation.												Review progress, gather feedback, and plan next steps for ongoing AI awareness and technology adaptation.			

Figure 8.12 – Phase 5 timeline

Through the continuous monitoring of Microsoft's technology roadmap and proactive adaptation to emerging AI solutions, the company will maintain a competitive edge, ensuring its Microsoft 365 environment remains at the forefront of digital innovation.

This phased strategy ensures a structured and effective implementation of Microsoft 365 with a strong emphasis on AI integration. Starting with a solid foundation, it gradually introduces AI capabilities such as Copilot, optimizing the digital workspace for future growth and technological advancements.

Summary

In this chapter, we explored the strategic blueprints necessary for creating a dynamic and sustainable Microsoft 365 and SharePoint environment.

We began by understanding the importance of building an implementation roadmap that aligns with organizational goals, using AI-driven insights to make informed decisions. We then delved into establishing a governance framework that ensures a secure and compliant environment, emphasizing how AI tools such as Microsoft 365 Copilot can automate data governance and access controls.

Change management techniques were also discussed, focusing on how to drive user adoption and ongoing engagement with AI-powered personalized experiences. Lastly, we examined how AI can revolutionize collaboration models, acting as a catalyst for seamless teamwork and communication within the digital workspace.

By mastering these strategic approaches, we have gained essential skills such as building implementation roadmaps, developing governance policies, managing change, and leveraging AI to elevate productivity and collaboration within the organization. These lessons are invaluable in establishing a Microsoft 365 environment that is not only efficient and secure but also future-ready.

In the next chapter, we will take these strategic insights a step further. We'll dive into hands-on recipes that will help put these strategies into action, covering tasks such as configuring settings, user provisioning, collaboration, development practices, IT management, and more. This will be the next natural step in the journey to fully mastering the Microsoft 365 and SharePoint ecosystem.

9

Implementing Microsoft 365 and SharePoint Solutions – Implementation Playbooks

In this chapter, you will explore how to take advantage of the powerful tools within the Microsoft 365 ecosystem to create solutions that drive productivity and efficiency in an organization.

You'll learn how to plan and execute successful development projects, from initial scoping to post-deployment support, and dive into the importance of strategic planning, choosing the right tools, and the need for structured phases to keep your projects on track.

Why is this important? Well, it's not just about writing code: it's about creating solutions that solve real business problems. By following a clear roadmap and adopting best practices, you'll be able to create scalable, maintainable applications that align with both technical and organizational goals.

In this chapter, you're going to cover the following main topics:

- Microsoft 365 application development process breakdown – understanding how to structure your projects for success

- Choosing the right tools for Microsoft 365 development – what to use and when to use it

- Streamlining your workflow with continuous integration and delivery with DevOps

By the end of this chapter, you'll have the confidence to take your enterprise development journey to the next level.

Microsoft 365 application development process breakdown

Microsoft 365 is a robust ecosystem of tools designed to transform how businesses operate. It's packed with features that, when used strategically, can significantly boost productivity and streamline workflows. But the real challenge isn't just knowing which tools are available; it's about figuring out how to combine them effectively to create solutions that make a real impact.

Figure 9.1 – Process breakdown for application development

To do that, it's important to step back and look at the bigger picture – delivering a successful solution, whether it is aimed at enhancing collaboration, automating business processes, or developing custom apps, follows a structured set of steps. These steps form the foundation of any well-executed project, ensuring that it doesn't only meet technical requirements but also adds genuine value to the organization.

Planning is crucial. Each solution has its own objectives and challenges, and jumping into development without a clear roadmap can lead to unnecessary roadblocks. By understanding the lifecycle of the solution, teams can work through challenges more methodically, make informed decisions on tools and strategies, and ultimately build something that not only works but is built to last.

This process isn't limited to big, complex projects. Whether we are rolling out a simple automation to handle a repetitive task or developing a large-scale intranet, the same principles apply.

It's essential to *break down the development process into well-defined, manageable stages.* This approach helps maintain focus throughout each step, ensuring that we tackle every phase with clear direction and confidence in the decisions. By organizing the process into smaller, more digestible parts, it becomes easier for us to manage complexity, address potential challenges as they arise, and keep the project on track.

The development plan overview

A **development plan overview** is a strategic roadmap that outlines how a software project will be developed, including its stages, timeline, roles, responsibilities, technologies, and methodologies.

Figure 9.2 – Development plan

In the context of a Microsoft 365 or SharePoint development project, a well-structured development plan helps to ensure that projects are executed efficiently and in alignment with organizational goals.

Let's break down the key components of the development plan and look at them closely.

Project scope

This defines the boundaries of the project, identifying what will and will not be included. For example, in a Microsoft 365 solution, this might involve specific services like SharePoint, Teams, and Power Automate. The scope outlines which functionalities will be developed, the expected outcomes, and any constraints, such as time or resources.

The key elements of project scope are as follows:

- **Objectives**: What the project aims to achieve
- **Deliverables**: The tangible outcomes (e.g., workflows, solutions, custom applications)
- **Constraints**: Time, budget, or technology limitations
- **Assumptions**: Key assumptions regarding the project's success (e.g., data availability, user adoption)

Project phases

Breaking the project into manageable phases is critical. Typical phases include the following:

- **Planning**: Define requirements, create design specifications, and set up governance
- **Development**: Writing the code or configuring tools in Microsoft 365
- **Testing**: Ensuring that the solution works as expected through functional and **user acceptance testing** (**UAT**)
- **Deployment**: Releasing the solution to production environments
- **Post-deployment support**: Maintaining and updating the solution

Each phase should have clear entry and exit criteria, so the team knows when it's complete.

Roles and responsibilities

The development plan should define the roles of everyone involved in the project, from project managers to developers and testers. For a Microsoft 365 or SharePoint project, specific roles might include the following:

- **Project manager**: Oversees timelines, budgets, and project coordination
- **Solution architect**: Designs the solution's architecture and ensures alignment with enterprise guidelines
- **Developers**: Write and configure code for the solution, whether it's custom web parts, workflows, or PowerApps
- **Quality assurance (QA) testers**: Conduct testing to identify bugs and ensure solution quality
- **Support team**: Provides ongoing maintenance and support post-deployment

Technology stack

This describes the tools, platforms, and frameworks that will be used. For Microsoft 365 projects, this could include the following:

- **SharePoint Online** for document management and collaboration
- **Power Platform (Power Apps, Power Automate)** for low-code development
- **PowerShell** for automation and governance tasks
- **Azure Functions/Durable Functions** for serverless computing scenarios
- **React** for modern web part development or extending SharePoint with custom user interfaces

Development methodology

The methodology defines how the team will manage development. Here are some examples:

- **Agile/Scrum**: Involves iterative development, sprints, and regular feedback loops, allowing for quick adjustments
- **DevOps practices**: Continuous integration and continuous deployment pipelines to ensure code quality and quicker releases

In the context of Microsoft 365/SharePoint, adopting a DevOps strategy can streamline processes such as version control for scripts or automation.

Timeline and milestones

This component outlines the schedule for completing the project, including key milestones. Milestones might include the following:

- Completion of the requirements gathering
- Completion of the initial solution design
- Successful implementation of a pilot or **minimum viable product** (**MVP**)
- UAT
- Go live of the final solution

Having a clear timeline helps manage expectations and track progress.

Risk management

Risks are potential issues that could derail the project. This section outlines the risks and mitigation strategies. In Microsoft 365/SharePoint projects, risks might include the following:

- **Integration challenges**: Difficulty integrating new solutions with existing systems
- **User adoption issues**: Users not embracing the new tools and workflows
- **Compliance concerns**: Data security or regulatory issues, especially in hybrid or multi-tenant environments

Mitigation strategies include thorough testing, stakeholder training, and compliance checks.

Testing and quality assurance

This section explains the approach to testing and ensuring quality. It may include the following:

- **Unit testing**: Testing individual components or features
- **Integration testing**: Ensuring all components work together seamlessly
- **UAT**: End-user validation to ensure the solution meets business needs

For Microsoft 365 and SharePoint projects, testing might involve both custom code and platform features.

Training and documentation

Proper documentation is key for long-term sustainability, and training ensures users can take full advantage of the developed solutions. This might include the following:

- End-user training for custom workflows or Power Apps
- Administrator documentation for managing and updating solutions
- Development of handover documentation, including code repositories and CI/CD pipelines

Post-deployment support and maintenance

After the solution goes live, a plan for supporting and maintaining it is essential. This can include the following:

- Monitoring system performance and availability
- Fixing bugs or issues that arise post-launch
- Regular updates and enhancements to adapt to evolving business needs

In Microsoft 365, this may include ongoing management of user permissions, monitoring service usage, and leveraging new platform updates.

To summarize, this development plan overview has provided us with a strategic roadmap for executing Microsoft 365 or SharePoint projects. We have learned how a well-defined scope, clear project phases, structured roles and responsibilities, and an effective technology stack contribute to the success of our development efforts.

As we move forward, it's crucial to build on these foundations, beginning with detailing the planning phase effectively, ensuring a well-organized approach for the rest of the project.

Mastering the planning phase

Before jumping into the code or even selecting tools, we need a solid plan. The planning stage is where we define the problem, gather requirements, and outline the solution.

Understanding the requirements

It's critical to have a clear understanding of the problem we are trying to solve. This is where gathering requirements comes into play.

Figure 9.3 – Gathering requirements

We need to know the pain points we're addressing.

Ask the right questions, involve stakeholders, and map out the business objectives that our solution should meet. What pain are the users facing? What processes are causing inefficiencies? This ensures that the final product not only functions well but also provides real value.

> **Important note**
>
> Get input from the actual users: it's way too easy to create a solution that sounds great on paper but misses the mark because we didn't understand their daily challenges. We need to gather feedback from the people who will use the app. In this way, we will save a lot of headaches down the road.

The more specific we can be here, the easier it'll be to create an app that solves real problems, not just shiny features that no one will use. So, we need to be as specific as possible.

Mock-ups as visual tools guidance

By incorporating user input early in the process and organizing objectives through visual frameworks like flowcharts, Kanban boards, and prioritization matrices, developers can align their efforts with user needs and business goals.

The following mockup suggestions serve as visual tools to guide developers in gathering essential feedback, defining clear objectives, and prioritizing tasks. These mock-ups help ensure that developers build applications that address real user problems, rather than just focusing on features.

Each mockup in this list illustrates a different aspect of the problem-definition and solution-planning process, from gathering user feedback to identifying key inefficiencies.

User input flowchart

The **user input flowchart** visually represents the critical steps in gathering input from users, which is the foundation of creating an application that effectively addresses user needs.

Figure 9.4 – User input flowchart

The flowchart walks through a logical progression of activities, helping teams to identify pain points, set clear objectives, and ensure alignment with user expectations.

The following are the flow elements:

- **Interview users**: Start by conducting interviews with potential users to understand their needs, preferences, and challenges. This could involve one-on-one discussions, surveys, or focus groups. The goal here is to obtain qualitative insights directly from the people who will be using the app.

- **Visual representation**: A person icon with a speech bubble.

- **Gather feedback**: After collecting input from user interviews, consolidate the feedback into actionable insights. This step involves analyzing responses to uncover common themes, such as usability issues, feature requests, and areas of inefficiency.

- **Visual representation**: An icon showing a clipboard or document with feedback notes.

- **Identify common pain points**: Once the feedback is gathered, it's essential to map out common user pain points. These could include repetitive manual processes, lack of integration, or poor user interface experiences. Identifying these pain points provides a starting point for creating a solution that directly addresses real-world problems.

  Visual representation: A puzzle piece or warning icon symbolizing issues.

- **Outline specific app goals**: Based on the identified pain points, define clear and specific goals for the app. These goals should align with users' needs and address the problems highlighted in the previous steps. Clear objectives ensure that the development team knows what success looks like and that the final product meets user expectations.

  Visual representation: A target or dartboard icon symbolizing setting goals.

- **Validate with users**: Before finalizing the app's objectives, take the time to validate them with the users. This ensures that the proposed solutions address the correct pain points and that no crucial elements have been missed. Validation may involve presenting users with prototypes or mock-ups and collecting further feedback.

  Visual representation: A group of people icon or checklist, symbolizing validation and approval from users.

The user input flowchart emphasizes the importance of engaging users in the early stages of development to gather actionable input that drives the app creation process. By systematically gathering feedback, identifying pain points, and outlining specific objectives, the development team ensures that they are solving the right problems and creating an application that adds value to users, and we can maintain a user-centric approach, ultimately leading to a more successful and functional application that solves real problems rather than just incorporating trendy but unnecessary features.

Kanban problem definition

A **Kanban-style board** is a highly visual and flexible tool for managing and organizing tasks throughout the development lifecycle. For problem definition, this board becomes essential in breaking down complex user needs into more actionable and digestible components.

• KANBAN STYLE •

Figure 9.5 – Kanban problem definition

By using specific columns to categorize different aspects of user pain points, desired features, and objective priorities, developers, and stakeholders can collaboratively assess and prioritize the most important tasks for application development.

The board is divided into three key columns to organize and visualize the problem definition phase. Here is the mockup structure (columns):

- **User pain points**: This column lists the primary problems users are facing. These are issues that negatively affect user experience and efficiency, such as *Approval workflow delays*, *Form validation errors*, or *Mobile accessibility challenges*. The goal here is to capture these pain points based on user feedback and research.

- **Desired features**: This column represents the features that would directly address the identified pain points. For example, *Automated approval workflows*, *Enhanced form validation*, and *Mobile-responsive design*. These features form the basis of the solution that the development team will implement.

- **Objective priorities**: In this column, the team organizes the identified features based on priority. High-priority items should be those that have a significant impact on user satisfaction or business goals. For instance, *Reduce approval delays by 80%* or *Ensure seamless mobile access for 90% of users.*

The Kanban-style board provides a streamlined and structured approach for organizing and prioritizing user needs, ensuring that development efforts focus on the most critical aspects of the application.

This visual representation allows both developers and stakeholders to stay aligned on objectives, track progress, and adjust priorities as new user feedback emerges, ensuring a continuous focus on delivering high-value features that address real problems, rather than developing features in isolation without user context.

User journey map

The **user journey map** is a visualization tool designed to trace the steps a user takes when interacting with a specific process, such as manual approval workflows or data entry systems.

Figure 9.6 – User Journey Mapping

By mapping out each stage of the journey, developers and stakeholders can identify where inefficiencies, delays, and miscommunications occur. This mockup emphasizes the importance of tracking user pain points to uncover opportunities for optimization and automation, ensuring that the final solution addresses the most pressing issues.

Here are the stages in the user journey:

1. **User submits request**: This is the initial stage where the user triggers the process by submitting a request or initiating an action, such as filling out a form or making a data entry.

    *   **Common issues**: Confusing interfaces, missing fields, unclear instructions
    *   **Opportunity for improvement**: Simplify the user interface, add real-time field validation, and provide clear prompts.

2. **Manager's approval**: After the request is submitted, it moves to the next stage for managerial approval. This is often where bottlenecks begin as managers might not have a streamlined way to review and approve requests.

    *   **Common issues**: Approval delays due to manual workflows, high workload, and lack of visibility in priority requests.
    *   **Opportunity for improvement**: Implement notifications, automate reminders, and introduce an approval dashboard to provide better visibility.

3. **Request stalled in process**: At this stage, requests may stall in the process due to a lack of follow-up or oversight, causing significant delays in reaching completion.

    *   **Common issues**: Lack of tracking, missing updates, no escalation mechanism when requests are overdue.
    *   **Opportunity for improvement**: Automate tracking and escalation alerts and provide real-time status updates to users and managers.

4. **Manual email follow-ups**: Often, users or managers resort to manual email follow-ups to check on the status of a request. This introduces more delays and communication breakdowns.

    *   **Common issues**: Inefficient communication channels, missed emails, and no clear ownership of the follow-up process.
    *   **Opportunity for improvement**: Replace manual follow-ups with automated notifications and reminders through a centralized system, such as Power Automate.

5. **Completion**: The final stage where the request is resolved or completed, but this stage may still face issues related to tracking whether the request was fully addressed or if it fell through the cracks.

    *   **Common issues**: Unclear closure status, no confirmation provided to the user, incomplete resolution.
    *   **Opportunity for improvement**: Send automated completion notifications, request feedback from users, and provide a resolution summary.

This user journey map visually represents the user's experience within a broken process, making it easy to identify where improvements can be made, and showcasing how spotting inefficiencies at each stage of the user journey can help build targeted solutions. By visualizing these stages and pain points, developers can prioritize what to automate or optimize, ensuring the final product provides value by solving the real issues users face.

These mock-ups help readers visualize the problem definition process and demonstrate how to use these tools effectively before starting app development.

The mock-ups are invaluable because they ensure that developers focus on solving real-world problems rather than just building features in isolation, and by incorporating these tools, teams can create user-centric applications that align with business goals and enhance user satisfaction, setting a strong foundation for a more strategic and organized development process, helping to avoid common pitfalls and misalignments.

Enhancing the problem definition workflow with Microsoft Teams

Integrating Microsoft Teams into the app development process enhances communication, collaboration, and the overall feedback loop. In the early stages of app development, particularly during the problem definition phase, it's crucial to ensure that developers, stakeholders, and end users are aligned on the key pain points, requirements, and objectives.

Figure 9.7 – Streamlining the problem definition with Microsoft Teams

Using Microsoft Teams in this context helps streamline the process and ensures that feedback is collected efficiently and in real time.

Here's why it's important:

- **Streamlined communication and collaboration**: Teams allows us to create a centralized space for discussions related to app development. By dedicating specific channels for app feedback, testing reports, or idea-sharing, everyone involved in the project can contribute, review, and respond to feedback efficiently, reducing the need for back-and-forth emails and keeping all relevant information in one easily accessible location.

- **Improved collaboration with prototyping and iteration**: Live demo and brainstorming sessions within Teams provide an interactive platform for refining objectives. Developers can screen-share prototypes while gathering real-time feedback through chat or voice calls, creating a dynamic environment where issues are discussed, and solutions are formulated on the spot. Stakeholders and users can point out areas for improvement as they experience the prototype, helping developers adjust before the project moves forward.

- **Centralized feedback and documentation**: With Teams, all feedback, decisions, and changes are documented in one place. This transparency is key to avoiding misunderstandings and ensuring that all participants are on the same page. The documented discussions, testing reports, and feedback can be easily referenced throughout the app development lifecycle, ensuring nothing is lost or overlooked.

- **Boosting accountability and ownership**: Having a dedicated space for feedback and problem definition in Teams creates a sense of ownership and accountability. Developers, testers, and stakeholders are all part of the collaborative loop, encouraging more active participation. Stakeholders feel heard, developers are clear on expectations, and the project moves forward with clarity.

- **Extending the impact**: By leveraging Teams to its full potential, organizations can make the problem definition process not just more efficient but also more inclusive. Stakeholders from different departments, regions, or time zones can collaborate seamlessly, ensuring that the app addresses a diverse range of needs and pain points.

This collaborative approach fosters a culture of shared ownership and commitment to the project's success, reducing the risk of missed requirements or misunderstandings.

Let us now look at an example workflow:

1. **Create a Teams channel**: Set up a dedicated *App Feedback* channel where stakeholders can contribute feedback and ideas

2. **Host live prototyping sessions**: Organize regular meetings in Teams to showcase prototypes, using screen-sharing and chat to gather real-time feedback

3. **Automate notifications with Power Automate**: Use Power Automate to create workflows that notify developers whenever new feedback is submitted, ensuring a prompt response

So, using Teams as a framework for problem definition enhances collaboration, improves the feedback loop, and ensures that the app development process remains agile, transparent, and user-focused.

By integrating real-time feedback and collaboration, teams can address issues early, align on goals, and ensure the final product delivers maximum value.

To wrap things up, we have covered why the planning phase is such a crucial part of building a successful application: we've talked about how understanding user pain points, gathering detailed feedback, and involving stakeholders early on helps ensure that the app actually solves real problems and doesn't just look good on paper.

Using tools such as user input flowcharts, Kanban boards, and journey maps keeps everything focused on what matters most: meeting user needs and business goals. Plus, integrating Microsoft Teams into the mix makes collaboration and feedback easier, ensuring the whole process stays smooth and on track.

Now that you've got a strong foundation for planning, we're ready to dive into the next important step: *Choosing the right tools for Microsoft 365 development*. This is where we'll learn how to pick the best tools to bring all these ideas to life within the Microsoft 365 ecosystem.

Choosing the right tools for Microsoft 365 development

When it comes to developing custom solutions in Microsoft 365, having the right tools in our toolkit is half the battle. The good news is that Microsoft offers a wide range of tools to help us build apps, automate workflows, and integrate, but let's face it, picking the right tools can sometimes feel like picking the right tool from a toolbox that's packed to the brim.

In this section, we'll break down some of the must-have tools for Microsoft 365 development, including why they're useful, how they fit into the development workflow, and some insider tips to get the most out of them.

Visual Studio versus Visual Studio Code – which IDE should we use?

First things first, we need an **Integrated Development Environment** (**IDE**) to write and manage the code.

Figure 9.8 – Choosing the right integrated development environment

Visual Studio and **Visual Studio Code** (**VS Code**) are two of the most popular options, but they serve different purposes:

- **Visual Studio** is a heavy-duty, full-featured IDE that's perfect for large-scale, complex solutions. If we are working on enterprise-level projects with deep integrations, microservices, or server-side applications, Visual Studio is probably the best bet. It supports everything from C# to ASP. NET and comes packed with debugging and testing features.

- VS Code, on the other hand, is the leaner, more flexible alternative. It's perfect for frontend development, especially when we are working with SharePoint Framework, React, TypeScript, or PowerShell scripts. VS Code is lightweight, fast, and highly customizable through its massive library of extensions. Whether we are building web parts for SharePoint or custom apps for Teams, VS Code is a go-to choice.

> **Important note**
>
> For most Microsoft 365 development work: such as building SharePoint Framework web parts or Power Automate scripts, VS Code is the tool we want. It's lighter, integrates seamlessly with Git, and offers tons of extensions for things such as linting, auto-completion, and debugging.

React – the backbone of modern web development in Microsoft 365

React is the go-to JavaScript library for building user interfaces in Microsoft 365, especially within SharePoint Framework solutions.

Figure 9.9 – React

It's component-based, meaning we can build small, reusable pieces of UI and stitch them together into larger, more complex applications.

Why React?

React is lightweight, well-documented, and comes with a huge ecosystem of tools and libraries. Plus, if we are already working with the SharePoint Framework or Microsoft Teams Toolkit, React is built into the framework, making it the natural choice for UI development.

> **Important note**
>
> Use hooks in React to simplify the code and manage state effectively. Hooks such as *useState* and *useEffect* allow us to build more powerful components without the need for complex lifecycle methods.

While React is the most common choice for building solutions with the SharePoint Framework, it's not a requirement. The SharePoint Framework is flexible and allows us to use any other JavaScript framework, or even no framework at all, depending on your project needs.

The SharePoint Framework – the go-to for SharePoint solutions and customizations

The **SharePoint Framework** is specifically designed to extend the capabilities of SharePoint, enabling developers to create custom solutions using modern web technologies such as React, TypeScript, and Node.js.

Figure 9.10 – The SharePoint Framework

It allows us to build powerful, interactive components that can be deployed seamlessly across the SharePoint environment, making it perfect for enhancing the user experience. Whether we are creating dashboards for document management or developing custom forms, the SharePoint Framework will be at the core of the process.

Microsoft has developed accelerators to help us get started quickly, offering pre-built templates and tools that streamline the initial setup. We will be working with React and TypeScript, a dynamic duo for SharePoint development. React helps us build fast, interactive user interfaces, while TypeScript adds type safety to JavaScript, making projects easier to debug and scale.

> **Important note**
>
> The SharePoint Framework is a client-side framework, so everything runs directly in the browser. This means we need to pay extra attention to performance: optimize our code, minimize dependencies, and leverage caching where possible.

Microsoft Teams Toolkit – building collaborative apps

Microsoft Teams has become a central hub for collaboration within organizations, and **Microsoft Teams Toolkit** is our key to building apps that live directly within Teams.

Figure 9.11 – Microsoft Teams Toolkit

With Teams Toolkit, we can develop custom tabs, messaging extensions, and bots and even integrate with Power Apps and Power Automate for deeper workflow automation.

The toolkit simplifies the development process by offering pre-built templates and debugging tools, making it easier to get started even if we're new to Teams app development:

- **Custom tabs**: These allow us to embed web content or apps directly into Teams, providing a more streamlined workflow for users who spend most of their day in Teams.

- **Messaging extensions**: These enable users to interact with the app right from the Teams message composer, whether they're pulling up data or initiating workflows.

- **Bots**: We can create intelligent chatbots that interact with users, answer questions, or automate routine tasks: all within the Teams interface.

> Tip
> If we are building for Teams, always consider the user experience. The goal is to add value without cluttering the interface. Keep things simple, responsive, and easy to navigate.

The SharePoint Framework versus Microsoft Teams Toolkit – what is the best approach?

When comparing the SharePoint Framework and Microsoft Teams Toolkit, it's important to understand how Microsoft has streamlined both platforms with predefined accelerators to simplify the development process.

These accelerators allow developers to quickly build apps, bots, and solutions integrated into both SharePoint and Teams environments.

If we are just starting, it's tempting to use these accelerators as they help us hit the ground running. They simplify many tasks such as authentication, app packaging, and deployment, allowing us to focus more on the core goals rather than infrastructure and configuration details. For many initial use cases, using these predefined tools can be very effective, especially when the focus is on delivering business value quickly.

However, for long-term development strategies, it's wise to think beyond just using Microsoft's predefined tools. These accelerators, while helpful, may limit us in terms of flexibility, especially when we are looking to leverage the full power of modern development stacks such as React, Node.js, or other frameworks.

By shifting the mindset toward building full-fledged web applications, we are open to broader possibilities, such as integration with non-Microsoft services, more flexible deployment options, and full control over technology choices.

> **Tip**
> The key takeaway is to start with the accelerators if they help us to achieve our immediate objectives quickly. But, as we evolve, consider transitioning toward building web apps independently, allowing us to fully leverage the best tools, frameworks, and platforms for our needs, rather than being constrained by the limits of Microsoft's development accelerators.

PowerShell – automation for admins and developers alike

No Microsoft 365 development setup would be complete without mentioning **PowerShell**. Whether we are an admin managing user configurations or a developer automating deployment tasks, PowerShell is the scriptable glue that binds it all together.

Figure 9.12 – PowerShell

With Microsoft Graph API integration, we can use PowerShell to automate everything from user management to Teams provisioning. Need to set up SharePoint sites in bulk? PowerShell's got us covered. Want to automate the deployment of SharePoint Framework web parts? Write a PowerShell script to do it.

> **Important note**
>
> Check out PnP PowerShell, a module that simplifies working with SharePoint and Microsoft 365. It abstracts away many of the complexities involved in using native cmdlets and offers a more developer-friendly way to interact with Microsoft 365.

Azure Functions – serverless computing for Microsoft 365 integrations

When our project needs to interact with external services or handle background tasks, **Azure Functions** is the perfect tool.

Figure 9.13 – Azure Functions

Azure Functions is serverless, meaning we don't have to worry about infrastructure; we just focus on writing the code.

Common use cases for Azure Functions in Microsoft 365 development include the following:

- **Webhook integrations**: Trigger actions when changes occur in SharePoint or Teams

- **Data processing**: Process large datasets from SharePoint or other data sources in the background

- **Custom APIs**: Build lightweight APIs that can be consumed by Power Apps, Power Automate, or other Microsoft 365 services

Azure Functions allows us to scale an application without having to manage a server, making it a great choice for lightweight integrations or tasks that don't require a full-blown web service.

> **Important note**
> Pair Azure Functions with Logic Apps or Power Automate to create powerful automation workflows that respond to triggers and events across our Microsoft 365 environment.

Choosing the right tools for Microsoft 365 development is all about understanding our project's needs and picking the tools that will help us get the job done efficiently. Whether we are building sleek user interfaces with React, automating processes with PowerShell, or integrating external services with Azure Functions, there is a tool in the Microsoft 365 ecosystem to fit every need.

As we get more familiar with these tools, we will start to see how they can complement one another. For instance, we might build a custom web part using the SharePoint Framework and React, automate its deployment with PowerShell scripts, and trigger data updates with Azure Functions. The possibilities are endless, and as we continue our development journey, these tools will become second nature.

So, whether we are just getting started or looking to refine our process, remember that picking the right tools is key to delivering efficient, scalable, and maintainable Microsoft 365 solutions.

By now, we've covered some of the essential tools we will need to build, automate, and customize our Microsoft 365 solutions: whether we are leaning toward Visual Studio for larger projects or prefer the flexibility of VS Code for frontend work, we've got a solid foundation to start developing smarter, more efficient solutions.

And remember, PowerShell, React, and Azure Functions aren't just side tools: they're key players in delivering fast, scalable, and robust solutions across the platform.

Why is all this important? Because the right tool not only simplifies our work but also ensures the solutions are maintainable, future-proof, and aligned with best practices. The tools we pick now will shape our development experience and ultimately the quality of the solutions we deliver.

As we move forward, it's essential to embrace practices that ensure the seamless integration of development and operations within Microsoft 365 and SharePoint environments. The next section lays the groundwork for adopting DevOps methodologies that streamline workflows, enhance collaboration between teams, and drive continuous innovation.

Streamlining your workflow with continuous integration and delivery with DevOps

When we are working on a project involving Microsoft 365 or SharePoint solutions, **DevOps** is a game changer. It's not just a buzzword but an approach that can genuinely enhance the way our team develops, tests, and deploys solutions.

DevOps is a set of practices, methodologies, and cultural philosophies that aims to bridge the gap between software development (Dev) and IT operations (Ops) teams.

Figure 9.14 – DevOps

The goal of DevOps is to enable faster development, more reliable releases, and improved collaboration by automating and streamlining the processes of software development, testing, and deployment.

The core principles of DevOps are as follows:

- **Collaboration and communication**: DevOps fosters a culture of collaboration between development and operations teams. By working together, these teams can share knowledge, reduce bottlenecks, and eliminate the traditional silos that exist in software development.

- **Continuous integration and continuous delivery (CI/CD)**: DevOps practices emphasize automating the integration of code changes and their testing. CI/CD pipelines allow for continuous testing, building, and deployment, ensuring that code is always in a deployable state and allowing for rapid release cycles.

- **Automation**: A key tenet of DevOps is the use of automation to streamline tasks such as testing, deployment, infrastructure management, and monitoring. This reduces human error and increases consistency and speed.

- **Infrastructure as code**: DevOps encourages managing infrastructure in a version-controlled, automated way, just like application code. Using tools such as Terraform, Ansible, or Azure ARM/Bicep templates, teams can define and deploy infrastructure through code, making it reproducible and scalable.

- **Monitoring and feedback**: DevOps promotes continuous monitoring of applications and infrastructure. Tools such as Prometheus, Nagios, and Azure Monitor are used to gather metrics and logs, providing real-time feedback to teams. This helps in identifying issues quickly and improving performance.

- **Agility and flexibility**: DevOps supports an agile approach to development, where smaller, iterative changes are preferred over large, infrequent releases. This agility allows teams to react more quickly to business needs and customer feedback.

- **Security integration**: In modern DevOps practices, security is integrated into every phase of the development lifecycle rather than being treated as an afterthought. This approach ensures that security practices are automated and integrated into CI/CD pipelines.

Implementing DevOps properly can lead to faster releases, higher quality, and better collaboration across teams. But before jumping into DevOps full throttle, we need to get the basics right.

Here's a step-by-step breakdown of how to prepare our environment for CI/CD.

Version control – the bedrock of DevOps

Before anyone on our team writes a single line of code, there's one essential tool we need in place: **version control**.

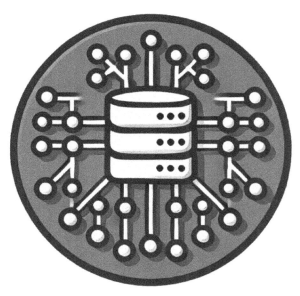

Figure 9.15 – Version control

Git is the gold standard here and for good reasons. It allows us to track every change made to projects: whether it's PowerApps, SharePoint Framework solutions, PowerShell scripts, or Azure Functions. By using Git, we ensure that the entire team is always in sync and has a full history of every change. This makes collaboration easy, whether we are working solo or with a larger group of developers.

Why does this matter so much?

Imagine we are tweaking a PowerApps component for days, only to realize our changes have introduced a bug. With version control, we can easily roll back to an earlier, stable version, saving us from pulling our hair out.

Git enables collaboration through features such as pull requests, allowing team members to review code changes before they're merged into the main project.

Git and branching – version control best practices

Git is the backbone of our development and DevOps process, ensuring every line of code is tracked and recoverable.

Let's break down how to use Git effectively in our development cycle:

- **Main branch**: This is our production-ready code. Only stable, thoroughly tested changes should be merged into the main branch. Avoid pushing experimental features directly to the main branch: treat it as the golden version of the project.

- **Development branch**: This is where the magic happens. The development branch is where new features and bug fixes are integrated before they're tested and eventually merged into the main branch. It acts as a buffer zone, allowing it to validate changes in a more controlled environment.

- **Feature branches**: For every new feature or major fix, create a separate feature branch. This isolates changes and makes collaboration easier. Once the feature is complete, we can merge it back into the development branch. Feature branches should be short-lived, existing only for the duration of the work being done.

Branching strategy example

Let's say we are working on a new feature for a SharePoint Framework solution:

1. **Create a feature branch**: Start by creating a branch from the development branch, for example, *feature/new-navigation-component*.

2. **Develop locally**: Work on the feature in a local environment, and test the code locally. Instead of waiting until the end of the development, push changes to the remote Git repository every time a block of code is tested and ready. This ensures that no work is lost in case of hardware failure. The use of a dedicated feature branch maintains isolation from other team members, so frequent commits do not affect their workflow.

3. **Collaborate and review**: As changes are frequently pushed, other team members can periodically review the code via pull requests. Automated tests can be triggered through the CI pipeline to ensure code quality at every step.

4. **Merge into development**: Once the feature is complete and reviewed, we can merge the feature branch into the development branch. The CI/CD pipelines will kick in to ensure everything builds and tests correctly.

5. **Deploy**: After the feature is fully tested, we can merge the development branch into the main branch and deploy the update.

Automated testing – quality control, on autopilot

Automated testing is like having an extra set of eyes on the code 24/7.

Every time someone makes a change, we want to be sure it hasn't broken something else, and that's where automated tests come in.

For Power Apps, we can use Power Apps Test Studio, which lets us create test scripts that validate app functionality as new code gets added. If we are working on PowerShell scripts, Pester is the go-to testing framework. It allows us to write unit tests that ensure the scripts work as expected, helping us to catch bugs early in the process.

For Power Apps, we can use Power Apps Test Studio, which lets us create test scripts that validate app functionality as new code gets added. This ensures that critical app features continue to work as expected even as the app evolves.

If we are working on PowerShell scripts, Pester is the go-to testing framework. It allows us to write unit tests to verify that scripts perform as intended, helping us catch bugs early in the process and maintain script reliability.

For React and TypeScript projects, Jest is typically included by default for unit testing. The React Testing Library is often used alongside Jest to test React components by simulating user interactions and verifying the UI behaves correctly.

Playwright, a powerful end-to-end testing tool, is also commonly used to automate browser interactions and validate full application flows in multiple browsers.

Think of it like this: without automated testing, we are essentially playing a game of whack-a-mole with bugs. We fix one, only for another to pop up somewhere else. Automated tests allow us to confidently move forward with new features, knowing that any critical issues will be caught early, long before they can affect users.

CI – catching problems early

CI is the next crucial piece of the puzzle. With CI, every time a developer commits new code, it's automatically built and tested. Whether we are using Azure DevOps or GitHub Actions, we can set up a pipeline to ensure that no change goes untested: this helps catch issues early in the development cycle, instead of letting them snowball into bigger problems down the road.

Imagine this: one of the team members adds a new feature to our SharePoint Framework solution. Without CI, that new code might introduce a conflict that isn't caught until much later, creating a bigger mess to untangle. But with it, the moment that code is committed, it's built and tested automatically: any problems are flagged immediately, allowing the team to address them right away.

CD – automating deployments

Once we have CI in place, it's time to think about CD.

CD takes things a step further by automating the deployment process. For example, if we're working on PowerApps or SharePoint Framework projects, we can set up a pipeline in Azure DevOps that pushes changes directly to our environments – whether it's development, staging, or production.

Here's how this plays out in real life:

- Our team has finished developing a new feature, and it passes all the automated tests in the CI pipeline.

- With CD, that feature can be automatically deployed to a staging environment, where it's further tested before going live.

- Once everything checks out, it's seamlessly pushed to production without anyone having to manually upload files or run scripts. This reduces human error and ensures that our deployment process is consistent every time.

CD using PowerShell and Bicep for Azure asset creation

When we talk about CD in the context of web app development, particularly within Microsoft 365 environments, it's not just about deploying the app itself. It also includes automating the creation and management of cloud resources that our app depends on. This is where PowerShell and Bicep come into play for Azure.

Figure 9.16 – Continuous delivery

Both PowerShell and Bicep provide powerful tools to define and manage Azure assets as code, helping ensure consistency and efficiency throughout the deployment pipeline.

PowerShell – automating infrastructure creation

PowerShell is a versatile scripting language that works well for automating Azure asset creation as part of a CI/CD pipeline. By using PowerShell scripts, we can interact with Azure services, automate routine tasks, and create infrastructure in a consistent manner across different environments.

Here are some common use cases for PowerShell in Azure automation:

- **Provisioning resources**: Create Azure services such as virtual machines, databases, storage accounts, and more.
- **Managing Azure resources**: Update, scale, or remove assets as needed.
- **Configuration management**: Ensure that services are properly configured, including setting up networks, firewalls, and security policies.

In a CD pipeline, PowerShell can be used to deploy these assets in real time, making the pipeline more efficient by automating manual processes. We could trigger a PowerShell script as part of the pipeline using tools such as Azure DevOps or GitHub Actions.

Bicep – infrastructure as code, simplified

While PowerShell is excellent for scripting and managing Azure resources, **Bicep** takes things a step further by offering a declarative approach to Infrastructure as Code.

Bicep is the newer, streamlined version of Azure Resource Manager templates, but it's easier to read and write. It abstracts away a lot of the complexity that was present in ARM templates, making it much simpler to define resources.

Where PowerShell allows for procedural automation, Bicep defines the desired state of the infrastructure. Bicep files are designed to be reusable, modular, and version-controlled, making them perfect for CD scenarios.

Key advantages of Bicep include the following:

- **Declarative syntax**: Define what resources should exist rather than how to create them, making code cleaner and easier to manage.

- **Modular design**: Break down infrastructure into reusable components, making it easier to manage complex environments.

- **Idempotent**: Re-running the same Bicep file will not result in duplicated resources: it will simply ensure the infrastructure matches the desired state.

Integrating PowerShell and Bicep into CI/CD pipelines

Both PowerShell and Bicep fit naturally into modern DevOps pipelines.

Here's how we can integrate them into a CI/CD pipeline:

- **Pipeline triggers**: The CI/CD pipeline triggers when changes are pushed to the repository

- **Infrastructure setup**: A PowerShell or Bicep script runs during the build or release process, creating or updating Azure infrastructure

- **App deployment**: Once the infrastructure is in place, the pipeline moves to the next step: deploying our web app or service

For example, using **Azure DevOps**, we could have a pipeline with steps like the following:

1. **Run Bicep**: Deploys the necessary infrastructure
2. **Run PowerShell**: Configures any specific resources or policies
3. **Deploy app**: Deploys the web app to the newly created infrastructure

By combining PowerShell for procedural tasks and Bicep for defining infrastructure, we can create a robust continuous delivery pipeline that automatically provisions and configures the resources our app needs without manual intervention.

Why use both?

- PowerShell is great for managing specific, granular tasks and configuration changes

- Bicep is ideal for describing the broader infrastructure in a readable and maintainable format

When used together, they ensure that our Azure assets are created, managed, and deployed as part of our pipelines, ensuring faster, more consistent delivery of both applications and their underlying infrastructure.

In a modern CD setup, leveraging PowerShell and Bicep together allows us to automate the entire process of provisioning and managing the Azure infrastructure. This makes the pipeline faster, more reliable, and much easier to manage at scale, providing the foundation for a truly streamlined DevOps workflow.

> **Note**
>
> A critical part of our DevOps pipeline is having a *staging environment*. This is where we can test new features before they're deployed to production. Think of staging as a safety net. By deploying to staging first, we catch any last-minute issues before they affect our live environment. It's a way to keep our production tenant stable and avoid the embarrassment of pushing buggy or incomplete features to users.
>
> For example, we might deploy a new SharePoint Framework solution to staging, run the final tests, and have stakeholders review it. Once everyone gives the green light, the CD pipeline takes over, and the feature goes live with minimal hassle. Without staging, we are taking a big risk every time we push a change, as we won't know if something's broken until the users start complaining.

As we've explored, integrating DevOps into our Microsoft 365 and SharePoint projects introduces a new level of efficiency, collaboration, and automation. From leveraging version control with Git to automating testing and infrastructure deployment using PowerShell and Bicep, these practices not only ensure smoother development but also help us deliver high-quality solutions faster. Understanding these foundational concepts is crucial, as they form the bedrock of successful continuous integration and delivery. The importance of this approach lies in its ability to reduce errors, foster better teamwork, and maintain agility in a fast-paced environment.

With these tools and methodologies in place, we are well-equipped to implement best practices that will optimize the development and operational aspects of our project.

In the next section, we'll take a closer look at how to structure and optimize the various environments involved in the development lifecycle for Microsoft 365 and SharePoint solutions.

Windows development environments

When building and deploying solutions in Microsoft 365 and SharePoint environments, it's important to have a well-structured development setup. From local development on our machines to deploying live in production, each stage comes with its own tools and processes.

Here's an overview of the key tools and techniques to optimize our workflow, with a focus on using Windows as the core operating system for local development.

Local development – why WSL 2 is a must-have

The Windows file system and frontend tools are notoriously slower in certain operations, particularly when handling tasks that involve heavy file system access, such as managing large numbers of files, running package managers such as *npm*, or executing build processes for frontend projects.

This performance bottleneck can significantly impact development speed, especially in modern web development environments such as the SharePoint Framework, where frequent builds and file changes are common.

This is one of the reasons why many developers turn to Linux-based environments, which offer faster file system performance and better handling of tasks that Windows struggles with, improving overall efficiency and reducing delays during development cycles.

Windows Subsystem for Linux 2

Windows Subsystem for Linux 2 (**WSL2**) is a feature in Windows 11 that allows developers to run a full Linux kernel directly on Windows, providing a powerful and lightweight environment for running Linux-based development tools without the need for a virtual machine.

Figure 9.17 – Windows Subsystem for Linux

It offers significant improvements by providing faster file system performance, better compatibility with Linux apps, and full system call support, making it ideal for developers working with technologies such as Node.js, Docker, and other Linux-native utilities.

Here's why WSL 2 is a must-have for Windows local development:

- **Faster performance**: WSL 2 runs on a real Linux kernel, which leads to faster file system operations, critical when working with Node.js and package managers such as *npm* or *yarn*. These tools perform significantly faster compared to running them natively on the Windows file system.

- **Better resource usage**: WSL 2 is lightweight compared to traditional virtual machines, using fewer resources by running directly on the Windows kernel. This means our machines can handle heavier workloads while maintaining smooth performance.

- **Seamless integration**: We can access both Linux and Windows file systems seamlessly, allowing us to use our favorite Windows-based tools (such as Visual Studio Code) in conjunction with the powerful Linux-based development utilities. This hybrid environment is ideal for projects that require multiple platforms to work together efficiently.

Installing WSL 2

To install WSL 2 using the Windows Package Manager (`winget`), follow these steps:

1. Open **Windows Terminal** or **PowerShell** as Administrator:

    A. Right-click on **Windows Terminal** or **PowerShell** and choose **Run as Administrator**

    B. Run the `winget` command to install WSL:

    ```
    winget install --id=Microsoft.WSL -e
    ```

2. Once the installation is complete, set WSL 2 as the default version by running this:

    ```
    wsl --set-default-version 2
    ```

3. Install a Linux distribution such as Ubuntu by running this:

    ```
    winget install --id Canonical.Ubuntu
    ```

4. It is recommended to restart the computer after installation to ensure all changes are applied.

PnP.Wsl2

To fully leverage WSL 2 in Microsoft 365 and SharePoint development on the Windows operating system, using **PnP.Wsl2** is highly recommended.

Figure 9.18 – PnP.Wsl2

PnP.Wsl2 is an open source, community-driven project aimed at streamlining and optimizing the management of WSL 2 instances, specifically for developers working with Microsoft 365 and SharePoint on the Windows operating system. It promotes collaboration and the adoption of best practices within the development community, helping to create a more efficient and consistent development environment.

By automating the deployment of essential tools and environments, such as SharePoint Framework development tools, Git configurations, PowerShell, and Python core, PnP.Wsl2 makes it easier for developers to efficiently set up and manage their WSL 2 instances.

Goals and key features

The main goal of PnP.Wsl2 is to simplify WSL 2 instance management and automate the deployment of extra features, including the following:

- **Pre-configured development environments**: Automate the setup of SPFx, PowerShell, and other development tools inside a Linux distribution

- **Effortless instance management**: Simplifies the process of creating, copying, exporting, importing, and deleting WSL 2 instances

With PnP.Wsl2, we gain powerful tools for managing and enhancing our WSL 2 instances:

- **Create and copy instances**: Easily create new WSL 2 instances or clone existing ones

- **Export/import WSL instances**: Transfer instances between machines or save them for future use with TAR file exports

- **Delete and list instances**: Manage and view all WSL 2 instances running on our system

- **Create/restore WSL 2 checkpoints**: Though WSL doesn't natively support checkpoints, PnP. Wsl2 uses timestamped TAR files as backup points

- **Enable/disable WSL**: Quickly toggle WSL functionality on or off

- **Install development tools**: PnP.Wsl2 automates the installation of tools such as SPFx, PowerShell, Node.js, and Python within WSL instances using customizable bash scripts

Open source and community-driven project

PnP.Wsl2 is a community-driven project that fosters collaboration and best practices within the developer ecosystem. It will soon be officially integrated under the *Microsoft Patterns and Practices* umbrella, ensuring broader support and easier access for developers looking to enhance their workflows using WSL 2. This integration will provide wider community involvement and improved resources for managing and optimizing WSL 2 instances for Microsoft 365 and SharePoint development.

Installing PnP.Wsl2

To install PnP.Wsl2, ensure that you have PowerShell Core installed on your system.

Next, follow these steps to install PnP.Wsl2 and set up a fully optimized environment for WSL 2:

1. Open **PowerShell Core** as Administrator:

    *   Right-click on **PowerShell Core** and choose **Run as Administrator**

2. Install the PnP.Wsl2 module:

    *   Run the following command in the PowerShell window to install the PnP.Wsl2 module:

        ```
        Install-Module -Name PnP.Wsl2
        ```

In conclusion, PnP.Wsl2 is an important tool for developers working with Microsoft 365 and SharePoint on WSL 2, simplifying instance management and automating essential development environment setups. As it integrates with the Microsoft Patterns and Practices community, it will continue to enhance workflows and provide a more streamlined, efficient development process for teams.

Summary

In this chapter, we focused on practical approaches to implementing Microsoft 365 and SharePoint solutions, highlighting key strategies for success: we explored the importance of structured development processes, from planning to deployment, ensuring solutions align with business goals. We also emphasized using DevOps methodologies, along with version control (Git), to streamline development, automate testing, and speed up deployments with continuous integration and delivery (CI/CD).

Key tools such as Visual Studio, the SharePoint Framework, Microsoft Teams Toolkit, PowerShell, and Azure Functions were discussed, with guidance on selecting the right ones to enhance productivity.

We also introduced Windows Subsystem for Linux 2 (WSL2) and PnP.Wsl2. They provide an optimized development environment for Microsoft 365, allowing developers to leverage Linux's performance advantages on Windows.

Overall, the chapter underscored how these tools and methodologies improve collaboration, increase efficiency, and ensure successful project outcomes by delivering high-quality, maintainable solutions that meet real business needs.

Final thoughts

As I wrap up this book, I can't help but reflect on how this is a *reasonable snapshot* of the experiences, lessons, and trials I've gone through in my journey as an enterprise developer.

Over the years, I've navigated the ever-shifting landscape of Microsoft 365, SharePoint, and enterprise development in general, and while technology continuously evolves, some core principles remain the same: focusing on what's important and learning from the bumps along the way.

Throughout my career, I've seen how quickly tools and platforms change. New frameworks come in, old ones fade out, and today's "best practice" could be obsolete tomorrow.

But rather than get bogged down by the rapid pace of innovation, I've found it essential to embrace the growing pains of technology. Each new challenge is an opportunity to grow and rethink how we approach problems, whether that's rethinking a project's architecture, automating workflows, or improving how teams collaborate.

What I hope readers take from this book is that enterprise development isn't about finding one perfect solution: it's about *adapting, learning,* and *staying curious.* Yes, there are specific skills and tools discussed, but more importantly, there's the underlying message: have fun with it.

Don't be afraid to experiment, make mistakes, and *leverage those experiences to become better.* Every project teaches something new, and as technology keeps changing, so do we.

In the end, this book is an invitation to approach *enterprise development not as a rigid, rule-bound activity but as an evolving craft.*

Enjoy the process, embrace the challenges, and keep pushing forward, because that's where real growth happens.

If you need any help, just let me know – I'm happy to jump in.

Index

packtpub.com

Subscribe to our online digital library for full access to over 7,000 books and videos, as well as industry leading tools to help you plan your personal development and advance your career. For more information, please visit our website.

Why subscribe?

- Spend less time learning and more time coding with practical eBooks and Videos from over 4,000 industry professionals

- Improve your learning with Skill Plans built especially for you

- Get a free eBook or video every month

- Fully searchable for easy access to vital information

- Copy and paste, print, and bookmark content

Did you know that Packt offers eBook versions of every book published, with PDF and ePub files available? You can upgrade to the eBook version at packtpub.com and as a print book customer, you are entitled to a discount on the eBook copy. Get in touch with us at customercare@packtpub.com for more details.

At www.packtpub.com, you can also read a collection of free technical articles, sign up for a range of free newsletters, and receive exclusive discounts and offers on Packt books and eBooks.

Other Books You May Enjoy

If you enjoyed this book, you may be interested in these other books by Packt:

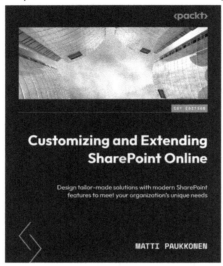

Customizing and Extending SharePoint Online

Matti Paukkonen

ISBN: 978-1-80324-489-1

- Discover the diverse capabilities offered by SharePoint Online
- Organize and classify documents with Microsoft Syntex AI models
- Add automation capabilities using SharePoint's REST APIs with Power Automate
- Enhance the user experience by connecting SharePoint data to Canvas apps
- Design custom solutions using SharePoint Framework and Microsoft Graph
- Understand how to use ready-made solutions from the developer community

Microsoft PowerPoint Best Practices, Tips, and Techniques

Chantal Bossé

ISBN: 978-1-83921-533-9

- Plan your PowerPoint presentation content and know your audience
- Prepare PowerPoint masters to speed up the development process and maintain consistency
- Add and modify visual and multimedia elements
- Use transitions and animations efficiently
- Build flexibility and interactivity into your presentations
- Practice your delivery with Presenter Coach
- Leverage Presenter View during delivery to increase your confidence
- Use PowerPoint Live in Teams for easy-to-manage remote presentations

Packt is searching for authors like you

If you're interested in becoming an author for Packt, please visit `authors.packtpub.com` and apply today. We have worked with thousands of developers and tech professionals, just like you, to help them share their insights with the global tech community. You can make a general application, apply for a specific hot topic that we are recruiting an author for, or submit your own idea.

Share Your Thoughts

Now you've finished *Mastering Microsoft 365 and SharePoint Online*, we'd love to hear your thoughts! Scan the QR code below to go straight to the Amazon review page for this book and share your feedback or leave a review on the site that you purchased it from.

`https://packt.link/r/1835463657`

Your review is important to us and the tech community and will help us make sure we're delivering excellent quality content.

Download a free PDF copy of this book

Thanks for purchasing this book!

Do you like to read on the go but are unable to carry your print books everywhere?

Is your eBook purchase not compatible with the device of your choice?

Don't worry, now with every Packt book you get a DRM-free PDF version of that book at no cost.

Read anywhere, any place, on any device. Search, copy, and paste code from your favorite technical books directly into your application.

The perks don't stop there, you can get exclusive access to discounts, newsletters, and great free content in your inbox daily

Follow these simple steps to get the benefits:

1. Scan the QR code or visit the link below

https://packt.link/free-ebook/9781835463659

2. Submit your proof of purchase

3. That's it! We'll send your free PDF and other benefits to your email directly

www.ingramcontent.com/pod-product-compliance
Lightning Source LLC
Chambersburg PA
CBHW080607060326
40690CB00021B/4619